3-31

Something More Than Night

Something More Than Night:
The Case of Raymond Chandler

Peter Wolfe

Bowling Green State University Popular Press
Bowling Green, Ohio 43403

To
the loving memory of Margaret Salius Duffy (1907-83)
and to
Lucille Miraglia,
another who has come a long way from Torrington

Contents

Acknowledgments

The author and publisher join hands in expressing thanks to those whose time and energy went into the preparation of this book: Sylvia Stephens, who typed the manuscript; Marla Schorr, who helped with proofreading; Francis M. Nevins, Jr., who furnished me with important out-of-print material by Chandler; the University of Missouri-St. Louis Graduate School, which gave me a generous grant to move forward with the book without having to worry about the rigors of the classroom for a summer; Mrs. Helga Greene, Raymond Chandler's literary executrix and copyright holder; Chandler's American publishers, Alfred A. Knopf and Houghton Mifflin and his publisher in the United Kingdom, Hamish Hamilton.

The combined help of the following people amounts to a major contribution: Lewis J. Loria, Eileen Walsh, Christine McIntyre, Ernest Mono, Harold Siu, Gordon Slepyan, Gertrude Cavallo, Grace Kennedy, Reama Brownlee and Lin Yu K'Eng.

Chapter One

The Legend and the Man

RAYMOND CHANDLER'S EMINENCE as a mystery writer is unchallenged. Somerset Maugham and George Grella both rate him above Dashiell Hammett; Eric Partridge deems him "a serious artist; and a very considerable novelist"; while praising him as "one of the finest novelists of his time," his biographer, Frank MacShane, calls him "a prophet of modern America." Finally, Jon Tuska believes him to be "the most important author of detective fiction in the history of the genre."[1] Buttressing these accolades is the variety of goodness readers have found in Raymond Chandler (1888-1959); any writer who can be read and enjoyed for so many reasons will often acquire a grandeur. Jerry Speir is correct in calling him "a figure now assuming legendary proportions."[2] Those who have helped build the legend include S. J. Perelman, for whom Chandler is "the major social historian of Los Angeles, along with Nathanael West," and Stephen Knight, who prizes Chandler as "the most literary, and so the most respectable of the crime writers." His art includes the ability both to create and maintain flexibility of tone. Thus W.H. Auden judges his "extremely depressing books" as "works of art," and MacShane ends his 1976 biography by calling him one of his era's "most delightful" writers.[3]

Some legends take on a reality more useful than facts; some ignore facts. Though Chandler forswore any pretense to profundity, he displays, in his work, a spectrum of unusual skills, shored up by his understanding of many of the basic elements of life. But these elements also made demands on him that he couldn't satisfy concurrently. Something would always slither from his grip. Several times in his life, he discarded prizes he had fought hard to win. After scoring third in a field of 600 who took a

1

Civil Service exam in England, he rejected a career in The Admiralty. He threw away a career as an oil executive by boozing and wenching. Rude, uncooperative, and late in meeting script deadlines at both Paramount and Warner Brothers, he riled his Hollywood co-workers. His first American book publisher, Alfred A. Knopf, had to drop him because of his undependability. Then there was his unfairness. He would impose standards upon others he never met himself. "He strongly resented adverse criticism from others," recalls Julian Symons, "although he was prepared to make it himself." Another Englishman, John Houseman, who worked with Chandler on the film *The Blue Dahlia* (released 1946), observed of him the same moral blindness: "He uttered . . . juvenile obscenities at which he would have been the first to take offense, if they had been spoken by others."[4] The decades preceding *The Blue Dahlia* were marked by the restlessness of a man looking in vain for privileges he knows he doesn't deserve. In the years from 1924, when they got married, to 1934, Ray and Cissy Chandler moved nine times, ranging as far from Los Angeles as Cathedral City, in the desert near Palm Springs, to Big Bear Lake in the Sierra Madre Mountains. The years after *The Blue Dahlia* were even more frenzied, especially those following Cissy's death in 1954. Using phrases like his "self-punishing conscience" and "this persecution from within,"[5] Natasha Spender describes Chandler as a devious, self-pitying man who plagued his friends with his alcoholism and threats of suicide.

Why he became such a nuisance may never be known. He kept his motives so dark that he may have also lost touch with his deepest self. "No one I have spoken with who knew Chandler has the foggiest notion of what he wanted from life,"[6] claimed Tuska in 1978. Though important, his work didn't fulfill him. Being a mystery writer, in fact, probably brought him as much embarrassment and hence anger as it did satisfaction. His letters bristle with self-conscious references to literary detection. A writer of mysteries, he feared, could never rival serious mainstream novelists; by working in a suspect, if not despised, subgenre, the mystery writer either confirms his own triteness or goes slumming artistically. For all Chandler's heavy talk about making literary detection important writing, he would have preferred practicing some other art. But which one? He lacked the outgoing personality, the sense of social reciprocity, and the faith in others undergirding drama; it's no surprise that the play he wanted to write and see produced in London in the 1950s never got written. Writing to him was always a solitary rather than a communal activity; he loathed the story conferences he had to attend as a screen writer. A man who seldom looked at the person he was talking to and who disliked shaking hands[7] would only surrender artistic control reluctantly; voicing his disbelief in artistic collaboration was his claim that the meddling of studio executives has stopped screenwriting from rising to an art. In Philip Marlowe, he invented a narrator-detective he could trust not to spring awkward surprises. The superiority of his first-person stories over those told in the third person, culminating in the emergence of Marlowe, his continuing detective, as the voice of the novels, expresses his need to maintain control.

Other aspects of his work stress the apartness of the writer. The creation of literature is as lonely as it is private, believed the decadent poets, who were popular in Chandler's London boyhood and whose languid strains seep into Chandler's youthful verse. From the outset, both the writer in Chandler and his stand-in, Marlowe, project isolation. In "The Pioneer," published in London's *Westminster Gazette*, 17 November 1909, a poet says of his songs, "I know they made men fellows,/But they left me alone." Like those songs, Marlowe's detection aids social cohesion without rewarding him with fellowship, cash, or a sense of accomplishment. Marlowe has other forebears. The title figure of "The Hermit" (*Westminster Gazette,* 28 February 1910) walks alone in a gloomy, deserted place. The speaker in "The Clay God" (*Westminster Gazette*, 5 January 1911) also lives apart from his kind; his addressing an image rather than a person completes the abstraction from flesh into lifelessness. The alcoholic, adulterous novelist, Roger Wade, in *The Long Goodbye* (1953), published more than forty years later, puts forth as stark an image of driven isolation, working in his remote study while his wife entertains friends in the living room and patio of their large, expensive home. Completing Wade's estrangement is his wife's shooting him to death.

Chandler's wife wasn't homicidal or she might have shot him, too, for being unfaithful. Perhaps she knew, as a woman seventeen years his senior, that she couldn't win his sexual loyalty. Perhaps she could afford the sacrifice. The tenderness and devotion with which he spoke of her in his letters ("She was the light of my life, my whole ambition," he wrote in January 1955, some three weeks after her death) indicates a deep emotional dependence. His marriage to Cissy was the most important relationship of his life. But how much of his truest inner self did this relationship claim? Chandler wrote most of the letters declaring his emotional loyalty to her after her death and late at night. Like alcoholism, insomnia besets the lonely, the unfulfilled, and the guilt-ridden. It beset Chandler most of his adult life. His failure to sleep alongside his beloved implies her inability to quiet his self-doubts or his wish to be somewhere else. Other evidence argues that, like his writing, marriage frustrated Chandler as much as it gladdened him. As an oil executive, he would disappear from work and home for days with a secretary. His orneriness on the lots of Hollywood discloses the same discontent; while many of his colleagues went romping after work with the fillies browsing Paramount Studios, he would trudge home to his old mare. No wonder he took out his resentments during business hours. Self-consciousness about Cissy's age continued to fret him. Both at their La Jolla home, where they moved in 1946, and in England, which they visited in 1952, he would either decline or cancel social outings to sidestep the embarrassment of introducing Cissy as his wife. That not one happy marriage brightens the Chandler canon sounds the depth of this embarrassment. His craving for maternal approval, protection, and warmth might have cost him more than he anticipated. But, like the American protagonist of "English Summer" (written in 1957), he continued to support a woman after his ardor for her had waned.

If sentiment or duty is a poor substitute for love, it can still exert force, especially upon someone like Chandler, who perceived the beloved as a stricken older woman. His father's abandoning the family in 1895 left Raymond the only male in the home and then led to his assuming the role of protector to his mother, after Florence Chandler took him to London. Although Chandler the adult may have rejected intellectually the stereotype of Galahad-like protector, he never shed it. Writing about his life in London after Cissy's death, some sixty years after his first glimpse of the city, Natasha Spender tells how his concern for the welfare of his female friends went beyond normal solicitude. He wanted to protect and rescue so badly that he would trump up distress in order to relieve it: "His highly dramatized view of our lives," Spender writes, "was often totally wide of the mark, and it was useless to argue against his strong desire to impose his interpretation."[8] She might have shown less surprise. Strongly responsive to early influences, Chandler always linked going to London with disaster having befallen the woman closest to him. His apparently willful misreading of his female friends' welfare stems from survivor's guilt; the drive to compensate both for his mother's being abandoned and his wife's dying prodded him to envision heroic deeds. Spender does trace this anxiety to his mother, within weeks of whose death he married Cissy: "One wondered how much the idolized saintly mother had given to him of the warmth and reassurance he had needed,"[9] she notes wryly. He needed nursing himself when fabricating ailments in her and her circle of women. Tending Cissy, who lived till age eighty-four, for many years brought some needed comfort; the physician who heals others also heals himself. Whether it also aggravated in him the incest craving often ascribed to him can't be known.

But the patterns formed by recurrences in his life make it a safe surmise. The transformation of mother into lover could have easily prefigured the healer-patient reversal in a psyche as romantic and sensitive as Chandler's. In addition, his interest in both dancing and pornography after Cissy's death betokens a sexual reawakening, even if it brought no renewal. (Those like Natasha Spender who knew him in his widowhood speak of his irritability, distrust of others, and secretiveness.) The pattern of courtship had formed and set, and he was too tired to break it. Like Marlowe at the end of *The Long Goodbye*, he reverted to what he knew. And what he knew of sexual love consisted of female flesh dishonored or damaged and seeking redemption through his knight errantry. The code proved stronger than self-interest or the profit motive. Thus he kept sending money to an Australian woman after dropping his idea of marrying her. His response to a more serious candidate for marriage, Helga Greene, slanted the code to his private needs. Twenty-five years his junior, Helga Greene reaffirmed in his psyche the pattern of intergenerational marriage. Next, Chandler's demand that he get the approval of her father, a man his own age, before undertaking the marriage reveals the chivalry he had extended to his mother and his wife.

But this act of chivalry defeated him. Or did it? Chandler may have exaggerated the rules of courtship both to dash his hopes for marriage and to rid himself of a stereotype he had disclaimed nearly twenty years earlier in *The Big Sleep* (1939), a novel which yokes knightliness to waste and ineffectuality. Nothing jolted Don Quixote, western literature's most famous knight, more than his encounter with the Knight of the Mirrors. Faced by Helga Greene's father, his own mirror image, across a dinner table, Chandler must have perceived his old man's folly. Poetic truth must eventually confront hard facts. Artist enough to depress and delight his readers, Chandler both created and starred in a scenario concocted to defeat him. But at age seventy, he could no longer rebound from setback. The paradigm reactivated by Helga had made him its own. Fed by the same deep sources as his mother fixation, it possessed him so completely that, in rejecting it, he also reaffirmed it. It would not be shed, Chandler having forced a painful, futile confrontation that confirmed his enslavement. But the self-contempt issuing from this bondage didn't rank him with the lost. Like Marlowe, who championed decency and justice while surrounded by venality, he fought great odds. His defeat doesn't dull the splendor of his efforts. The dreadful music he makes struggling in his chains sends out strains of bleak hope amid the distress and melancholy.

I

Insight into this barely relieved desolation comes from a maverick source—a minor character in a tired, undistinguished work, Chandler's last novel, *Playback* (1958). Ceferino Chang is a pot-smoking garage attendant; he lives alone in a "one-unit slum" near San Diego; the second time he appears in *Playback*, he's hanging by his neck in a converted privy. Besides proving that Chandler wrote himself into characters other than Marlowe, the one memorable speech delivered by Chang discloses his tendency to hide his most illuminating self-revelations in unlikely places. The speech, "I'm part Chinese, part Hawaiian, part Filipino, and part nigger. You'd hate to be me," refers to Chandler's discomfort with his own mixed background. Born in Chicago of an Irish mother and an American father, Chandler grew up in England, studied in France and Germany, and served in the Canadian army before settling in California. This fragmentation informs both J.B. Priestley's description of him as "very much a divided man" and Eleanor Anne Ponder's belief that he was "a curious mix of contradictions."[10] Other discussions of Chandler touch upon the deep self-division caused possibly by his multinationalism. William Ruehlmann's statement, "Chandler had a paradigm love-hate relationship with Hollywood," Gavin Lambert's view of Chandler as a "man without a country" and Russell Davies' reference to "the struggle between soul-bearing and reticence in Chandler's mind"[11] all reflect the same truth—that Chandler lacked the conviction and self-esteem to resolve the different impulses colliding in his psyche.

His dual nationality points up this ambivalence. Part of Chandler values tradition and order. There is also that face that looks to the wild side. Though admiring American vitality, he deplored his native country's alleged crudeness and vulgarity. At the same time, though, he knew that the English taste and refinement needed to civilize new world energy encroached upon snobbery and suburban gentility. Let us approach the problem of his cultural ambivalence by invoking that piece of goods from *Playback,* Ceferino Chang's appearing alive only once let Chandler unleash his creativity while freeing him of the drudgery of smoothing Chang into the plot; Chang is a lyrical, not a narrative, challenge. He also spells out another important truth about his creator. Minor, off-key works often say as much about Chandler as his minor characters do. More suddenly and revealingly than the Marlowe novels, for instance, the posthumously published (1976) "English Summer" describes Chandler's psyche rushing into the open. This flight is the happy product of unconstraint. Falling outside the category of detective fiction, "English Summer" freed Chandler's imagination of the shackles imposed by the hardboiled formula. What is more important, this literary diversion took shape in a genre which allowed him to disregard the verdict of posterity. He knew that his reputation would be formed by his detective fiction.

His gift of freedom releases, among other energies, his feelings about his national identity. Now the English strain ran strong in Chandler. His living for months at a time, after Cissy's death, in the London where he grew up represents a return to the consoling, nourishing maternal bosom. England always mattered to him. He never forgot the names of England's leading public schools, and it was as one English public school man to another that he approached John Housemen, producer of *The Blue Dahlia*, with his problems at Paramount Studios. Priestley believed him "more English in manner than American,"[12] and Chandler often spoke in his letters about the influence exerted by his public school education upon his style, an instrument that referred to the trunk of a car as the boot and to a phone booth as a phone box. Yet in his column, "Crosstown with Neil Morgan," in the *San Diego Evening Tribune* for 4 June 1957, he defended the United States against an attack made by a London journalist. He might have defended England just as stoutly against a similar attack by a fellow American. Obviously, the forty-five continuous years he had lived in America hadn't destroyed his English roots. Trying to sort out early influences, he wrote "English Summer" two years before his death from the standpoint of an American whose summer visit to England threatens to prolong itself into a lifetime stay—behind bars.

At the outset, John Paringdon is besotted with the customs, traditions and landscapes he identifies with the cottage where he is staying, even though he finds the place uncomfortable and inconvenient. This ambivalence gives way to others just as characteristic of Chandler. Like his author, Paringdon becomes so Anglicized that he is sometimes mistaken for English. But his acculturation belies an inner malaise. His attraction to English taste, poise and breeding hasn't smoothed his fears about being tricked and perhaps destroyed. Radiating from the cottage where he is staying, these fears take an Oedipal form. He is baffled by the rift between appearance and reality. The Crandalls' cottage, so charming on the surface, is poorly built and cheaply maintained. And whereas dark, passionate Lady Lakenham, a neighbor, has the strong, sinewy hands of a horsewoman, symbolic tamer of male sexuality, it is pale, delicate Millicent Crandall who commits murder. The death she causes shocks Paringdon. First, the sight of his dead host, Millicent's husband, sprawled, significantly, on a bed, chills his heart. Although he has loved Millicent from a distance, he turns down the chance to make love to her and to marry her. His restraint shows wisdom. He assumed Crandall to be drunk, not dead, when he saw his host inert on his eiderdown. The shock accompanying his discovery of Crandall's death summons up a transference he can just stop from running its destructive course. He soon learns that, like himself, Crandall had sex with Lady Lakenham while sharing a deeper, more enduring bond with Millicent. His reaction to this news, "So even there he had to be first," casts Crandall in the role of his father. But, as his failure to survive middle age shows, he is a flawed father, just as his rickety cottage puts forth a flawed image of home and tradition.

Like other Chandler heroes, Paringdon, in shrinking from Millicent's embrace, rejects an impulse he had nearly acted upon. The claims of self-preservation, and even of morality, outrank that of appetite in Chandler. The idea is acted out by Buzz Wanchek (played by William Bendix) of *The Blue Dahlia*, another atypical but revealing Chandler work. Though fiercely loyal, the primitive Buzz, like Moose Malloy of *Farewell, My Lovely* (1940), another creature of impulse, comes close to being mentally retarded. Chandler had originally designated him as the killer, but, because Buzz was serving in the wartime Navy during the movie's shooting, the Navy Department in Washington vetoed the idea. The plot lines of the 1946 film still imply Buzz's guilt, the culmination of which would have been death, as in the cases of both Moose Malloy and his prototype, Steve Skalla of "Try the Girl" (*Black Mask*, January 1937). The sad examples of Steve, Moose and Buzz confirm John Paringdon's wisdom in bridling his instinct. Yet the analogy between Paringdon and the three primitives breaks down. He is more subtle and complex than these predecessors and his moral problem is more delicate. Chandler has undercut the wisdom of his restraint with a typical ambiguity. Although Paringdon helps Millicent win a plea of innocence by making Edward's death look like suicide, he won't follow Edward's example of marrying her. What he does instead expresses his self-division. After leaving the cottage, he takes a walking tour of Devon and then stops in London. He only decides to leave England after being snubbed by her at the inquest. The snub is a welcome release. So exaggerated was his sense of duty that, to protect her, he told a policeman that he had killed Edward himself. Luckily, the policeman didn't believe him.

But some of the policeman's colleagues at Scotland Yard might have been less trusting. Had not Lady Lakenham testified in his favor, he could have gone to the gallows. He thanks her for her help and makes a date with her when he accidentally sees her in Piccadilly. The date he may not keep, having made plans to leave England the next day. What has his English summer taught him? His name reflects Chandler's own wish to refine his morality to a few simple precepts by which he could rule his life. This paring-down has bedeviled him. A dark, mysterious stranger gave him sex and then helped save his life, while the blonde representative of the cheerful daytime world has committed murder. But he shrinks from the transforming power of Lady Lakenham. As her name implies, an acceptance of her would constitute a drowning into life; his only time alone with her culminated in sex. But water distorts as well as reflects; its depths conceal dangerous currents and, perhaps, sea monsters. Her decaying mansion, Lakeview, could portend a destructive sea change. He probably won't find out if it does. Like Henry James' Winterbourne of *Daisy Miller*, he has lived too long in foreign parts. His English sojourn has widened a split in his psyche. Having had his Yankee spontaneity dulled by English reserve and caution, he is still American enough to regret his restraint. Yet, when scrutinized, the celebrated English charm he has prized amounts to sexuality, betrayal, and murder. Symbolizing

England's surface appeal, the two houses in the story exude decay and devastation. The path between them, where horses gallop and where adulterers wage trysts, is a wild erotic landscape rather than a garden of civilized joys.

Chandler's ending the story before Paringdon decides whether to face the challenge posed by Lady Lakenham or to board his homebound ship reflects authorial anxiety. At stake is self-trust; everything connected with Lady Lakenham has worked in Paringdon's favor, whereas everything connected with the stereotypically English Millicent Crandall smacks of death. The kindness of the investigating policeman who rejects Paringdon's panicky declaration of guilt, symbol of authority, hasn't raised Paringdon's confidence. Nor did the writing of "English Summer" resolve Chandler's contradictory impulses toward the land where he grew up. And since he wrote the story two years before his death, he probably never healed his inner division. Miriam Gross has her own list of the unresolved tensions vexing him at this time. Noting "the split between outward circumstances and inner fantasy," she observes "plenty of other paradoxes in Chandler: the mixture of toughness and sentimentality, for instance; the antiliterary stance which coexisted with intense literary ambition .... And if he is a moralist, his morality seems at odds with his relish for violence."[13] These paradoxes echo the main conflict underlying "English Summer"—the pull between instinct and precept and, by extension, between the demands of the moment and those of tradition. Ambivalence turns out to be Chandler's dominant trait. Had he been blessed with a better physique and more new world self-reliance, he'd have followed his instincts and kicked Paringdon into the arms of Lady Lakenham.

The conflict between rebellion and obedience to a hollow code of behavior also pulsates through Marlowe. The detective who says, "To hell with the rich. They make me sick," and "Women make me sick," in *The Big Sleep*, makes love to a millionaire's daughter in *The Long Goodbye*, agrees to marry her in *Playback*, and emerges as her husband in the unfinished "Poodle Springs Story" (1962). He has mellowed. The trappings of wealth he finds both beautiful and useful. Forgetting the angry pride he took in being poor, he enjoys foiling some would-be extortionists with his wife's big luxury sedan: "A cheap car would have stalled, but not the Fleetwood .... There might be a small scratch or two on the front bumper." Scratched or not, the car trails ambiguity along with exhaust fumes as it leaves the collision. The same king-size convertible that insures his escape from gangsters piqued him in the work's opening scene. Here, he is a passenger and his wife of three weeks is driving. Pulling into the driveway of the Palm Springs mansion she has rented for the season, she brims with confidence, calling him "darling" the first two times she addresses him and using a simile. He, meanwhile, feels threatened, voicing his caution and reluctance in self-protective sarcasm. The improvement of his opinion of Linda's Cadillac symbolizes the process by which both he and his creator grew more friendly to the rich. Supporting this idea is the contrast between the solid, intelligent policemen of the rich community of Esmeralda in *Playback* (1958) and the corrupt, vicious Bay City police in *Farewell, My Lovely* (1940). Also the Marlowe of *The Long Goodbye* (1953), now living in the suburbs, displays a new fascination with money, putting in much more time at the Wades' estate (Chapters 25-30 alone take place there) than he did in other houses owned by the rich, like the Sternwoods' in *The Big Sleep*, the Grayles' in *Farewell, My Lovely* or Elizabeth Bright Murdock's in *The High Window* (1942).

It is easy to credit Marlowe's growing attraction to money. Neither money nor power necessarily impedes love in Chandler. The dying millionaire, General Dade Winslow, shows the same tender concern for his missing son-in-law in "The Curtain" (*Black Mask*, September 1936) that General Guy Sternwood will direct to Rusty Regan in *The Big Sleep*. Both works show the detective responding in kind to a loving heart by risking both his license and his neck. And if the rich make him sick, the inventiveness and the energy that won them their fortunes also compel his admiration. Eddie Mars of *The Big Sleep* and Derace Kingsley of *The Lady in the Lake* (1943) have regal-sounding names; that of Lewin Lockridge Grayle of *Farewell, My Lovely* evokes religious associations. Though prosperous, these three men have a void in their private lives that matches a void within. Millionaires like General Guy Sternwood or the newspaper tycoon and caring father Harlan Potter of *The Long Goodbye* have simple names. Performance outranks pretense for them. In open, democratic America, where industry reaps dividends, any guy can acquire military honors if he applies himself. Staying at the potter's wheel, i.e., working hard, will also help every guy attain business leadership.

The self-employed Marlowe will win no such laurels. Though one of the most famous adventure heroes in American fiction, he achieves little. Davies says correctly of him, "He is not, after all, a hyperactive hero .... Indeed, it is true that Marlowe is more easily defined by what he will not do than by what he will."¹⁴ The knight on the stained-glass panel over the entrance of the Sternwood mansion casts a foreboding shadow. Chilled in time, he will never loosen the ropes binding the lady. From him, Marlowe is to learn that *all* knights are ineffectual; that chivalry is dead; that everything, justice included, is for sale; and that women, far from needing protection, often act decisively. Yet he doesn't act on his knowledge. Chandler won't let him. As early as *The Big Sleep*, his first novel, Chandler overturns all the courtly conventions he has invoked—knight errantry, the romantic quest, the damsel in distress, mortal combat with the dragon as a proving ground of knightly valor. Yet his having resurrected these conventions in nearly all of his later books certifies his ongoing belief in them.

His failure to shed the stereotype soured him. The chasm between his heroic ideal and the moral devastation around him accounts for the impression he sometimes gives of not having fought and suffered for the truth. The following sentence, which ends the second paragraph of *The Little Sister* (1949), shows him giving in to facile cynicism: "The call houses that specialize in sixteen-year-old virgins are doing a land-office business." Assuming the worst about people, such cynicism causes regret. It is doubtful that Chandler had personal knowledge of brothels featuring teen-agers. His smuggling the invented detail into his novel and recording it tonelessly shows him ignoring depth and expansiveness in favor of a schoolboy's desire to shock. It's a cheap shot. The knowing generalization, usually phrased at somebody's expense, cheapens his art generally. Marlowe says at the close of the first chapter of *The Long Goodbye*, "I had an impulse to ... take the scotch bottle away from him. But it wasn't any of my business and it never does any good anyway. They always find a way to get it if they have to have it." Like the romantic stereotypes he invokes against his better judgment, such inductive leaps save him the trouble of judging things and people on their merits. He strews the book with cynical blanket statements: "Tijuana is nothing; all they want there is the buck," Marlowe says in Chapter 6, adding in Chapter 24, "Every cocktail party is the same, even the dialogue." Perhaps the most embittered moment in the novel, allegedly Chandler's richest in heart knowledge, comes at the end of Chapter 38, after Marlowe has slogged through a long, tiring day:

Out there in the night of a thousand crimes people were dying, being maimed, cut by flying glass, crushed against steering wheels or under heavy tires. People were being beaten, robbed, strangled, raped, and murdered. People were hungry, sick, bored, desperate with loneliness or remorse or fear, angry, cruel, feverish, shaken by sobs. A city no worse than others, a city rich and vigorous and full of pride, a city lost and beaten and full of emptiness.

Such diatribes neglect the great majority of Marlowe's townsfolk. Remote from violence, they're preparing coffee for the next day's breakfast, reading, hearing the late news, saying goodnight to friends on the phone, making love, or praying. Chandler's tendency to distort and degrade vitiates his artistry because it robs people of their individuality; mudslinging causes facelessness. In *Farewell, My Lovely*, Marlowe calls a psychic consultant he hasn't yet met "a fakeloo artist, a hoopla spreader." That his judgment proves correct is no vindication but, rather, a stroke of authorial manipulation *cum* self-fulfilling prophecy. Marlowe has been there before; he knows all about it and nothing can surprise him. Passages like the ones ending Chapter 38 of *The Long Goodbye* recall the catalogs of Walt Whitman. But whereas Whitman's catalogs celebrate America's splendor and strength, Chandler's (Los Angeles is a "city no worse than others") expose taint, squalor, and moral plunder.

Chandler's practice of typecasting can mar his treatment of minorities. Chiding the young homosexual Carol Lundgren of *The Big Sleep*, Marlowe says of his dead lover, "He was like Caesar, a husband to women and a wife to men. Think I can't figure people like him and you out?" The same smugness blurs his reaction to Lundgren's strength. Although Lundgren's punch lands flush, it's harmless: "I took plenty of the punch. It was meant to be a hard one, but a pansy has no iron in his bones, whatever he looks like." Then in one of his vilest moments, Marlowe tosses his pistol at Lundgren's feet, in order to give himself the chance to punish Lundgren for reaching for it. The rest of the scene shows him using unnecessary violence on his victim while continuing to goad him sarcastically. Yet it is Lundgren, not Marlowe, whom Chandler describes as a beast, balanced on all fours like a quadruped and flashing "an animal brightness in his . . . eye." But how representative is this cruelty? And how accurately does it reflect Chandler's views of homosexuality? An approach to some answers lies in *Black Mask* aesthetics. Even though Chandler said in a February 1957 letter that homosexuals lack emotion, he had no quarrel with gays. The subject was one he preferred to leave alone. Lundgren is probably his only gay male, and he owes more to Wilmer Cook, the "gunsel" of Hammett's *Maltese Falcon*, than to Chandler's creativity. Bullied as he is, he gets no scurvier handling than do any number of male gays in Ross Macdonald, who also wisely omitted homosexuals from his later work. Perhaps to atone for the abuse dealt out to Lundgren, Chandler has novelist Roger Wade of *The Long Goodbye* say without being contradicted that gays have flourished in ages of great artistic activity, like the Renaissance. Personal experience may have accounted for the improvement in attitude toward gays that Wade's remark implies. Uneasy around others, Chandler nonetheless enjoyed swimming in the Santa Monica pool of Christopher Isherwood; Miriam Gross' *The World of Raymond Chandler* includes a snapshot of him diving into the pool. Had he bridled at Isherwood's homosexuality, the shy, sometimes petulant Chandler wouldn't have visited his home as a guest.

Chandler's slurs against Jews and blacks generate a different sort of ambiguity. Some critics have branded Chandler a bigot. Dennis Porter cites "Chandler's racist innuendo," while the Australian Clive James only absolves Chandler from racism by calling him a crypto-sociopath: "His race prejudice would amount to outright fascism if it were not so evident that he would never be able to bring himself to join a movement."[15] Reasoning more soberly but agreeing in principle with James and Porter, Stephen Pendo complains that Chandler ruined *Farewell, My Lovely* with his "very definite bias against blacks."

Not only does Marlowe label blacks "niggers" but also the novel contains the stereotypic black who rolls his eyes. All the book's blacks are loud dressers ... and we never meet an admirable black although the other characters, no matter how unsavory, usually have some admirable side.[16]

This argument has at least two flaws. The black bouncer of Florian's turns away Moose Malloy gently and courteously. His friendly dismissal, "No white folks brother, Jes' fo' the colored people. I'se sorry," hardly merits the battering Moose gives him; he'd have been denied far less courteously had he tried to drink in an all-white bar. Several chapters later, a black hotel clerk calls Marlowe's attention to the city directory, an aid the detective should have thought of himself as a professional searcher for missing persons.

These flaws weaken but don't destroy the spirit of Pendo's argument. Beyond *Farewell, My Lovely*, it also applies to the

Hispanic Dolores Gonzales, a blackmailer and murderess in *The Little Sister;* to the treacherous Jewish gangster, Ikky Rosenstein, of "The Pencil" (*London Daily Mail,* 6-10 April 1959 as "Marlowe Takes on the Syndicate"); and to the abrasive Palm Springs nightclub owner, Manny Lipshultz of "The Poodle Springs Story." Chandler libelled minorities his whole writing career. Also germane in this context is Marlowe's move from his city apartment to a house in the suburbs in the early 1950s; the move reflects the massive out-migration by urban whites from 1946 to 1960. But Marlowe's contribution to the White Flight doesn't prove by itself that Chandler was a bigot. For if the author was accused of anti-Semitism by two readers of *The High Window,* he also refused to join a beach club because it wouldn't admit Jews.[17] What is more, he doesn't buy Marlowe's outlook completely. His nearly chronic self-consciousness and passion for secrecy could make him as ironical as Jonathan Swift. Though he sympathizes emotionally with Marlowe, he withholds assent intellectually. Ross Macdonald has noted, "It is Marlowe's doubleness that makes him interesting .... Part of our pleasure derives from the interplay between the mind of Chandler and the voice of Marlowe."[18] But the same countertension that pleases also clouds. Examples from the canon show Chandler's position on the matter of race and religion to be darkly ambiguous.

The ambiguity existed from the start. To fend off any accusations of anti-Semitism, Chandler renamed the blackmailer and smut merchant Harold Hardwicke Steiner (the final *e* of whose middle name implies that, were he Jewish, he'd rather not be), of "Killer in the Rain" (*Black Mask,* January 1935), Arthur Gwynn Geiger in *The Big Sleep.* Chandler's first novel also includes a smirking, gaudy Jewish credit jeweler whose shop stands near Geiger's. But Chandler offsets any offensiveness the jeweler emits by quickly introducing an intelligent, observant Jewish woman who helps Marlowe. A variation of the same pattern found in Chandler's first novel recurs in the very late story "The Pencil," where Marlowe says of a Jewish client, "He had a rusty voice. I didn't like it any more than I liked his clothes, or his face." Three pages from the end of the story, he reverses his snap judgment, saying of his client, "He grows up in the mob, but he's not rotten. He's not rotten enough." The question asked Marlowe by a Hollywood film executive in *The Little Sister,* "Anti-Semitic, huh?" can't be answered. Nor can Chandler's opinion of blacks be ascertained. Words like shine, dinge and smoke appear in *Farewell, My Lovely* in dialogue. Marlowe will only say them to ignoramuses like Police Lieutenant Nulty and the alcoholic widow, Jessie Florian, who use them routinely. By intentionally using language he disapproves of to lower the guard of Jessie and Nulty, though, Marlowe is resorting to base means to establish justice. He also miscues when he calls Jessie's greeting "as weak as a Chinaman's tea," and when he says of "a Jap gardener," "He was pulling a piece of weed . . . and sneering at it the way Jap gardeners do." Such blanket judgments are always hostile in Chandler. They should have been left out. They undermine the novel as badly as does Marlowe's saying of a shabby old man in *The High Window,* "He had a sort of dry, musty smell, like a fairly clean Chinaman." Such descriptions carry a nasty implication. If Chandler used racial slurs to shore up his hero's hardboiled pose, then he might have been patronizing his readers just as his hero did Lt. Nulty and Jessie Florian.

Chandler's ambivalence extends to narrative technique. The same man who insulted both his readers and his art by settling for stereotypes would also fight past ordinary discourse to seek the truth. Lambert says that "the authentic Chandler overtone" fuses the casual and the bizarre. He's not alone in this belief. Referring to "Chandler's rich digressive effects," Porter claims that "the most characteristic mark of a Chandler novel is . . . a quality of extravagance."[19] Chandler's fiction looks inward and outward. Reaching out to comprehend southern California society, it also compresses society to the shape of Chandler's obsessions. This obsessiveness provides much of the interest, Chandler caring little about politics, economics, or social change. Paul F. Ferguson says that he gave his people names like Lois Magic (*The High Window*) and Orfamay Quest (*The Little Sister*) to inject wonder into the journalistic realism dominating the *Black Mask* formula.[20] Distortion and magnification are what the romantic uses to cope with violence. A highly wrought, vigorous language declares itself in *The Big Sleep,* whose opening chapters mingle different voices. Cutting across Marlowe's dry wit and self-mockery is Chandler's flair for the absurd and the grotesque, those legacies of Gothic fiction. Buildings are important. Besides including a symbolic castle, Chandler wrings fear from a dark house, inside of which materialize a corpse and a naked woman. Further portents of sin and depravity come from the rain, always ominous in Chandler; from the powerful, enigmatic Eddie Mars, owner of a casino; and from General Sternwood, the figure of the dying king.

Patricia Highsmith likens Chandler's attraction to the bizarre to her view of him as a misfit. "One sees Chandler as not really fitting in anywhere," she says in connection with the wild humor generated by his similes.[21] The mood of stress and striving imparted by his prose stems from his urge to belong; by parading his linguistic virtuosity, he hopes to impress the literary establishment. Yet the sense of shame ignited in him by the main realities of his life—his detective writing and his much-older wife—ruled out belonging as a goal. He lacked the self-acceptance to feel comfortable anywhere. Using humor to mask both his anger and his insecurity, he writes as a man depleted. He resents having done without the protection, assurance, and warmth he extended to both his mother and his wife. He also resents having been denied a young wife, dismissed by the literati as an entertainer, and robbed of the freedom to test his creativity as a film writer. To compensate for feeling lonely and ransacked, he would show his detective heroes brandishing firearms, symbols of male force, with their rigidness and explosive discharges of power. The nameless sleuth of "Killer in the Rain" shoots a gunman in the shoulder while outnumbered, three to one. Often, it will suffice for the detective merely to hold weapons. In "The Lady in the Lake" (*Dime Detective*, January 1939), John Dalmas holds two guns after having been unarmed by his foes in a mountain cabin; even after being divested of his male force, a true man can recover it twofold, runs Chandler's self-conscious joke. The holding of guns buoys up Marlowe in *The Big Sleep*. Although he enters grifter Joe Brody's apartment unarmed, he holds three pistols later in the sequence, during which he also disarms Carol Lundgren. This compulsion to have firearms literally in hand recurs throughout the canon. Marlowe appropriates a shotgun and a .38 automatic from a bartender in *Farewell, My Lovely*; in Chapter 28 of *The Little Sister*, he's holding three pistols.

His need to claim and control these tokens of virility sorts well with his hard drinking, his dangerous job, and his attractivenes to women, all of which male swagger implies Chandler's need to compensate and act out; stereotypes comfort the indecisive. The sexual insecurity he was fighting comes from a smothered family identity aggravated by dual citizenship. Maleness sat uneasily on him. An only child of divorced parents of different nationalities, he fathered no children. He may have even married a woman of fifty-four to dodge the challenge of paternity; Julian Symons explains his marriage to Cissy as a reaction to "psychological injury."[22]

But did the healing of one psychological hurt inflict others? Marrying Cissy might have offered the promise of maternal affection and security. But by reinforcing the patterns of domesticity evolved with his mother, it also deepened his deprivation. Repetition, claims Dante, Nietzsche, and Freud, indicates enslavement; the individual who keeps doing the same deeds lacks the freedom, wit, and courage to try something new. With his finely tuned sense of moral ambivalence, Chandler must have viewed his marriage as a regression, a trap, and, in view of the certainty of childlessness, a sham. Life's most important realities, like good health, usually confirm themselves in absentia; only the sick and the maimed know the joys of being healthy. Emotionally responsive to stereotypes and possessing a semi-outsider's heightened awareness of native values, Chandler couldn't ignore that face of the American dream featuring a home with children. The blocked drive to fatherhood gets into his work persistently. Not surprisingly, it asserts itself as denial. Chandler was a late starter. He married at thirty-six, published his first novel at age fifty, and didn't gain the satisfaction of being appreciated as a serious artist till his 1952 trip to England, when he was sixty-four. Other blessings, referring to the family, never graced him, and he knew they never would. Thus he either downgraded them or pretended that they didn't exist.

The emotional climate in which Chandler's anger unfolds enhances the mood of depletion. His fiction endorses the truth that the people who touch us most deeply are our immediate families. All his work grazes the classic family drama set forth in Ibsen's *Ghosts,* Lawrence's *Sons and Lovers,* and Arthur Miller's *View from the Bridge*—any hurt inflicted upon an individual will send shock waves through his/her family. But the drama is underdeveloped. In *The High Window* and *The Long Goodbye,* Chandler's imaginative shortcomings or faintheartedness blunts its force. It is too narrowly based. Childless and an only child, Chandler couldn't or wouldn't create a family unit consisting of children and their young to middle-aged parents; the one preadult in the canon, psychopathic Dade Trevelyan of "The Curtain," is more monster than child. The parents in Chandler are usually old and widowed, like Elizabeth Bright Murdock (*The High Window*), Harlan Potter (*The Long Goodbye*), Henry Cumberland (*Playback*) and General Guy Sternwood, who first knew fatherhood at age fifty-four. Though married several times, his daughter, Vivian, has never had children. American crime fiction had to wait for Ross Macdonald before describing the family drama memorably.

Though oblique and unformed, Chandler's insights into the American family strike home. People living under the same roof hardly notice one another. No member of the Sternwood family appears with any other in *The Big Sleep*. In fact, no two Sternwoods appear together in the same chapter. The action opens with Marlowe talking to the Sternwood sisters and their father in individual chapters, and it ends the same way, in separate interviews, each of which gets its own chapter. A similar breach divides residents of the same home in *The High Window*. "I like your being devoted to your wife," says Marlowe to Leslie Murdock, who defied his mother to marry a nightclub singer. Yet Murdock is never seen together with Linda; nor do Bill Chess and Derace Kingsley of *The Lady in the Lake* appear with *their* wives. Most encounters between married couples occur offstage in Chandler, even the violent ones. Elizabeth Bright Murdock of *The Little Sister*, Eileen Wade of *The Long Goodbye*, and perhaps Betty Mayfield of *Playback* all kill their mates while Marlowe is somewhere else; the detective is on the scene but unconscious when Al Degarmo slays his ex-mate in *The Lady in the Lake*. Communication between husband and wife is so feeble in Chandler that the description of brutality involving couples went against his sense of artistic propriety.

It hardly needs saying that the corpus bristles with bad marriages. Already noted have been the hate-filled ties joining the Lakenhams and the Crandalls in "English Summer." Another little-read story Chandler wrote a great deal of himself into is "A Couple of Writers" (c. 1951; 1962). As in "English Summer" and the equally atypical "Pearls Are a Nuisance" (*Dime Detective*, April 1939), drink mars a close tie between a man and a woman. Hank Bruton not only follows Chandler in his tippling; he also writes fiction, keeps a cat, smokes a pipe and enjoys swimming. As guilt-raked as Chandler's most notable writer, Roger Wade of *The Long Goodbye*, he prepares and serves his wife's morning coffee. The story's first sentence finds him doing this chore with the same dedication that impelled John Paringdon to cover up Millicent Crandall's murder of her husband in "English Summer." But it adds a note of special pleading. Though Bruton drinks, he always recovers sufficiently the next morning to make Marion's coffee and, as is shown later, to swim in the cold river near the house: "No matter how drunk he had been the night before Hank Bruton always got up very early and walked around the house in bare feet, waiting for the coffee to brew," the story begins. His polite care reaps no gratitude. Whereas he is gentle and accommodating, his wife, no demure Maid Marian, squawks neurotically about his drinking.

Yet he can't be pitied as a victim. He feels guilty because, beyond tending to Marion's creature comforts, he gives little of himself. He drinks furtively. He views her hysterical outbursts as bravura performances rather than expressions of pain or bids for attention. When she prepares to leave him, he doesn't try to discourage her. Instead, he offers to drive her to the train station. He also asks her if she wants to make the morning train, revealingly announcing its departure time six minutes ahead of schedule. He can afford to press the issue of her leaving him because he knows she will stay. If she's a shrew, his quiet brutality (Bruton-brute) aggravates her shrewishness. Both his casual dismissals of her tirades and his hard drinking heighten the frenzy of her demands to be noticed. For all her wildness, he controls the marriage; she lacks the courage to break away. More actress than playwright, she wants an audience. He risks nothing by casually supporting her decision to leave him. The fictional frame he has imposed upon their marriage outlasts hers. He is the better writer. But he doesn't vibrate any more keenly. As Chandler demonstrated with his mother and foresaw demonstrating with his fast-sinking wife, only Marion's death could change Bruton's life markedly.

Another drinker who controls a bad marriage is Helen Morrison of *The Blue Dahlia*. (Very rarely in Chandler will a wife's tippling hurt a marriage.) As with the Brutons, the husband is apologetic and biddable, whereas the wife loses grip. The marriage suffers its first shock when Johnny is called into the Navy. Helen accidentally kills their small son in a car crash while Johnny is serving overseas. The accident warps and coarsens her emotions. She begins carousing with other men. More devastation follows. Within hours of the time of Johnny's surprise homecoming, she is murdered. Johnny's response to the murder typifies the heroes of Chandler's minor fiction. Although he doesn't love Helen any more than Hank Bruton loves Marion or John Paringdon of "English Summer" loves Millicent Crandall, he can't shrug off her murder. A sense of moral obligation prods him to find her assailant. But his isn't the only shaky marriage in the 1946 film. Joyce Harwood wants to divorce her husband, Eddie. A figure with many counterparts in the Marlowe-narrated fiction, Eddie owns a nightclub and a parts plant. Cementing the bond Chandler usually makes between power and corruption, Eddie also committed murder in New Jersey before moving to California. Voicing Chandler's cynicism toward marriage is Joyce's wish to divorce Eddie, which has nothing to do with his wrongdoing. Rich, successful, and sometimes even accomplished husbands in Chandler get little joy from their wives. Both Lewin Lockridge Grayle of *Farewell, My Lovely* and Alex Morny of *The High Window* married cabaret singers who deceive them with other men. Derace Kingsley of *The Lady in the Lake* hires Marlowe to find a missing wife addicted to both shoplifting and adultery. A more striking example of the castrating wife, Eileen Wade of *The Long Goodbye*, murders her husband. From the outset, Chandler's men and women found little happiness together. "I'll Be Waiting" (*Saturday Evening Post*, 14 October 1939) centers on a woman waiting for a husband she loves to finish a jail sentence she herself engineered. In *The Big Sleep* Mona Mars loves her racketeer husband, Eddie, but, because of his shady dealings must express that love by living away from him.

The figure of the public success who has everything in order but his marriage suggests either cynicism or self-pity in Chandler. In its bogus romanticism, it looks ahead to a Chandler motif, the love that can only come once in life. It also calls to mind the truth that most of his views of sexual love stem from stale romantic conventions. In a letter written in March 1957 he claims, "I do have a strange sort of instinct for understanding people, especially women." This claim is moonshine. His writing conveys but little understanding of females. In the column "Crosstown with Neil Morgan," in the *San Diego Evening Tribune*, 12 June 1957, he says "At the bottom of his heart every decent man feels that his approach to the woman he loves is an approach to a shrine." This religious adoration fades quickly away from the bedroom. The same man who reveres the woman of his heart dismisses others as tramps, hustlers, or gold diggers. It doesn't matter that decent men may love them. Chandler saw women as sluts or saints. When Marlowe meets likable, independent Anne Riordan in *Farewell, My Lovely*, he rejects her because she doesn't belong on a pedestal or in the gutter. He shunned challenging relationships with women because his author couldn't put him in one. Chandler's exacting moral code concerning women sidestepped the responsibility of coping with human ambiguity. What is most damaging, it also sidestepped his responsibility to himself.

Although obsessions can sustain a writer, they also limit him, clouding his sense of justice and fairness. Chandler they seem to tie in knots as well. The frequency with which people like John Paringdon of "English Summer" reject impulse for prudency discloses his lack of self-confidence. The impression that Chandler neither knew nor trusted his feelings gains strength from his having returned time after time to conventions and stereotypes he knew to be empty. As much as he despised the hackneyed, he would invoke it to spare himself the anguish of choice. Also germane is the regularity with which primitives like Moose Malloy of *Farewell, My Lovely* came to grief. The writer who denies his feelings will withhold happiness and fulfillment from those driven by emotion and impulse. In his letters, Chandler sought refuge from the instant and the immediate by feigning superiority. A letter dated 11 February 1937, for instance, reveals him describing himself as both a conqueror and protector of women. He is showing off. His self-proclaimed loyalty to a courtly code amounts to a denial of his feelings, as is made clear in his last sentence:

There was a time in my life as a young man when I could have picked up any pretty girl on the street and slept with her that night. (Bragging again, but it is true.) I didn't do it because there has to be something else and a man like me has to be sure he is not hurting anyone . . . . Because one doesn't love in order to hurt and destroy.

The following letter, written 19 March 1957, contains even more blatant press-agentry. (Since when did anyone claim that a one-night stand had anything to do with love?) First, Chandler's statement that he was faithful to Cissy is a lie; according to MacShane, he chased and bedded women frequently for fifteen years starting about 1930. What is more shocking in the letter is its disregard of Chandler's feelings for the wife he deceived. Love can't be automatically inferred from reverence; in fact, reverence often erects barriers that inhibit communication, let alone intimacy. Since Cissy was the most important person in his life, his prayerful words show him once more hiding from himself; the most he says about his alleged faithfulness to Cissy is that it was practical and expedient:

I wasn't faithful to my wife out of principle but because she was completely adorable, and the urge to stray which afflicts many men at a certain age, because they think they have been missing a lot of beautiful girls, never touched me. I already had perfection.

II

Chandler's concealment operation came all too naturally. Believing that everything carries a price tag, the self-made man will underrate love, which is free. Although he grew up in England, Chandler enacted the American drama of self-creation. He did it first when he went to England at age seven as his mother's protector. Protection his mother needed, having lost her husband to another woman and then, unable to support herself, falling back upon her "stupid and arrogant" (letter, 15 July 1954) mother; MacShane speaks of the "extraordinary sense of loyalty to his mother"[23] Chandler cultivated in childhood. Other acts of self-creation followed, some of which concerned writing. He defied a "rich and tyrannical uncle"[24] by resigning from The Admiralty in London in order to practice journalism. At age forty-five he published his first detective story. The other major preoccupation of his life, women, also promoted resurgence and self-renewal. Some of these moments have already been mentioned, like his marriage to Cissy right after his mother's death and his having learned dancing and considered remarriage after Cissy's death in 1954. But this activity hewed to the curve first traced in 1895 when he and Florence Chandler crossed the Atlantic. In 1916, Florence began living with him in California. The 1924 marriage to Cissy again cast him in the role of protector to an older woman. He couldn't break the pattern. Seconding Natasha Spender, Speir tells how he "would invent imaginary dangers from which to protect"[25] the women he befriended in his widowhood.

His willingness to maim healthy flesh in order to preserve the archetype shows the strength of the archetype. Chandler had both the wit and the intellectual honesty to know he was trapped. His never having lived in the same home with another male after the age of seven had mangled his outlook on male-female relationships. As has been seen, his feeble rebellion against his entrapment took the forms of drink, extramarital sex and writing. Writing, though the least harmful of his protest mechanisms, fostered deprivations of its own. John Houseman explains that, rather than complaining in person to director Billy Wilder, when the two men were working on the film *Double Indemnity* (1944), he put his objections and demands in writing; his letter of complaint, moreover, he sent, not to Wilder, but to a studio head, who was to mediate between the two men. In addition, the exemplar of the writer in the Chandler canon, Roger Wade of *The*

Long Goodbye, wenches and boozes besides earning a living as a novelist. Wade's asocial behavior, consequent guilt, and death by murder all yoke him to the classic figure of the artist as formulated by Schopenhauer, Freud, and Mann, all of whom saw the artist as society's enemy—a misfit and an outlaw. What is more, each of these men was dyed deeply enough by nineteenth-century German dialectic to call for the artist's punishment. Although there is no way of knowing if Chandler, too, read Hegel, who dominated nineteenth-century European thought, his retributive morality endorses the dialectic; any violation of the law entails redress. Chandler's characters only get better than they deserve when the detective suspends man's law by bestowing grace upon an evildoer. (Sherlock Holmes freed murderers in "Charles Augustus Milverton" and "The Abbey Grange"; murderers also go unpunished in Agatha Christie's *Murder on the Orient Express* [1934] and *Dead Man's Folly* [1956].) But these rare godlike acts are often foiled by the evildoer's own sense of guilt.

Retribution enters Chandler's writing with the same defensiveness that colors most of his shows of feeling. His imaginative transformation, in his late years, of the women close to him into invalids suggests both a compulsion to control women before they controlled *him* and a possible reason for the compulsion. Damaged people inflict damage; were Chandler not maimed inwardly by his mother and his mother-wife, he'd not have been so eager to maim other women. His treatment of mothers in his work discredits his frequent claim that his mother was a saint. As has been seen, *The Big Sleep* (1939) includes no mothers; General Sternwood's wife is dead, and his daughter, Vivian, unlike her prototype in "The Curtain," is childless. An ageing mother of an only child does appear briefly alongside her husband in *The Lady in the Lake* (1943), but the child, a daughter, is dead. Exerting a greater force than Mrs. Grayson of *The Lady in the Lake* is the harsh, denying mother of the Quest children in *The Little Sister*: "Mother never let Father smoke in the house, even the last two years after he had his stroke," says Orfamay Quest. "She said she couldn't afford to give him money for useless things like tobacco. The church needed it much more than he did." But this rigid puritan, ruling her roost in distant Kansas, never appears in the action.

The only amply developed character study of a mother in the canon is invasive Elizabeth Bright Murdock, Marlowe's client in *The High Window* (1942). Pendo notes her "pent-up hatred and total disregard for everyone but her son . . . . She stands out as the perfect Chandler villainness: an over-possessive rich woman far more evil than the blackmailer with whom she deals."[27] Tough and nasty she is; Marlowe calls her "the old dragon" and refers to "the elephant hide of her cheeks." She has bullied her secretary-surrogate daughter, Merle Davis, into believing herself a killer, and she tells Marlowe both how to investigate the case of her missing coin and whom to blame for the coin's theft. Her tippling and her practice of cheating at solitaire both direct her wrongdoing back to herself. Mrs. Murdock savages those closest to her. She wants Marlowe to help her wreck the marriage of her son, Leslie, who, like Chandler at the time of his own marriage, significantly, to a woman his mother wouldn't have picked for him, is a well-dressed, somewhat Anglicized pipesmoker in his thirties who hides his shyness behind wisecracks. (So total is his mother's domination over Leslie that he changed his last name to that of his stepfather when his mother remarried, even though he was in his twenties at the time). The death of Horace Bright, Leslie's father, further explains Chandler's fears of the mother-wife. To end his womanizing, Mrs. Murdock pushed her husband through the high window of the novel's title. Now Chandler doesn't chronicle lives, but moments. One of his recurring motifs is the inextricability of loss and gain; triumph contains the seeds of downfall for Marlowe in his encounters with Mona Mars of *The Big Sleep* and Terry Lennox of *The Long Goodbye*. Horace Bright enacts the same drama, but more explosively, as the hope for sexual union with Merle Davis ends with his fatal drop from an open window. The swift reversal of his expectations is conveyed symbolically. Identified with female sexuality, the window represents for Bright a deathly exit rather than an access to life-enhancing joys.

Little is known of this first husband of Elizabeth, whose behavior and ironical front name brand her a false queen, mother and wife. Every attempt has been made to wipe out both his name and memory; even the missing coin Marlowe has been hired to find belonged, not to him but to his successor, Jasper Murdock. But the attempt to erase his existence, in which Chandler collaborated, perhaps unconsciously, was doomed. Elizabeth's middle name, Bright, came from her first husband. The line from Thomas Nashe, "Brightness falls from the air," used to describe Lucifer, also refers to him. Intent on enjoying the dark riches of sexuality, he hurtled to his death through a blaze of daytime air some ten years before the recorded time of the novel. In a sense, he acted wisely, i.e., brightly, to defy Elizabeth. Life lived in her proximity is no life at all. His defiance gives new meaning to MacShane's summary of Chandler's childhood crisis: "Chandler rarely spoke of his father except occasionally to call him 'an utter swine.' His complete disappearance from Chandler's life and his failure to provide support for his former wife made him reprehensible."[28]

Reprehensible but also enviable for his boldness? To deny one's father is to deny one's roots and, by extension, one's own self. Thus the denial can never be complete. This ambivalence may have explained Chandler's punishing the sexual offender and false father, Horace Bright, by plunging him into a fatal flood of brightness. It also explained his failure to make his revenge perfect. Success would have identified him with the nasty Mrs. Murdock, who had the most to gain by killing her husband and then blaming the death on Merle Davis. Yet Chandler stands closer to her son, Leslie, and to Marlowe, both of whom followed Bright's lead by defying her. How much closer? one is tempted to ask. His self-division shows in his very collaboration to blot out an absentee father. The same open window through which people fly to their deaths admits the air and light that sustain life. Before killing Bright, Chandler, sadistically perhaps, misled him with false hope.

Why? Had he driven out all memory of Maurice Chandler, he'd have had no need to repeat the act imaginatively. Aggravated by his divided national loyalty, his ambiguous attitude toward his father could well explain his swings in mood between arrogance and shyness. His perception of his mother's inadequacies also ruled out any final judgment of his father. "This aspect of crime—the likable murderer—was one that interested Chandler,"[29] said Dorothy Gardiner and Katherine Sorely Walker. Though Maurice Chandler murdered nobody, his desertion of his family caused an upheaval so powerful in his son that the son never recovered from it. The "recurrent ambivalences between over-confidence and anxiety, generosity and apprehension"[30] noted in Chandler by Spender took fictive shape as resentment, admiration, and the wish to under-stand.

Chandler was torn by opposing drives. Yet he knew that the same tension that racked him as a man enriched his art. Achievement and frustration, loss and gain, always had a common root for him as well as for Marlowe. If his father was a wenching alcoholic, so would he and his three self-projections in

The Long Goodbye drink heavily and chase women. Chandler took on his father's vices to know both Maurice Chandler and himself. Assuming the life stance of his father came easily to an imaginative man who disliked saying goodbye and whom circumstances had forced several times to improvise a self. But his improvisations brought suprises. He insulted his mother by replacing her immediately with Cissy, and he insulted Cissy with infidelity. As was shown by his father and Horace Bright, he believed that men kick against the restrictions imposed by marriage.

The husband-father sometimes appears in Chandler's fiction as a corrupt figure of power who exacts strict obedience. Divested by authorial fiat of children because of his sins, he may be a physician, a policeman, or a cabaret owner, who, like Eddie Mars of *The Big Sleep*, Laird Brunette of *Farewell, My Lovely,* and Clark Brandon of *Playback,* enjoys political power. Mars' having married the singer Mona Grant before Marlowe can court her recurs in John Paringdon's anger in learning that Edward Crandall preceded him in having sex with Lady Lakenham. Paringdon's saying inwardly of Crandall, "So even there he had to be first," expresses both the son's resentment of the father and the upstart American's dismay at the guile of the older, more established culture. Eddie Harwood, the fugitive murderer turned cabaret owner and industrialist in *The Blue Dahlia*, approaches the primal family drama from the opposite side. Harwood invokes Maurice Chandler, or at least the author's idea of him. Although he may not drink much, he sells liquor at the Blue Dahlia, which dominates the movie it gives its name to, just as the drama of the high window accounts for most of the tension in Chandler's 1942 novel. "I get to own a war plant and a night club—I even marry a girl who oughtn't to have given me the time of day," says Harwood in an off-guard moment; women are always girls in Chandler, as well as being sluts or saints in the eyes of their vexed husbands. The esteem in which Harwood holds his wife Joyce typifies Chandler, too, who always exaggerated women's virtues and vices rather than recognizing their ambiguity. Reflecting his author's tendency to substitute reverence for love, Harwood never discourages Joyce from leaving him; he never deserved her, to begin with. She justifies this admiration by displaying outstanding loyalty—not to him but to Johnny Morrison, whom she protects while believing him his wife's killer.

Morrison, the Alan Ladd role, is also a father, albeit not a full-fledged one. Both his son and his wife have died violently. And if these crashing defeats weren't enough, Chandler also has him robbed, beaten, and threatened by arrest as Helen's killer. His innocence is established within the symbolism of the family, revealingly the seat of his pain, as well. The killer turns out to be one Dad Newell, the caretaker of the apartment court where Helen was living when she died. Newell's age, given by him as "going on fifty-seven," recalls the first sentence of the John Houseman memoir introducing the published version of the movie: "Raymond Chandler was fifty-seven when he risked his life for me."[31] This identification is important in the light of Newell's job, his fifteen years as a policeman, and his name. Whereas the names Dad and Newell imply rebirth, the caretaker has taken life. Though his guilt both releases Johnny from a debt of honor and affirms his innocence, the future looks grim. The end of the movie shows Johnny going into the Blue Dahlia with his mates after turning from Joyce, the woman who loves him. Boy doesn't get girl. Instead he joins his friends for a drink at the bar owned by his dead wife's lover. That the movie opened with the same three men drinking denies Johnny any moral growth or gain in self-knowledge despite his suffering. On the other hand, his very survival preserves the image of the father in Chandler's psyche. It would be good to know what Chandler had in mind by sending him to the nightclub of Helen's lover, a racketeer who virtually gave her the apartment in which she committed adultery and was later slaughtered. In view of the male comradeship evoked by the film's final shot, Johnny wasn't driven by anger or revenge. Responding to deeper impulses, Chandler may have intended to have one broken father shaking hands with another and thus creating a whole one.

The crypto-father recurs rarely but steadily. If "English Summer" resurrected it in the 1950s after *The High Window* and *The Blue Dahlia* featured it in the 1940s, the short story "Guns at Cyrano's" (*Black Mask* January 1936) pushed it to the fore in the previous decade, Chandler's first as a published thriller writer. Durham's summary of the action of "Guns at Cyrano's" shows some of the importance of the archetypal figure:

In "Guns at Cyrano's," Chandler used as a hero a man who had once been a private eye but was living on the money—dirty money—inherited from his father. The story is distinguished by the hero's attempt to make up to society for his father's acts against it.

As in *The High Window* and *The Blue Dahlia* (and in "English

Summer," too, if England, the tale's setting, counts as a fatherland, or *patria*), two broken fathers steer the action. It's noteworthy that neither one has the first name of Eddie or Edward, as with Eddie Mars, Eddie Harwood and Edward Crandall. In fact, Marcus Carmady, the former underworld czar and father of the detective, bears the same initials as Chandler's father, Maurice; the second corrupt father is Senator John Myerson Courtway. Besides fronting for the mob, Courtway disclaimed his illegitimate daughter, who then poisoned herself out of grief. Chandler's making an adult daughter rather than a small son the story's fatherless victim preserves the archetypal figure as a worldly success who fails morally and then suffers the sting of his failure.

III

A rehearsal of familiar Chandler motifs will again reveal the writer's ephemera as more expressive of his creative unconscious than his novels. The Marlowe of *The Long Goodbye* calls saying goodbye a form of dying because cutting oneself from the past also denies the people and/or events that have formed one's character. Marlowe needn't have viewed the past so sentimentally. As Chandler's treatment of family life shows, the past can never be shed. Marcel Proust, who is mentioned in *The Big Sleep*, believes that experience acquires meaning, not at its moment of occurrence, but in reflection. Chandler's Proustian streak cuts deeper tracks than is usual in action writers. The little-read fantasy "Professor Bingo's Snuff" (*Park East*, June-August 1951; *Go*, June-July 1951), records the supremacy of adult moral conditioning over the instincts. By inhaling magical snuff, the story's main character can make himself disappear. He vanishes once in order to murder his wife; an invisible murderer can't be arrested. Nor can he enjoy the fruits of his villainy, he learns. Although his murder plot succeeds, he turns himself in to the police and confesses his guilt. Chandler's other fantasy, "The Bronze Door" (*Unknown*, November 1939), also poses a wild and ultimately unworkable solution to marital conflict. In the Proustian sense, it describes the corrosion caused by achieving one's hopes. The morality implicit in his warning also captures Chandler's conservative, elitist faith in civilized conduct.

The traditionalism that the story will question before vindicating shows in the story's English setting. Timid James Sutton-Cornish follows the main figures of "Professor Bingo's

Snuff" and "A Couple of Writers" in being henpecked. Within hours of brassy Louella's walking out on him, he buys a huge oriental door, through which things vanish forever. Though promising renewal, the carved door defeats Sutton-Cornish. His undoing begins immediately. He lets himself be fleeced by the seller of the door, buying at the quoted price rather than bargaining; he wastes more money by paying for the drayage and then tipping the drayman. His degeneration in the presence of the door continues. So neglectful and slovenly does he become after buying the door that his butler, parlormaid, and cook all resign. His beautiful ancestral home grows dirty and dilapidated. Reflecting this decline, Sutton-Cornish drinks more and more and locks his door to visitors. His excursions outside the dark home take him to low dives, where he eats his meals among other faded, twilit men. This process of self-negation ends with his disappearing through the bronze door.

Although an artistic trifle, the story says a great deal about Chandler. The split between an alcoholic husband and a shrewish wife that is threatened but not enacted in "A Couple of Writers" happens in "The Bronze Door." The story's English setting and fantastic narrative mode freed Chandler's moral imagination. Ironically, this freedom offended his conservatism while hampering, rather than whetting, his creativity. His values had already formed and hardened. His cutting of the cable with reality restored him to reality with a slamming recoil. The middle-class virtues of reason, property, and moral stability surpass dreams of freedom, surpass freedom itself for him. Dreams that come true end in grief, just as total freedom leads to madness and isolation. For the sake of sanity, controls must be maintained. The bronze door, with its promise of power and adventure, deserved to be smashed after claiming its last victim and owner. Sutton-Cornish, too, should have stayed married to Louella, scold that she was. By opting for freedom, even the false freedom of the bottle, he destroyed both of them.

"The Bronze Door" is one of Chandler's darkest stories, its author giving its weak hero two grim choices. Sutton-Cornish can die the drunkard's sad, slow death or he can dart through the bronze door. Although the alternative is never posed, he can also cut his drinking and try to win back his wife. The story puts meaning with the individual; Sutton-Cornish, the buyer of the bronze door, not the door itself, causes the havoc. Chandler keeps hope alive for him. Yet, alcoholic and wife-ridden himself, he also knows that Sutton-Cornish has annihilated hope. Marlowe notes at the end of Chapter 12 of *The Long Goodbye*, "There is no trap as deadly as the trap you set for yourself." Like Sutton-Cornish, most of Chandler's other people hurt themselves more than their enemies could; even Marlowe foils himself with his self-imposed fear of playing the sucker or patsy. Chandler will extend compassion to a humanity that defeats itself. Though less compassionate toward evildoers than Ross Macdonald, he nonetheless adopted a relativism that encompasses both primitive justice and his heart's craving for mercy.

A doctor in *The Long Goodbye* claims to embody the dialectic: "I am a mixed character like most people," says the doctor. He might have added that duress sometimes forces him to compromise; nobody in Chandler is as moral as he/she would like to be. The doctor's claim, "All I do is help people and all they do is kick me in the teeth," deepens the struggle. Though the doctor, an unsympathetic figure, is speaking out of blatant self-interest, his likable ex-patient admits to "feeling like a bastard" for withholding payment. The ex-patient's saying moments later of his unpaid $5000 debt, "Maybe I'll give it to him. He's broke," shows mercy tempering justice. It's significant that the speaker is Roger Wade, the novelist. By using an imaginative writer to express a morality, Chandler, no Brecht, endorses it. Although Wade is never seen writing a $5000 check to his dunning doctor, his desire to do so voices Chandler's faith in both generosity and the wisdom of extending others the benefit of doubt.

This charity operates at different levels. A sadist can disclose a tender heart. Al DeSpain, the brutal cop in "Bay City Blues" (*Dime Detective*, June 1938), deals out the most savage hammering in all of Chandler within moments of acting gently with a woman he rescues. Not only does he remove the tapes from the woman's mouth and wrists; encouraging the belief that her husband is still alive, he also tells her softly to spend the night with friends. The narrator-sleuth's final judgment of DeSpain, after the policeman dies following his unmasking as the culprit, is both tender and dignified: "I liked DeSpain. He had all the guts they ever made." Because of its persistence, however infrequent, such charity compels our attention. Chandler's sleuth also tells a morphine-peddling physician who helped cover up his wife's murder in the same story, "You in your quiet way have a lot of guts." Perhaps he can afford kindness; its recipient is under arrest, just as DeSpain had to die before being eulogized in the same scene. In both cases, evil-doing has sparked a dialectic that sorts well with Freud's view of criminal justice: Both to deter murder and to vindicate the law, lifetakers must be punished. But because they do in actuality what the rest of us merely fantasize about, their jail sentences will get reduced; this reduction is our tribute to their courage.

Dialectic can also occur within the felon. The drive that compels people to commit crimes also compels them to be punished. The lawbreaker's unspoken respect for the law runs high in the canon. Chandler could never explain the death of Owen Taylor, the Sternwood's chauffeur in *The Big Sleep*. But an explanation uncoils from his later work. That guilt over killing the pornographer Arthur Gwynn Geiger drove Taylor to suicide gains plausibility from the finale of Chandler's next novel, *Farewell, My Lovely*. Marlowe interprets Helen Grayle's suicide as an act of contrition and redemption. By shooting herself, Mrs. Grayle, the former Velma Valento, punishes herself for killing Moose Malloy. What is just as important is her committing suicide to shield the man she loved. The only way left for her to vindicate the rule of love is to spare her sick, ageing husband the ordeal of watching her being tried in court as Moose's killer. The ordeal would have crushed him, even though she'd have not been convicted. Her sacrifice shows that Chandler's most lethal figures—all of whom are beautiful women—have vulnerable, sympathetic sides. Another poisonous beauty, Eileen Wade of *The Long Goodbye*, has no husband to protect, having murdered him. But rather than facing a trial in which she'd have been acquitted, owing to her social clout, she kills herself. Like that of Velma before her, her act of primitive justice shows the law in Chandler to be intrinsic and not imposed.

A world in which destruction explodes so quickly offers little comfort or safety. Despite his money, his mansion, and his oil wells, General Sternwood will soon die. Lewin Lockridge Grayle, the millionaire who controls much of Bay City in *Farewell, My Lovely*, has bought, in Velma/Helen, something he can't control well enough to enjoy. As has been seen, Grayle ranks alongside other powerful figures who find marriage alienating. Nor can the alienation be healed. Dr. Vincent Lagardie of *The Little Sister*, a Sorbonne graduate, leaves his midwestern practice to peddle drugs in sleazy Bay City because he wants to be near the wife, or ex-wife, he later kills. Seized by the same kind of love-hate frenzy, Al Degarmo (like his prototype, Al DeSpain, of "Bay City Blues") kills his former wife in *The Lady in the Lake*. Dr. Albert Almore's dependence upon his office nurse in the same book intensifies the sour impression of marriage created by *Farewell, My Lovely*,

"The Bronze Door," and *The Blue Dahlia;* ex-wives and even lovers can bullyrag a man as completely as a wife. Characters like Moose Malloy, Dr. Lagardie, and Al Degarmo show that men love more recklessly in Chandler than women do; driven to wilder extremes both of loyalty and fury, Chandler's men put aside reason and safety to join with the beloved. The danger bred by this juncture helps explain Marlowe's ability to stay single into his forties.

The granite-like bleakness facing Marlowe as he travels alone deeper into mid-life is symbolized by the color gray. Gray almost always refers to death in Chandler. "The Bronze Door," that demonstration of protest-as-madness, begins on a gray day; Louella Sutton-Cornish, one of Chandler's most vicious women, has a "long gray stare"; her husband's degeneration makes him look gray. Gray even connects to death more dramatically in other works. A man dies in a gunfight at Gray Lake in "Trouble is My Business" (*Dime Detective*, August 1939), and the corpse of Edward Crandall in "English Summer" materializes in a "gray stillness." The grayness-as-death motif also appears in the novels. Eddie Mars, the gambler who causes most of the wreckage in *The Big Sleep*, enters the novel as a gray shape:

He was a gray man, all gray, except for his polished black shoes and two scarlet diamonds in his gray satin tie.... His shirt was gray and his double-breasted suit of soft, beautifully cut flannel. Seeing Carmen he took a gray hat off and his hair underneath it was gray .... His thick gray eyebrows had that indefinably sporty look.

Such harmony blocks the flow of oxygen. The "complete composure" Mars manifests in the scene suggests a corpse. Composed in the sense of having been dressed and groomed, this walking testimony to the undertaker's art harms old and young, rich and poor, outlaw and lawman. The grayness that signals his destructiveness recurs in *The Little Sister*, where a faded, out-of-work actor wears a gray homburg and where a gray-faced mortician owns a gray hearse.

Besides getting lost in the gray mists, Chandler's truthseekers are also misled by differences between appearance and reality. Things are not what they seem in Chandler. The modern criminal, for instance, has cultivated a talent for respectability; he dresses quietly, speaks softly and grammatically and surrounds himself with objects reflecting good taste; most of the elegant homes in the canon are owned by crooks. The physical toughness of an Eddie Mars or a Clark Brandon (*Playback*) describes the athlete, not the thug. Another sign of a criminal's power is his anonymity. Eddie Mars hires henchmen to do his killing; the gambler Laird Brunette of *Farewell, My Lovely* and the newspaper tycoon Harlan Potter of *The Last Goodbye*, though not equally villainous, both guard their privacy closely. Their ability to go against the Hollywood rage for publicity shows Yankee self-reliance encroaching upon wisdom. Justice works poorly amid shadows. When the big-time racketeer isn't hiding his villainy behind a genteel facade, he's burying it.

The appearance-reality rift which helps him prosper resembles, in its effects, the gulf created by the innocence-experience dualism. Usually deemed a virtue, innocence perpetuates tyranny in *The High Window*; moral seasoning commensurate to her age would help Merle Davis stand up to Mrs. Murdock. *The Little Sister* shows innocence scorning the family tie for material profit; the younger the Quest sib, the more mercenary and indifferent to others he/she is. Moose Malloy of *Farewell, My Lovely* dies because he believes he can recover the joy he knew with Velma eight years before, even though he hasn't heard from her for the past six. Innocence destroys most spectacularly in *The Big Sleep* in the person of that giggling, thumbsucking incontinent, Carmen Sternwood. Carmen's behavior bespeaks a homicidal idiot. Her morality is stark. The men she likes, and calls "cute," she wants to sleep with; those she dislikes, usually for rejecting her sexually, she tries to kill. But she does more than enact the destructiveness of innocence. Like Orfamay Quest, the littler of Manhattan, Kansas's sisters, she also helps point up Chandler's strident distrust of youth. That this distrust shows Chandler at his worse emerges clearly when contrasted with the generosity and courage displayed by the young in Ross Macdonald. Youngsters usually rebel in Ross Macdonald's fiction because their elders are withholding information they need to feel complete. The anti-social behavior manifested by youths in Chandler relates strictly to sex and money.

What is more, this behavior is usually female. Aside from minor figures, Chandler's fiction contains very few men under thirty; even the unformed Leslie Murdock is thirty. His marriage helps make him an aberration. Most of Chandler's other youthful males sport muscles, smooth, bronze California skin, and the animal good looks that help them live off women. Chandler shows his contempt for these tomcats by making them so alike; like poverty and death, immorality always similarizes in Chandler. Each of them lives and dies the same way and for the same reason. Not content to be gigolos, they pry secrets from their rich clients at unguarded moments and set up as blackmailers. Their ambitions undo them, vindicating both the general truth that characters who know too much often die in mystery stories and Chandler's particular belief that we can hurt ourselves more than any foe can. If the regularity with which Chandler kills off his blackmailing gigolos implies sexual resentment of the young and virile, it also dramatizes the problem he had all his writing career of matching surface glamor to the grim underlying reality. "He had a hard time controlling his exaggerated response to physical appearance," says Davies. His insightful reading continues: "The number of beautiful, worthless women and fine-looking men in his stories testifies to his lasting puzzlement over this matter, in particular whether beauty is truth or perfidy."[33] Others have found Chandler's beautiful women frightening. Referring to Helen Grayle and Eileen Wade, Michael Mason says, "The most brutal murders in the Marlowe novels are committed by women with whom the hero has had an erotically exciting contact."[34]

Even the sexually restrained Marlowe feels the lure of female beauty. But he also watches Helen Grayle ánd Eileen Wade carefully when confronting them with their guilt. As soon as the former's evil is unearthed, her glamor deserts her: "She leaned forward a little and her smile became a little glassy. Suddenly, without any real change in her, she ceased to be beautiful. She looked ... Grade B Hollywood." On the other hand, the stunning Eileen Wade, whom George P. Elliott has called "the blonde of blondes,"[35] never looks better than when Marlowe reconstructs her murder of her husband. Marlowe, in both these denouements, creates as well as observes. The man in him has driven out the moralist, the change in his reactions to the two murderesses voicing Chandler's willingness to be human, even at the cost of inner peace.

Sometimes the appearance-reality interplay generates less tension. Already noted has been the tendency of big-time racketeers to surround themselves with elegance; often, the more splendid a gangster's adornments, the more vicious he is. Aspiring to the carriage trade, racketeer Mendy Mendendez of *The Long Goodbye* owns a Bentley, two Cadillacs, and an MG; a butler, two maids, and a cook help maintain his Bel-Air mansion; his two children attend private schools in the east. Yet these signs

of privilege clash so jarringly with Menendez's ill breeding that
they accentuate his vulgarity rather than civilizing it. With less
irony, Chandler will match other characters to their
surroundings. Hotels, for instance, he identifies with
homelessness; the itinerant, the unsettled, and the lonely stay in
hotels in *The Little Sister, The Long Goodbye,* and *Playback.* The
hotel can also portend bloodshed. House detectives in "The King
in Yellow" (*Dime Detective,* March 1938) and "I'll Be Waiting"
(*Saturday Evening Post,* 14 October 1939) disclose the dark side of
the daytime bourgeois personality. Once set in motion, the
darkness rolls in quickly. Many of Chandler's more violent
stories begin in hotels, like "Smart-Aleck Kill" (*Black Mask,* July
1934), "Guns at Cyrano's" (*Black Mask,* January 1935), and "The
King in Yellow." Identifying oneself with hotels brings on death.
Two men in *The Little Sister* die in hotel rooms leased by them. In
Tony Acosta of "Guns at Cyrano's," the closeness of the
identification chokes off hope. Working as a bell captain in one
hotel while living in another, Tony gets murdered halfway into
the story.

A character even less equipped to survive than the hotel
person is the one who uses aliases. As Helen Grayle/Velma
Valento proves, multinymity denies the stability and wholeness
of a unified, continuous self. The contrast between her glamorous
present and her tawdry past explains her wish to start anew. But
people with something to hide in Chandler can't escape grief,
regardless of what they call themselves. A jewel thief in
"Goldfish" (*Black Mask,* June 1936), one of Chandler's top
stories, changes his name and moves to northern Washington,
just inside the national border. He gets killed, anyway,
appropriately by two other crooks who have come to his hideaway
to claim the pearls he stole twenty years before. The jewel thief's
death shows the futility of concealment, the appearance of his
two foils on his doorstep revealing that he can't hide from
himself. Other characters in Chandler point the same lesson. Six
different names and three different faces, two of them the result of
plastic surgery, don't shield Terry Lennox of *The Long Goodbye*
from grief. Chandler's *realpolitik* reads morality as a seamless
whole in which effects follow causes. Any attempt to wrench this
law brings on redress. Lennox will probably live out his patched-
up life in Latin America, away from his origins and friends. His
being shot to death by Marlowe in the 1973 movie version of *The
Long Goodbye* merely carries forward the process of self-negation
described in the novel.

A turnabout as sharp as that displayed in characters who change their names comes in Chandler's treatment of midwesterners. The tough, self-possessed Chicago detective, Mallory, of Chandler's first published story, "Blackmailers Don't Shoot" (*Black Mask*, December 1933), takes on vice and corruption in the film industry, the police force, and organized gambling. His half victory, the most Chandler will permit him, surpasses by light years the defeat awaiting other midwesterners who bring hopes to L.A., like Wichita's Merle Davis (*The High Window*), Orrin Quest of Manhattan, Kansas (*The Little Sister*), and the bumptious Kansas City detective Ross Goble (*Playback*). That Goble is thrashed by a gangster, Merle browbeaten by her employer, and Quest murdered shows the variety of hurt awaiting the naive midwesterner in morally ravaged Los Angeles. Belonging, perhaps, in this sad roster of beleaguered midwesterners is Steve Skalla of "Try the Girl," Moose Malloy's prototype, who committed a crime in Kansas that sent him to jail.

If Chandler reconsidered the midwesterner's lot in California, his view of blackmail remains the same from the time of his first published story. Blackmailers don't shoot their victims because they want to wring them as long as possible. In fact, as has been seen, the relationship between blackmailer and victim always ends in the former's death; the secret worth paying to scotch also merits murder to crush. Blackmail flourishes in L.A. because of the obsession with surface, sensation, and image haunting the area. The female craving for intimacy, as a deterrent to celluloid values, turns men like Lindsay Marriott of *Farewell, My Lovely*, Louis Vannier of *The High Window*, Lancelot Goodwin of *The Lady in the Lake,* Chris Lavery of *The Lady in the Lake,* and Larry Mitchell of *Playback* into gigolos and then into blackmailers. Perhaps Chandler put the letter L into each of these men's names to hint at the perversion of love into lust and lucre, a process that must end in loss to the sexual Victorian, Chandler. The process obeys an iron logic, since everything happens instantly in southern California. It also discloses the emptiness both of the gigolo's clients and of the clients' marriages. The disclosure can be extended. Chandler's people don't startle us. They're neither incalculable nor extraordinary, just drably acquisitive, frightened and vain, all of which makes them blackmailable. Blackmail awaits anyone who lives by his/her image; a preoccupation with surface dulls the inner planes of perception.

And where are images prized more to the detriment of adult feelings than in Hollywood? The dangers unleashed by the attempt to win, hold, and protect an image amid tinsel and celluloid can't be blocked. "Blackmailers Don't Shoot" describes the dangers. Mallory's client, an actress whose career at Eclipse Films is in eclipse, says, "Publicity, darling. Just publicity. Any kind is better than none at all. I'm not sure my contract is going to be renewed and I'll probably need it." Rhonda Farr's obsession with her image goes beyond her craving for attention. It also hurts others. Mallory has risked his life to help promote her foundering career; four other men have died scrambling for the letters she originally hired Mallory to recover. These letters she now calls worthless forgeries. His rebuke to her, "You're a nasty little rat. I don't like you," voices Chandler's disquiet with a mentality that trades on surfaces and appearances. Rhonda's treachery tallies some of the damage stemming from the need for darkness and bright lights. The aliases and disguises (even Marlowe does some impersonations) and the greed which misleads gigolos into blackmailing add to Chandler's criticism of Hollywood. The depredations created by the screen industry are contagious. The Chandler corpus bristles with self-blamers; besides Merle Davis of *The High Window*, men like Bill Chess of *The Lady in the Lake* and both Terry Lennox and Roger Wade of *The Long Goodbye* downgrade their virtues while playing up their failings. The terms of Derace Kingsley's appeal to Marlowe in *The Lady in the Lake* rests upon a distortion just as enticing to a blackmailer. Kingsley hires Marlowe to protect his job, not because he loves his missing wife.

Kingsley's rugged good looks, abrupt manner, and brusque self-assurance mask an inner void which the seasoned Marlowe quickly exposes. If the mainspring of satire is wasted effort, then Kingsley's male swagger quickly becomes the butt of Chandler's jest. Not only do his colleagues know him to be insecure and hollow; the wife Kingsley is worrying about has also been dead a month before he starts looking for her. The jest recoils upon Chandler. Besides using irony to mock someone nearing one of life's worst shocks, Chandler's resentment of handsome younger men violates a basic tenet of fiction—reverence for the individuality of the individual. Yes, the speed with which blackmailers in Chandler die at the hands of their victims describes blackmail as self-defeating. But his use of the biter-bit, that legacy of Renaissance drama, also betrays Chandler's tendency both to gloat and to scold by trivializing. Collective judgments in the canon usually convey moral disapproval, as is shown in his verismo catalogs of urban degradation. Derace

Kingsley, who Chandler hints wasn't man enough to win his wife's sexual loyalty, suffers more than any of Chandler's L-named blackmailers. His youthful build and handsomeness have unfairly earned him his author's contempt. His being in love with another woman while still married doesn't sink him to the level of Chandler's tomcat blackmailers. In his rush to blame and punish, Chandler has forgotten to distinguish degrees of sexual misbehavior. By the end of the novel, he has stripped Kingsley of dignity.

Such surrenders to prejudice give Chandler the look of a one-note writer. They also block his view of our deep and abiding drive to violence. The tawdriness he depicts seems contrived and mean-minded when directed to men who threaten him. It sometimes exists in his work to give him the chance to rail against it. What saves this special pleading from cheapening his art more than it does is the excellence of his prose. By writing well, Chandler creates an illusion of vitality from the posed and the calculated. But style can also deepen rather than mitigate the impression he sometimes gives of believing in the inherent badness of America. In Marlowe's journalistic diatribes, waste and depravity are everywhere. People have little fun together, withhold help in time of need, and exploit one another regardless of their tie. This squalor, couched as blanket judgments, reflects Chandler's tendency to reject what is most productive, but also perhaps most painful, in himself—the singing tension created by his ambivalence. His rejection causes regret. The struggle of warring impulses tires him, lowers his resistance to the facile and the prefabricated, and makes him sulk and scold. After such moments, romantic stereotypes offer refuge. Chandler could reject a fresh idea as summarily as he could youthfulness. Although his career as a novelist spanned 1939-58, his social views stem from the era of Prohibition and the Depression; these views had already calcified by the Marxist 1930s.

About the problems of the 1940s and '50s, during which time his novels unfold, he says little. His neglect of the cold war, of problems created by the lack of effective birth control, and of the impact of technology (especially upon the air of greater L.A.) makes him look rearguard in his own artistic heyday. Leigh Brackett, author of the screenplay of *The Long Goodbye*, finds his fictional Los Angeles dated: "The Los Angeles Chandler wrote about was long gone," she said in 1969, adding, "In a sense it never really existed outside his imagination."[36]

Brackett's disclaimer rests upon Chandler's fixation with the films of the early 1930s, his criminology, economics, social theory, and urban history all connect crime with power and money; the social and political elite comprise the biggest crooks. He ignores the complex mechanism of money, rank, and property. In that the effects of corruption and decadence interest him more than the dynamics, he's not a social novelist. But he never pretended to be one. Brackett's assessment, though astute, over-looks the truth that his technique is more pictorial and dramatic than analytical. Chandler wasn't a system builder but a social observer interested chiefly in the sounds of American speech. His observations filter through his narrator-detective Marlowe. The talk, color, and smell of L.A. both cling to and issue from Marlowe. If Chandler imagined the city into life, Marlowe helps make it memorable. The period feel and flavor of his L.A. stay with us. The city's rundown frame bungalows and elegant mansions encompass a social range that creates a map of society. What is more, the map includes more than streets, buildings, traffic, and people. Chandler relieves it with brilliantly observed details of natural scenery. Ruehlmann has said correctly of him, "No one has a sharper botanical eye."[37] In "No Crime in the Mountains" (*Detective Story,* September 1941), that eye promotes a lyricism whose haunting details contrast admirably with the informational tone: "The knolls...were covered with ironwood trees.... Ironwood grows to about eighteen or twenty feet high and then dies. When it dies the limbs strip themselves and get a gray-white color and shine in the moonlight." *The Lady in the Lake* also yokes his eye to other faculties. Driving north from L.A., Marlowe goes out of his way to enjoy the scenery: "We'll switch over to Foothill Boulevard and you'll see five miles of the finest grevillea trees in the world." Earlier, his botanical flair had gained him the upper hand in an interview with a balky witness:

I pointed to the spray of manzanita in the fireplace. "You pick that up at Little Fawn Lake?"
"The hills around here are full of manzanita," he said contemptuously. "It doesn't bloom like that down here."

The health of any community can be gauged by the way people in the community interact both with their environment and with one another. Frederic Jameson's view of L.A. in 1970 as an urban sprawl lacking both a purpose and a principle of unity credits Chandler with the gift of prophecy:

Los Angeles is already of a kind of microcosm and forecast of the country as a whole: a new centerless city, in which the various classes have lost touch with each other because each is isolated in his own geographical compartment.[38]

Because it peddles hollow values and inflates them to the size of a movie screen, Los Angeles is America writ large. Chandler's L.A. describes American rugged individualism gone berserk, the exercise of the will defeating, rather than serving, the self. Marlowe knows he can't afford to yield to the lures of sex and money; no gigolo or blackmailer he. His survival depends on his tempering the will with reason and restraint. Will denotes striving, often a blind craving. As Moose Malloy discovers, the will can crush everything in its path, including the instinct to survive. The same American individualism extolled by Max Lerner in *America as a Civilization* (1957) threatens to recoil upon and destroy itself in Chandler:

> As the children of the reformation, Americans took over not only its dominantly Protestant heritage but also its deep individualist strain . . . . Each man was the judge of his own religious convictions . . . . The result has been an American religious tradition which is at once deeply individualistic, anti-authoritarian, concerned with sin and salvation, yet secular and rationalistic in its life goals.[39]

Chandler's social philosophy opposes the American middle-class drive to get ahead. Rejecting politics, business and technology, it rests on the belief that all human transactions are poisoned. The creed of self has blocked all avenues of negotiation. An honest man can't earn a decent living now that power has become concentrated in ever fewer hands, all of which are soiled. Crime has taken over so much of our daily life that a young man in *The Big Sleep* gives his girl friend a handgun for her birthday. The rich sicken Marlowe because they've been dulled to the finer things, they don't care about the problems facing the world, and they have no thought of man as a complex individual. The control they exert over politics, public welfare, education and the corporate structure frees them to smash and grab at will. Chandler's early working title for *Farewell, My Lovely*, "Law Is Where You Buy It," implies the power of the rich to take what they want while protecting themselves legally; selfishness is the most conservative political creed of all. But in Chandler, often one of the safest; Peter J. Rabinovitz shows how power, once entrenched, can work its will without check:

Evil cannot be uprooted by logic alone: there is simply too much of it; it is too well organized and too well protected by "legitimate" institutions. It is hard, sometimes impossible, to capture the wrongdoers—and even if you can, society ... will continue to spawn them.[40]

The cancerous effects of power and wealth are recorded in a short but telling exchange between Marlowe and a policeman in *The Long Goodbye*. A man can't earn an honest dollar, the exchange implies, because vested interests have leached free enterprise of its freedom:

"Organized crime is just the dirty side of the sharp dollar."
   "What's the clean side?"
   "I never saw it."

The Little Sister uses narrative structure to convey Chandler's belief that power has made life sordid and brutal. Chapter Eighteen, the central chapter in this novel about Hollywood, introduces the god figure or celebrant. Handsome and dapper, Sheridan Ballou has adorned himself with the trappings of culture—a grand piano, bookshelves, and fine French brandy. But he is an agent, not a star. And he has a headache so bad that he's lying on a couch. Tired and cranky, this groaning man has no wisdom to impart. He won't even look at Marlowe when introduced to him. Chandler includes Ballou in his anatomy of Hollywood for a reason. The movie industry consists of more than actors, directors, and shooting sets. The entourage of aides and retainers whose names never appear on credit lists exert real control. Though the public may never hear of effete, ill-mannered Sheridan Ballou, it watches the films he selects and the performers he wants to loft to stardom. His obscurity proves once again that power works most effectively and most ruthlessly when it works invisibly. Invisibility gives the magnate license while freeing him of accountability. With his henchmen running interference for him and the law supporting him, he can do what he pleases. His pleasure, it scarcely needs saying, adds no whit of beauty, knowledge or happiness to anyone but himself. Sometimes, pleasure eludes even him; the whining Ballou acts more confused by his power than pleased.

   Some policemen would try to stop the industrial mogul were their chiefs not on his payroll. The scorn Chandler accords doctors, describing them as charlatans or needle pushers, he tempers in his treatment of the police. Yes, cops do take bribes, shut off investigations when ordered to from above, and lure the innocent into crime in order to arrest them. The Marlowe of *The Lady in the Lake* is forced to break the speed limit to escape a pursuing squad car in a lonely spot; once caught, he has liquor splashed on his clothes to give the impression at the station house that he was driving while drunk. Then he is beaten up for allegedly resisting arrest. Stupid, sadistic policemen appear throughout Chandler. In "The Man Who Liked Dogs" (*Black Mask*, March 1936), three people with weapons drawn and a killer dog nearby manage to avoid violence, which only erupts when the police enter the scene. Aside from breaking the peace they're pledged to protect, the police commit numerous other wrongs in the story. The detective reviews some of these for the local police chief:

"*You* had me doped until I was half goofy and stuck me in a private jail. When that didn't hold me *you* worked a plant up ... to have my gun kill ... your helper, and then have me killed resisting some arrest."

The evil is squelched. In a rare concluding summary, Chandler begins the story's last paragraph, "By that time the County Grand Jury had indicted half the police force of the little beach city." Similar reforms take place at the end of *Farewell, My Lovely* in Bay City, i.e., Santa Monica. This housecleaning redeems much of the squalor undermining police activity in Chandler. The removal of Anne Riordan's father as chief of police for being too honest had turned the force over to local racketeers. Most of the graft and brutality in the canon comes from stooges installed by the mob after the Riordan firing. The L.A. police are usually honest and cooperative. An L.A. police captain in *The Long Goodbye* not only shows Marlowe restricted material; he also lets the detective remove it from the station house. The Esmeralda, i.e., La Jolla, police of *Playback* are exemplary in appearance, training, and moral fiber. The reform of the Bay City Police at the end of *Farewell, My Lovely* leaves the police in Chandler no worse than any other cross section of people. Though a cop may still take the odd bribe or even pound a drunk, he also faces the pressures caused by low pay, job insecurity and dangers far surpassing those accompanying most other lines of work.

Chandler's sensitivity to these pressures modulates his descriptions of police brutality. Al Degarmo, the cynical, violent police lieutenant in *The Lady in the Lake*, cares enough about his home to kill anyone who violates it, including the wife who divorces him. His putting his personal morality above the law leads to crime. But even though it destroys, his vigilante justice resembles the conduct of Marlowe, who also breaks the law to satisfy his conscience. Chandler's recognition of this resemblance may have prompted him to spare Degarmo the degradation of arrest, trial and conviction. Marlowe's asinine statement in *The Long Goodbye*, "In a way cops are all the same. They all blame the wrong things," represents but one side of the detective. Another, just as important, spurns the knee-jerk judgment in favor of recognizing ambiguity and accepting the burden of choice. He remarks inwardly, also in *The Long Gooodbye*, "That's the trouble with cops. You're all set to hate their guts and then you meet one that goes human on you." Marlowe goes human himself when he decides in favor of the police in *Playback*. Rather than returning or keeping a $5000 fee given him by a racketeer, he gives the money to the Police Relief Fund.

IV

Many of his other choices come less easily. Neither he nor Chandler ever decided whether sexual love brings out the worst in people and has to end in ruin. Knight speaks of Chandler's sexual anxiety, identifying his "ultimate villains" as sexy women and their victims as foils of Marlowe.[41] The murderesses in *Farewell, My Lovely* and *The Long Goodbye*, as others beside Knight have noted, are outstanding beauties with whom Marlowe has had sexual contact. Marlowe will resist sex when he can. In *The Big Sleep*, he denies Vivian Regan sexually after a session of heavy kissing because she's his client's daughter. The sexual provocation and arousal he shares with Helen Grayle stops short of intercourse because her husband could interrupt them at any moment. The years weaken his resistance. In *The Long Goodbye* he has sex with Linda Loring and would have also bedded Eileen Wade ("I was as erotic as a stallion") but for the intrusion of the Wades' houseboy. His sexual integrity vanishes in *Playback*, where he sleeps with one client and with the secretary of another.

The "vehement disgust about female sexuality"[42] Mason finds in Chandler distorts and trivializes. If women didn't excite Marlowe, he'd not have needed to devise a sexual code; nor would he have violated the code as he got older and developed a need for other people. The hostility Mason refers to but overstates counterweights an attraction just as strong. In fact, it affirms the attraction, which preexisted it. The sexual revulsion Marlowe shows in the following passage from *The Long Goodbye*, for instance, implies conditions under which it could become attraction. Marlowe is describing a laughing woman seen at a swimming pool: "She opened a mouth like a firebucket and laughed. That terminated my interest in her. I couldn't hear the laugh but the hole in her face when she unzipped her teeth was all I needed." Although the woman's laugh was audible, its sound dissolved in the threatening image of her bright red lips and postgate teeth. The threat is that of the *vagina dentada*; Marlowe is afraid of being bitten and chewed. But female sexual cruelty also entices him. His many references to long red fingernails reveal his fascination. The first time he meets Linda Loring, she has the reddest nails he has ever seen. Red polish on long, well-manicured nails either makes a woman sexy or enhances her sexiness. The clawing abandon of swift red talons expresses the destructive passion men crave and fear. Chandler may have craved it more than most, coming home each night to a wife who offered little erotic enticement. The relief of not having to worry about birth control as he embraced Cissy must have given way to needs she couldn't satisfy as she aged and faded.

But sex remains secondary. Marlowe's sexual behavior shows that Chandler only prized the excitement represented by flashy young sirens (many of his male characters—*The High Window* has two—marry nightclub singers) as a temporary release. Once mannish lust was appeased, the boy's need for safety took over. It's doubtful that any woman could satisfy his craving for both excitement and security. The pain caused by his family's breakup and relocation in faraway England may not have encouraged him to be monogamous, but it always brought him back home for nurture. To satisfy appetite both kills appetite and allows other needs to move to the fore. The deepest loyalties of Chandler and Marlowe, conservative men both, bypassed the boudoirs of young beauties. Marlowe has sex with three women that we know of. If his having had one-night stands with two of them denotes fear to give deeply of himself, it also shows him using sex as an escape rather than a confrontation. (John Paringdon also has sex with Lady Lakenham in "English Summer" but once.) The evasiveness and instability that drive a man to casual sex bespeak a fear of commitment. The fear will declare itself in a need for control. The sexual overture or even the declaration of availability offends Marlowe. Preferring more shadowy, stylized contacts, he flinches from the overt. The woman in *The Long Goodbye* with the firebucket mouth and the gated teeth upsets him because her uninhibited laughter leaves nothing to the imagination; the woman who laughs forfeits the ability to charm with a smile. The surmised and the whispered can also charm a sensitive artistic personality long after physical desire has waned. MacShane believes that Chandler's dream girl persisted in his heart because she remained a dream. Perhaps the

knowledge that the dream could never become gross flesh kept it
alive:

He dreamed of a romantic fulfillment, union with the girl with the
cornflower blue eyes. All along—and this was his torture—he knew it
could never happen. Nevertheless, it remained the central vision of his
life.[43]

Chandler's juvenile verse rates the remote and the
unattainable over the here-and-now. No yarnspinner or social
critic, the early Chandler invokes omens and portents; the
imaginary grips him more tightly than the real. Prefiguring
Marlowe's sex life (the detective only married after Chandler
became a widower), he severed poetry from sensuous reality as
most of us know and live it. His subjects include the impalpable
and the evanescent. Following other romantic poets, his response
to them endows them with importance. The title, "An Old House,"
captures his fascination for what is decrepit and twilit. In the
poem (*Westminster Gazette*, 15 November 1911), he turns from
"smoothest lawn,/Trim hedges, and . . . posies neat" to the goblin
gloom of damp cellars, rusty walls, and ancient, sagging gates
(the climax of *The Big Sleep* takes place near some disused,
abandoned oil sumps). His preference for collapse over growth
looks forward to the novels, where the response of the perceiver
outranks the factual reality of the perceived. This transvaluation
proclaims the supremacy of Marlowe's purposes, fleeting and
selfish as they may be, over women's feelings. His unfitness for
the sacrifices of an ongoing relationship grounded in sex
announces itself in poetry written thirty years before *The Big
Sleep*. Avoiding the pragmatic world of cares, deeds and
compromises, the poet in "A Woman's Way" (*Westminster
Gazette*, 22 April 1909) describes himself and his beloved as "a
boy and girl in a playroom land." Early Chandler often
withdraws from the everyday to woo the ineffable. This mode of
courtship has advantages. His ladylove can be summoned and
loved at his convenience. Because she's a fantasy projection, she
can be invested with his hopes and dreams. She can also be
dropped. "The Unknown Love" (*Chamber's Journal*, 19
December 1908) recounts how she appears but once to the poet; a
more extended, continuous acquaintance, it is tempting to say,
would have dulled her luster. Her absence recommends her for the
same reason that the laughing woman in *The Long Goodbye* is
dismissed. Best of all, perhaps, is that the absence is permanent;
the beloved acquires value inversely to her availability. The
speaker in "A Lament for Youth" (*Westminster Gazette*, 9
February 1911) claims that his sweetheart died because she was

too good for the world. How can he be argued with? Like the wry, wistful Marlowe, another outsider, he has devised a mode of loving which enables him to be both apart from and together with his lady. But the negation of the lady as an independent center of significance has perverted love. Chandler is really talking about masturbation, and the firebucket woman is laughing both at him and Marlowe.

The laughter may have pained him. Twenty years after the appearance of "Trouble is My Business" (*Dime Detective*, August 1939), his last story of the decade featuring Marlowe, he gave the form, which he always found alien to his talents, one more try. Perhaps he wrote "The Pencil" (*London Daily Mail*, 6-10 April 1959) to give Marlowe a chance for an honorable alliance with Anne Riordan. The same twenty-eight-year-old virgin she was in *Farewell, My Lovely*, Anne has made very little impact upon the detective's heart. She couldn't. Marlowe doesn't value intelligence and kindness in women. To appreciate such virtues would entail an appreciation of their source. Having waited in her car outside the Grayle mansion while Marlowe was kissing and fondling Helen Grayle, Anne says, "Probably you'd like me to mind my own business .... And not have any ideas you don't have first." The censure is valid; Marlowe denies women room in which to grow. The ending of "Nevada Gas" (*Black Mask*, June 1935) prefigures Anne's censure. Marlowe frustrates Anne because of his suspicion that a sexual relationship doesn't afford growing room for two; she can scale whatever heights she likes, but not in his presence. As his name implies, Johnny DeRuse, the detective in "Nevada Gas," shares Marlowe's need to protect himself. Self-interest, he believes, not sharing, governs all human ties. The last three speeches spoken to him by his sweetheart consist of the same words: "Yes, honey." Anne Riordan's indictment of Marlowe has hit home. The Chandler hero wants a woman to agree with and to follow him. Only after Francine's last "Yes, honey," does DeRuse fall asleep—referring to himself as a "pigeon." He knows that lowering his guard in Francine's, or any woman's, presence will undo him. The story's closing image justifies his fears; the man of ruses falls prey to the ruse of another, partly because he wants to. Chandler says of Francine, "She sat very still and watched him, her face cupped in her long delicate hands with the cherry-colored nails." Francine's patience, her holding her own face and not that of her lover, and her mesmerizing red talons convey a real threat. DeRuse should sleep while he has the chance.

Marlowe's policy of keeping his defenses in place promises no better than DeRuse's grudging trust, and Chandler knew it; being on one's guard against possible enemies defeats pleasure. Yet his very act of resurrecting Anne Riordan from *Farewell, My Lovely* nineteen years later (twenty-two years later really, in that her prototype, Carol Pride, appeared in "Mandarin's Jade," in the November 1937 issue of *Dime Detective*) reflects the hope that she and Marlowe could have gotten together. But Marlowe walks away from her into a technicolor cliche. Eileen Wade of *The Long Goodbye*, a book that mentions F. Scott Fitzgerald, speaks of "the wild, mysterious, improbable kind of love that never comes but once." This notion, which is sharpened by making itself felt only after the death of the beloved, always appealed to the romantic in Chandler. He had already dramatized it in "Red Wind" (*Dime Detective*, January 1938) and *Farewell, My Lovely*. By the time he was drafting *The Long Goodbye*, Cissy's decline both restored and strengthened his faith in it, even though Gatsby, Anson Hunter of "The Rich Boy," and his own Moose Malloy had already shown the attempt to recover lost love to be fatal. In *Playback*, the notion plays itself out. Not only can't the bygone hero-lover be resurrected; the unique, overmastering love Eileen Wade spoke of can't be rekindled with the same person once the golden moment passes. No wonder the book shows Marlowe indulging in cheap sex; brought up on a diet of romantic stereotypes, he has never learned to trust his heart. As he did in the poems he wrote forty years before, Chandler put forth a sexual ideal so rarefied it was unlivable. Cynicism followed inevitably.

Chandler's sexual cynicism hinges on the notorious, self-demeaning division of women into sluts and saints. Because the Chandler hero wouldn't spoil a virgin, he finds sex in the gutter. Perhaps to punish himself for slumming or to charge sex with a mystery beyond the reach of his intellectual scorn, he connects it to fear and violence: the self-made man attaches his own surcharge to what is freely given. This imaginative connection has impressed Chandler's readers. In *The Dangerous Edge* (1976), Lambert says that "Chandler equates sexuality ... with danger. His novels are a notable addition to the popular mythology that represents death as a woman." Cawelti shows sex combining attraction and fear in *Black Mask* fiction generally. His remarks apply as strictly to the ambivalence-ridden Chandler as to any of his hardboiled counterparts: "Sex tends to be represented in a double-edge way in the hardboiled story," Cawelti writes. "It is an object of pleasure, yet it also has a disturbing tendency to become a temptation, a trap, and a betrayal."[44] Those two female sexual symbols, the door and the window, become the undoing of husbands in "The Bronze Door" (*Unknown,* November 1939) and *The High Window.* The merging of female sexuality and death undoes other men in the canon, both married and single. Within an hour or two of enjoying sex,

John Paringdon of "English Summer" discovers a male corpse; he leaves the vicinity where the carouse and the murder took place that same afternoon. Chandler juxtaposes sexual radiance and savagery in all his work. The second stanza of "Song at Parting" (c. 1941) begins, "He left a rose beside her head,/A meat axe in her brain." A woman in "I'll Be Waiting" says of her husband, "I played him a low trick once. I put him in a bad place— without meaning to." As in Strindberg, the deadliness of sexual love is all the more deadly for being involuntary and for exploding so suddenly. Horace Bright gets pushed through a high window because he makes a sexual pass at another woman in his wife's presence. Tony Dravec of "Killer in the Rain" (*Black Mask*, January 1935), Steve Skalla of "Try the Girl" (*Black Mask*, January 1937) and Moose Malloy, all of whom die for the love of a beautiful woman, show that the purer the love a man feels for a woman in Chandler, the more lethal the result.

Stunners like Helen Grayle and Eileen Wade also convey Chandler's belief that the most beautiful women are the deadliest. They have several counterparts. The flaxen beauty alluded to in the title of Chapter 8, "Poison Blonde," which concludes "Mandarin's Jade," has not only committed murder; her husband also enters the action a page and half from the end to say, "Shoot me .... I'm only your husband." He must be well acquainted with her homicidal ways. Of a movie actress in *The Little Sister* who slew her lover rather than share him, Marlowe says, "She was exquisite, she was dark, she was deadly." The same woman had kissed him, drawing the length of her body against his, while holding a gun in her hand. The destructive siren is often a redhead, red being Chandler's obsessive color. Carol Donovan of "Goldfish" (*Black Mask,* June 1936) combines youthful beauty and murderousness: "Her face was fresh and young and delicate, and as hard as a chisel," Marlowe says of her while looking into the bore of her automatic. The beauty of Helen Grayle is so magnetic that it controls men as different as the apelike Moose Malloy and her sick elderly husband. Helen Matson, Dr. Austrian's office nurse in "Bay City Blues" (*Dime Detective*, June 1938), who becomes the murderous Mildred Haviland in *The Lady in the Lake*, is called "a red-headed man-eater" for her practice of sacrificing men to her selfish purposes. Marlowe himself isn't safe from beautiful redheads. His attractive red-haired client in "Finger Man" (*Black Mask*, October 1934), his debut, is betraying him while supposedly relying on him to shield her from the syndicate.

Chandler's fear of beautiful women grew with the years. This heightening shows in the evil he fastened upon heretofore innocent female characters when he turned his short stories into novels. *The Big Sleep* introduces two such changes from a leading source, "The Curtain" (*Black Mask*, September 1936). The introduction of Harry Jones into the novel displays the meanness of Agnes Lozelle, Jones' live-in girlfriend. Rather than supporting Jones during a crisis, the glamorous Agnes leaves town. Also, the killer in "The Curtain," a male, becomes female in *The Big Sleep*. The expansion of "The Lady in the Lake" (*Dime Detective*, January 1939) into *The Lady in the Lake* includes the same kind of change; the transformation of Howard Melton to Derace Kingsley shifting the identity of the felon from Marlowe's male client to a woman. A darker manifestation of Chandler's sexual fears is the recurrence in his work of violence directed to women. Implying that women drive the best men wild are the batterings Chandler's detectives inflict on women. The nameless sleuth in "Killer in the Rain" punches two women. In "Try the Girl," Ted Carmady disarms a woman carrying two pistols by knocking her over with a bodyblock. Violence connects him to women. In order to help the story's heroine escape sentencing for the accidental death of her blackmailer, he makes her look as if she had killed the blackmailer in self-defense. To give the impression that she has just fought a death match, he tears her clothes and bruises her flesh: "I tore her coat off, tore it up plenty, put hard fingers into her arms and neck and used my knuckles on her mouth." Whether this slugging and mauling gives Carmady pleasure is never said. But his act of punishing the woman in order to protect her reflects the love-hate interplay general in Chandler. Further, Carmady's recollection of the incident implies that the beating gave his victim, not himself, sexual pleasure. Note the fusion of sexuality and contempt: "I hadn't even kissed her. I could have done that at least. She wouldn't have minded any more than the rest of the knocking about I gave her." Carmady's own highly figured description of his rough justice, with its references to food, betrays the fascination he has tried to ascribe to his victim. The contempt he feels is self-contempt, were he to admit it: "She had a lower lip the size of a banana and you could have cooked steaks on the bruises on her arms and neck, they were so hot."

From the start, Marlowe used violence to punish female wrongdoers. Perhaps intuiting the treachery of his client in "Finger Man," he restores her to consciousness more roughly than would seem appropriate. He punches the beautiful murderess Carol Donovan's jaw in "Goldfish." He will slap Carmen Sternwood to revive her or to silence her in *The Big Sleep*; the same novel finds him twice thumping Agnes Lozell's head with his pistol. Even in hardboiled fiction, such violence is rare. It can't be explained by saying that the detective's contempt for civil law has driven him to seek redress privately. Lew Archer never hit a woman, nor did Sam Spade. In a shocking image, Hammett's Continental Op slugs a male jewel thief in "Tom, Dick, or Harry" both while the thief is dressed as a woman and while the reader believes him a woman. Perhaps Hammett made the victim of the Op's haymaker a man because he didn't have the same bitter grudge against women that Chandler did.

Though Marlowe's brutality with women wanes as he ages, some of his actions, both with women *and* men, have prompted readers to accuse him of sexual abnormality. The accusation isn't unfair. His butchering of the homosexual youth, Carol Lundgren, in *The Big Sleep*, discloses more sadism than any other scene Chandler wrote except for the one in which Al DeSpain tortures Moss "Big Chin" Lorenz in "Bay City Blues." Both scenes display a relish for violence. DeSpain's depravity, reflected in his having been reduced from police lieutenant to patrolman before being dismissed from the force altogether and, finally, in his being named the murderer, also shows Chandler's moral intellect warring with his naked impulses. Chandler probably had mild homosexual leanings. But his inward pressure to repress them, his chronic self-doubt, and his tendency to magnify any trait in himself he construed as a failing aggravated them. Like some of his most likable characters, he was a self-blamer. The person with a poor self-image may shun the traps set for him by others, but will ensnare himself. Chandler was probably more hetero- than he credited; otherwise his drive to self-disparagement would have sunk him. He approached homosexuality, i.e., intellectually rather than instinctively. If the joys of straight sex sometimes incurred penalities, then from the drawbacks of gay sex might be teased out some pleasure.

His career-long intrigue with homosexuality, like D.H. Lawrence's with his, he would have fiercely denied. The kindness that shows a salt edge in "Killer in the Rain" recurs with a man as its object in *The Long Goodbye*, again near the end. Throughout the novel, Marlowe had extended more protection and affection to Terry Lennox than to any woman in the canon. Yet he rejects Terry in the novel's finale to satisfy his sense of personal justice. Plenty of other evidence can be mustered to support Gershon Legman's belief that Marlowe is "clearly homosexual."[45] The statement's validity, in fact, extends beyond Marlowe. As so often happens in Chandler, a minor work will sound a major chord. The wooden diction and the rich young narrator of "Pearls Are a

Nuisance" (*Dime Detective*, April 1939) make that story as much of an anomaly in Chandler as "The Nails in Mr. Cayterer" (1926) and "A Man Named Thin" (1962) are in Hammett. The sexual innuendoes in "Pearls," though, make the story richly expressive of Chandler. Walter Gage, the narrator-sleuth, both reflects and prefigures Marlowe. Though he claims to relish the company of his fiancée, Ellen Macintosh, Gage spends most of his time with Henry Eichelberger. He visits Ellen in Chapters 1 and 8, the beginning and the end, whereas he is constantly with Eichelberger after meeting him in Chapter 2. His final words in the story, in fact, refer to Eichelberger and not her. This finale was foreshadowed, however unconsciously. At the start of Chapter 3, Gage wakes up with Eichelberger lying beside him in bed. He objects to Eichelberger's drinking nearly as vehemently as Ellen objects to *his*. Finally, Eichelberger proves treacherous, as the detective's intimate did in "Finger Man," "Guns at Cyrano's" and *Farewell, My Lovely*, works in which the intimate was a woman.

The Chandler detective (including Eichelberger, because most of the way he seems to be helping Gage) embodies other female traits. As Ted Carmady did with Joe Mesarvey's wife in "The Curtain," Marlowe kisses Mona Mars in *The Big Sleep* after she reveals that she's wearing a wig. His references to her as Silver-Wig don't hide the truth that, during their brief embrace, she could be reminding him of a boy. The ambivalence turns the mind back to "Pearls Are a Nuisance."

The psyche that reacts erotically to male traits in women also finds femininity in men. Lou Harger, Marlowe's friend in "Finger Man," has the full red lips and long eyelashes normally belonging to women. The story's female lead, the villainous Miss Glenn, who is "something less than beautiful and more than pretty," also has long lashes. Whether Marlowe is sensitive to female qualities in men, actively looking for these qualities, or wishing them into existence counts less than his strong reaction to them. His first meeting with handsome Chris Lavery in *The Lady in the Lake* finds him the female observer assessing her man, revealingly a gigolo, as a potential bed partner. The near-pornographic detail with which he realizes Lavery recalls his scrutiny of Vivian Sternwood Regan in Chapter 3 of *The Big Sleep*. Taking in Lavery's "terrific torso and magnificent thighs," Marlowe calles him "a nice piece of beef" (Helen Grayle had told Marlowe, presumably just before having sex with him, "You have a lovely build, mister"). But neither Lavery nor Terry Lennox moves Marlowe as much as Red Norgaard, an ex-policeman dismissed from the Bay City Police in *Farewell, My Lovely* for resisting in-house corruption: "He had the eyes you never see, that you only read about. Violet eyes. Almost purple. Eyes like a girl, a lovely girl. His skin was as soft as silk. Lightly reddened, but it would never tan. It was too delicate." One wonders if Marlowe weren't the wide-eyed girl; Norgaard has certainly made him feel girlish. The dynamism generated by his extravagant response to the ex-cop will color all their future dealings. Norgaard helps him board the gambling ship *Montecito*, where he leaves the message that will bring Moose to his apartment to meet Helen Grayle. This teamwork evokes the ambiguity so typical of Chandler when deeply stirred. In playing the traditional wifely role of helpmeet, Norgaard helps crush the most selfless, delicate love in the canon.

Is Marlowe crushing Moose to punish him for displaying finer feelings than he, Marlowe, could ever afford? Perhaps to mock the big man's hopes, Marlowe receives him both in bed and in his pajamas. It is material that Moose lets himself into Marlowe's apartment and that the detective's last waking thoughts had turned lovingly to Norgaard: "I thought of the giant with the red hair and the violet eyes, who was probably the nicest man I had ever met." What is less material is whether Marlowe foresaw Moose's impending death. Chandler both foresaw it and engineered it as a love-in-death consummation. Through Marlowe he butchers Moose for trying to transform poetic truth into fact. The dream must remain intact. Although Moose and Helen/Velma both die, Norgaard's image lives untarnished in Marlowe's heart. The negation called forth by the first syllable of the boatman's name (Nor—) implies the Keatsian sacrifice Chandler was willing to make to preserve the image. Norgaard is the male counterpart of the blonde with the cornflower blue eyes, an ideal unsmirched by the drabness of every day. Chandler never forgot him. In his first appearance, "The Man Who Liked Dogs" (*Black Mask,* March 1936), as Red Norgaard, he impresses the detective immediately. Carmady's reaction to being told in "a soft, deep, sad voice" that Norgaard was bounced from the local police force anticipates the gentleness with which he and Marlowe will always respond to him: "I liked his telling me that. 'You must have been leveling,' I said." Later in the story, Carmady not only lends Norgaard $25 for a suit, but also closes the first-person narrative with a reference to the "big redheaded detective-sergeant," now reinstated on the force. The newspaper reference to a Captain William Norgaard of the General Robbery

Detail of the LAPD in "Pearls are a Nuisance" shows the persistence of Chandler's fascination. His hero has risen from Sergeant to Captain and from grubby little Bay City to Los Angeles. A throwaway reference in *The Lady in the Lake* to Al Norgaard, now a military policeman stationed away from home, shows the ideal retreating into the distance but also perhaps shining more brightly in the process. Norgaard's bigness, his absence, and his association with male authority all stir in Chandler the excitement originally called up by the missing father.

The inviolability of Norgaard in his imagination allowed Chandler to degrade other male characters whose sexuality moved him; ugliness and brutality always coexisted with tenderness and beauty for him. Ever mindful of Norgaard as a principle of balance, Chandler equated male sexuality with violence in the same kind of dialectic that linked violence with sexy women. An image from "Guns at Cyrano's" implies that the victim being described bled to death from the genitals:

Tony Acosta sat at the desk. His head was slumped forward on his left arm. Under the chair on which he sat, between the legs of the chair and his feet, there was a glistening brownish pool.

This image impacted deeply enough on Chandler for him to repeat it in "Trouble is My Business." Speaking of the story's first corpse, revealingly another detective, Marlowe observes, "He had an artery ... but I couldn't find it and he didn't need it any more anyway. Between his bloated legs on the carpet a dark stain had spread and spread—" Chandler's decision to end the sentence (and the paragraph) with a dash rather than a period invokes the motif of the spreading stain. The absence of a full stop implies the process by which crime rays out from the genitals to smirch all society.

The process perpetuates itself, crime in the story exuding a rank aroma of male sex. Marlowe describes few male characters as fully or as admiringly as he does the story's culprit. Noting the culprit's "nice black eyebrows," he phrases his approval of him, another big man, in overheated terms: "George looked nice with his cap off. His head was clustered over with wavy dark-brown hair and his teeth were very white and clean .... His snappy black eyes had a cool glitter in them." This attentiveness to male physicality pervades the story. Besides describing George in glowing detail, Marlowe says later that the younger and better looking of the two policemen questioning him threatened to beat him up. Did Marlowe lead the handsome young policeman on? The policeman's "tickling his upper lip with the end of his tongue" as he threatens Marlowe links violence to sexual provocation. Perhaps in response to some unreported act of Marlowe's, the policeman is flirting with his intended victim. The scene implies that sexual byplay is an attribute of police interrogation. A "fat and erotic" policeman, "with what looked like ... [a] cigar stub in his face," smiles a smile "broad as the door of a two-car garage" when he grips Marlowe's arm. Such bizarre formulations again link male sexuality to authority. To say that Chandler views policemen, with their rigid, battering nightsticks, as symbols of the male authority that punishes the nonconformist is to distort both his homosexuality and his masochism. Yet many of the policemen he wrote about hark to his father, whose leaving home robbed him of an authority model. The big, beefy policemen whose brutality drips sexual cruelty show how keenly he felt the loss.

The writing of hardboiled detective fiction answered a deep need in Chandler. Sadistic policemen like Lt. Copernick of "Red Wind" (*Dime Detective*, January1938) and Captain Gregorius of *The Long Goodbye* suited the image of society as urban nightmare set forth by *Black Mask* aesthetics. Chandler described such men in terrifying detail because he responded to them from a source deeper than that of social conscience. Police brutality both helps convey the pervasiveness of big city crime and provides an occasion for his remarkable style. It also symbolizes his disgust with that which precedes all awareness of rhetoric and social organization. Perhaps more than anything else, his ability to write from his presocialized self won him recognition as a literary artist.

Chapter Two

Margins of the Mean Streets

CHANDLER'S AMBIVALENCE carries into his artistic practice. Though his subject is often the trauma caused by vulgarity and crime, he shapes his responses to a pattern of literary detection dating from *Oedipus Rex*. Some of the pattern has already been filled in. Appearances deceive; a truth from the distant past (often referring to sex and violence) threatens the present; crime set into motion by efforts to bury the truth infects society, especially in its upper reaches. The tumescence spreads quickly, as an apparently small problem, like a missing coin, will give rise to more serious ones. Because the detective's client is often the criminal, important facts are suppressed. But the dodges of the guilty client help the detective in the long run, enabling him to weave a tighter fabric of proof. He must discover the truth alone. Enriching the narrative, his lone search both discloses a growing complexity of motives and brings in people of widely differing backgrounds.

I

In Chandler's mind, this process of discovery and analysis hadn't attained full artistic growth. In January 1951 he called detective fiction "one of the most parochial and overworked fields of writing there is."[1] What he had in mind was the artistic cramp imposed by both the nonstop action of American hardboiled detection and the rigorous logic featured in the English crime puzzle. The English, or what he called the cheesecake manor, school of detective writing riled him more than the American. He objected to both the social and the aesthetic assumptions of the cozy English mystery. Classic English literary detection, he complained, rates plot over character. Though the people can be fresh and lively, they always subserve the plot; their freedom is strictly monitored. The reader must care more about the process of mystification than about the people, including the detective. He/she must also share the

56

writer's rearguard ideas about rank, money, and property in order to feel that the naming of the felon serves the common good. The restoration of reason and justice, as these virtues are defined by an elitist morality, degrades the sleuth while appearing to elevate him. His splendid energies serve a snobbish and inequable status quo. What is more, they are narrowly defined. His ability merely to outthink the culprit confirms his superiority rather than any innate nobility he might possess. Its portrayal of the detective as reasoner, claims Chandler, has doomed the English mystery story. Any important human issue it stumbles upon it either lies about or reduces to a mechanical exercise. "The English novel of detection," said Chandler in a March 1948 letter, "is either transparent or it is in some sense a psychological fraud."

The psychological truth he tried to impart to literary detection he grounded in character, motivation, and style. The infusion of emotion and sensation into the genre, he felt, wouldn't block thought. His English schooling wouldn't let it. A traditionalist in matters intellectual, he credited Dorothy L. Sayers, perhaps the most hidebound Golden Age mystery writer of all, with giving detective fiction an integrity found elsewhere only in Hammett (*Selected Letters* [23 April 1949], p. 173). Rather than ignoring the conservatism underlying the classic crime puzzle, he helped to combine its logical rigor with the excitement and emotional impact of the hardboiled school.

A January 1946 letter to Erle Stanley Gardner puts "the mental quality of the detective story" on a par with "the movement of the mystery-adventure story" identified with *Black Mask.* What stopped him from using this blend to revolutionize the mystery were his own deepest impulses. First, his admirable style, an amalgam of English syntax and American vocabulary,[2] may have attained a purity out of keeping with an art form as social as prose fiction. Chandler's problem with the give-and-take of social interchange shows in his poor plotting: "As a constructionist, I have a dreadful fault," he confessed to James Sandoe in a May 1949 letter; "I let characters run away with the scenes and then refuse to discard the scenes that don't fit." Disasters of artistic form like *The High Window* and *The Little Sister* betray this self-indulgent tendency to write scenes and then try to squeeze them into the plot. Although detective fiction may not call upon all the skills of a writer, it does demand very exacting use of the ones it does invoke. Included in these is plot structure. Because all the energies of a mystery culminate in the naming of the culprit, the mystery needs a harder, more logical form than was understood by Chandler, who preferred to improvise rather than plan ahead. Even *Farewell, My Lovely*, his most admired work, includes scenes that either don't fit or occur at the wrong time.

Chandler also failed to revolutionize mystery writing because of his fixation with the past. The insecurity that was always dogging him after he was ripped from home and country both made him reluctant to let go and blurred his outlook on the future. On the credit side, his tendency to cling produced his wisest, maturest novel, *The Long Goodbye*, whose leading idea surfaces as an envoi to Chapter 51: "To say goodbye is to die a little." Some of the drawbacks caused by his reluctance to sever ties have been noted—his attachment to social norms belonging to the past, his imitating a father he either secretly worshipped or hated, and his basing the sexual tie upon the figure of the maligned mother; being older, the mother incorporates more of the past than he does. Artistically, his courtship of the past brought him closer than he admitted to Golden Age mystery fiction. For all his blather about the benefits of taking murder out of the Venetian vase and dropping it into the alley, he leaned upon many of the conventions of the English logic-and-deduction formula. If he Americanized the formula as many believe, he first had to fight inclinations to write in the Christie-Sayers tradition. As sharp a critic as Julian Symons explains him in terms of American life, tastes, and values: "Long before Raymond Chandler died in 1959, his private investigator, Philip Marlowe, was an American folk hero .... The violence is entirely local, the product of individual weakness and greed, and shabby, incorruptible Marlowe is there to see the crooked record set straight."[3] Symons needs to be reminded of two truths: Marlowe rights far fewer wrongs than Sherlock Holmes or Hercule Poirot; far from being local, the violence in *The Little Sister* reaches to Kansas and encompasses a family; that of *The Long Goodbye* extends to Montreal, London, and Hitler's Germany; and both North Carolina and Kansas City, Missouri, supply criminal motives in *Playback*, most of which unfolds about ninety miles south of Marlowe's usual L.A. beat, near San Diego. Finally, Chandler's having set "Goldfish" in Washington state and *The Lady in the Lake* some 100 miles away from Marlowe's Hollywood office makes the violence he recounts much less local than that of Christie or Sayers, whose small fenland villages, country houses, and vacation resorts tend to put a tight geographical frame around the action.

Always on his guard, the self-protective Chandler would mask his commitments in jest. But his flip dismissal of Sherlock Holmes in "The Simple Art of Murder" (*Atlantic Monthly*, December 1944) as "mostly an attitude and a few dozen lines of unforgettable dialogue" doesn't hide the truth that his boyhood reading of the Holmes stories influenced the fiction he wrote as an adult. In both practice and principle, he draws heavily upon the conventions of the received formula; Jacques Barzun's quip, "The name Philip Marlowe ... from first name to final *e* connotes Englishness, Elegance, and Establishment,"[4] refers to the elitism Chandler never shed. His aesthetic values had taken shape without his knowing it. The points made in his informal essay, "Casual Notes on the Mystery Novel" (written 1949; printed in *Raymond Chandler Speaking* [1962], pp. 63-70), agree with many of the strictures and attitudes found in R. Austin Freeman's "The Art of the Detective Story," S.S. Van Dine's "Twenty Rules for Writing Detective Fiction," and Ronald A. Knox's "Detective Story Decalogue."[5] Like Knox, Van Dine, and Freeman, Chandler favors plausibility, realism, and the mystery writer's need to play fair in both placing clues and giving the reader reasonable access to the detective's mind.

Nor is Marlowe as different from the sleuths featured in the country house mystery as his creator would claim. Most mainstream English mystery writers say little about their detectives' childhood, education and family for excellent reasons. They want to free the detectives of prejudicial influences, enhance their social mobility, and sharpen their individuality; the detective in Poe's "Thou Art the Man" is anonymous. Apart from the autobiographical crumbs he offers General Sternwood in Chapter 2 of *The Big Sleep* ("I'm thirty-three years old, went to college once"), Marlowe reveals little of his past. What he says about his present can hinder more than help. His description of his investigative technique, which he again offers General Sternwood (in Chapter 30), is positively misleading: "I'm not Sherlock Holmes or Philo Vance. I don't expect to go over ground the police have covered and pick up a broken pen point and build a case from it." This investigator who once introduces himself (in *The Lady in the Lake*) as Philo Vance does examine physical evidence and then reason from it, sometimes outshining the police as dramatically as Holmes did Inspectors Gregson and Lestrade. In *The Lady in the Lake*, perhaps his best reasoning effort, he discovers an anklet in a cabin already searched by a local sheriff, and, in the same sheriff's bailiwick, he later breaks the case by matching the gashes on the victim's body with the blood and cuticle trapped under the murderer's fingernails.

Such moments show that Chandler never delivered himself from scientific detection; the detective must detect. All of his sleuths sift clues and leads from the debris confronting them in order to make patterns, out of which the felon's identity will emerge. The systematic search for means, motive, and opportunity accounts for the presence of coroners, medical examiners, and fingerprint experts in much of the fiction. The detective in "The King in Yellow" (*Dime Detective,* March 1938) speaks of "the Lund test, with paraffin wax, to find out who did or didn't fire a gun recently." The corpus contains further proof of Chandler's belief that mystery fiction depends upon reason. In "Smart-Aleck Kill" (*Black Mask,* July 1934), Chandler's second published story, the private eye infers that a left-handed Hollywood director didn't commit suicide; the fatal round entered the director's skull from the wrong side and angle. Scientific detection also identifies the right-handed murderer. The arcane lore Chandler objected to in R. Austin Freeman and Dorothy L. Sayers unravels other knots in his own fiction. The knowledge that serial numbers on firearms appear both externally and internally helps the detective trace the murder weapon to its source in "Smart-Aleck Kill." In "Pickup on Noon Street" (*Detective Fiction Weekly,* 30 May 1936), the casebreaking lead appears on a memo pad whose top page bears the marks made upon a recently removed earlier one. The evidence resulting from this lead is set forth in a scene that occurred in a galaxy of Golden Age mysteries—the obligatory scene near the end where the detective rehearses the evidence and names the culprit in the presence of all the other suspects.

Other conventions Chandler borrows from classic literary detection include the idea that the murderer is a scurvy sort whose removal will sadden nobody ("Nevada Gas" [*Black Mask,* June 1935]). There are also the conventions, from Poe's "Purloined Letter," of the most obvious place ("Goldfish") and the least likely suspect; many of Marlowe's clients are also the murderers. The misdirection of the reader's attention in *The Big Sleep* rests on devices introduced by Poe and used by Agatha Christie in both *The Murder of Roger Ackroyd (1926)* and *The ABC Murders* (1936). "Mandarin's Jade" (*Dime Detective,* November 1937), *Farewell, My Lovely* and *The High Window* extend the convention of the hidden treasure, originating in Poe's "Gold-Bug"[6] and carrying forward in Conan Doyle's "Musgrave Ritual" and Hammett's *Maltese Falcon.* The device of the dying message, popularized by Ellery Queen, helps solve the mystery of "The Man Who Liked Dogs" and "Goldfish." "Goldfish" also finds Chandler breaking one of his own rules. While attacking the English mystery for smuggling farfetched materials like "hand-wrought dueling pistols ... and tropical fish" into crime-solving in "The Simple Art of Murder" (1944), he must have forgotten that, eight years earlier, in "Goldfish" the pearls that several grifters die for nestle in the bellies of some tropical fish. "Goldfish" marks just one of many instances in Chandler where the derived and the preplanned dominate. But the story shouldn't be indicted for violating Chandler's artistic credo. One of the best early Marlowes, it reveals Chandler's wisdom in obeying his artistic impulses rather than trying to play the social critic or literary firebringer. Besides taking Marlowe farther from home than he would go again on a case, to Washington state, "Goldfish" displays some of Chandler's richest prose. Chandler responds powerfully to the rugged landscape and the play of light along the Pacific northwest coast. And the following description of a fishtank combines sharp lyricism and, thanks to the inventive similes, sinister-edged humor in a passage as evocative as any Chandler wrote:

There were long slim fish like golden darts and Japanese Veiltails with fantastic trailing tails, and X-ray fish as transparent as colored glass, tiny guppies half an inch long, calico popeyes spotted like a bride's apron, and big lumbering Chinese Moors with telescope eyes, froglike faces and unnecessary fins, waddling through the green water like fat men going to lunch.

The distance between art and press agentry in Chandler can be distressingly close. The most famous and also the most misleading part of "The Simple Art of Murder" comes three paragraphs from the end. Its impassioned eloquence seems to have blinded Chandler himself:

In everything that can be called art there is a quality of redemption. It may be pure tragedy, if it is high tragedy, and it may be pity and irony . . . . But down these mean streets a man must go who is not himself mean, who is neither tarnished nor afraid. The detective in this kind of story can be such a man. He is the hero; he is everything. He must be a complete man and a common man and yet an unusual man. He must be, to use a rather weathered phrase, a man of honor . . . . He must be the best man in his world and a good enough man for any world . . . . If he is a man of honor in one thing, he is that in all things.

There is no way to read sense into the drum-and-bugle music. The truth can't be told in such an urgent, florid style or in such lurid strokes. Chandler, always too ready to be spellbound by his prose, sensed it, too. His creative self rebelled against this battle cry, hardly a word of which is true. Readers have faulted the passage, Ross Macdonald scorning it as a surrender to the trite, the stereotyped, and the out-of-date (which Chandler would sometimes resort to rather than judging things on their merits). But even here, Chandler's practice of writing himself into characters other than Marlowe revealed him a better artist than he took credit for being; Ross Macdonald's argument continues:

> While there may be "a quality of redemption" in a good novel, it belongs to the whole work and is not the private property of one of the characters . . . . The detective-as-redeemer is a backward step in the direction of sentimental romance, and an over-simplified world of good guys and bad guys.[7]

Lambert has also attacked the "he is everything" passage of "The Simple Art of Murder": "This paragraph . . . makes Marlowe seem a much simpler and more idealized character than he appears in the novels themselves."[8] Lambert's case rests upon the end of the paragraph: "If he is a man of honor in one thing, he is that in all things." Many of Chandler's finest moments show appearance at odds with reality and the part out of joint with the whole. Had he seen people as consistent, he'd not have rejected both optimism and despair. Searching for a way to know his kind, he investigates society through the medium of Marlowe. Marlowe is the eye that sees the action and the voice that comments upon it. He reflects his author's ambiguity, fear, disgust and hope. Living on the edge of sadness, he also welcomes the odd outburst of promise, as much as he hates to admit it. Speir has described this process of alternation. Marlowe, says Speir, wavers between the desire to preserve the self and the rival claim of social responsibility: "Always there is the double pull—between a hope for a just future and the reality of an unjust present, between a commitment to others and a desire to withdraw from that commitment ... between idealism and contempt."[9]

Some of this contempt is self-directed. The clarity, order and inevitability Marlowe finds in chess have no parallel in his heart. Yet the outside chance of winning love and justice from the ambiguity within and the chaos without keeps hope alive. This dim hope corresponds to Chandler's persistence in preserving his romantic ideal of the blonde with the cornflower blue eyes. Maintaining hope despite the near certainty of loss and defeat defines the existential hero. Often he soldiers on in defiance of common sense. Wasting effort on futility nettles Marlowe almost as much as would relinquishing the hope that sparks his effort. Lonely, displaced, and a mite self-pitying, he moves on society's fringes, partly to protect his honor. Society is a threat; its institutions are run by corrupt men; marriage limits the hero's freedom rather than providing refuge. The redemption Chandler hails in the "he is everything" passage lacks a reference point. His novels describe not nuances of character but moral clashes. If not swamped by cynicism, his detective is still too self-protective to rise to the tragic. He doesn't risk enough. There's not enough emotional outlay by the private eye to generate a tragic vision. In place of the Shakespearean hero's tragic farewell to the reader, Marlowe will bow out with either a wry joke at his own expense (*The High Window*) or an expression of futility (*The Big Sleep*). The bleakness and distress pervading Chandler make toughness look like the best way to fight the void. Although Marlowe protects the weak and the innocent, his inability to withhold judgment and his nagging self-consciousness both block the tragic drive. Redemption enters Chandler's fiction in other ways.

One of these is the avoidance of straightforward realism. Trying to convey a reality too brutal and sordid for rational discourse, Chandler used an idiom marked by distortion, intensification, and magnification. Marlowe's wisecracks serve the same end as Chandler's elaborate conceits, that of gaining and keeping control of an exchange with another person. The narrator's voice and the author's mind are working here in unison, some of the most bizarre similes in the canon coming near the start of the first two novels, *The Big Sleep* and *Farewell, My Lovely*. Through their highly wrought language, Chandler and Marlowe both impose a style that put a potential opponent off balance long enough to break his stride. But the author-narrator partnership isn't solid. Marlowe isn't "everything" because Chandler wouldn't permit it. The beatings he gets from policemen as often as from gangsters bespeak the corruption of our cities; the man of honor and integrity faces as much danger from the alleged defenders of the law as from the lawbreakers. Behind these beatings, too, is the intellectual's resentment of the man of action's candor and exuberance. Not only do the beatings serve little purpose; for all his posturing, Marlowe is one of the most ineffectual of private eyes. They also curb our admiration for him. Ralph Harper's comparing him to a rubber ball bouncing from one beating to another, like a slapstick comic,[10] points up his unreality. Even Chandler called him "a failure," "not a real person," and a "creature of fantasy" as late as 1951 (*Selected Letters,* p. 294).

In muted but recurring accents, the absence of authorial approval shadows Marlowe's career. Clive James sees Chandler as a parodist: "A comic style, always on the edge of parody—and, of course, sometimes over the edge," steers the action. Marlowe can't hide from the parody. Although he's "making fun of himself"[11] in the first paragraph of *The Big Sleep*, as Ross Macdonald has said, he is primarily the butt of Chandler's joke. R.P. Blackmur's remarks on parody in Thomas Mann's *Dr. Faustus* illuminate Chandler's intent. Parody, says Blackmur, is a legitimate descriptive and evaluative tool in an age without norms. The self either sinks into his job, flattens into a stereotype, or retreats from people. Besides lacking guidelines, he also falls short of his own moral standards. Marlowe fits Blackmur's formulation. Lacking friends and family and also ruled by a mechanical routine, he has little to look forward to in his low-paying, high-risk job. Blackmur's ideas about parody state both the terms and the tone of Chandler's qualified disapproval of Marlowe:

Parody is not caricature, not satire: it is a means of treating reality so as to come short of it either on purpose or through necessity . . . . In our day, every man is a parody of his moral self. Parody is our ordinary means of judging men and events.[12]

Chandler only pretended to think that trouble was Marlowe's business. Marlowe wasn't created to face dangers so the rest of us could be spared from them. Rarely will Chandler offer, through him, ways to cope with the rottenness of modern life; a city consisting of Marlowes would be unlivable. Chandler sends Marlowe down the mean streets of greater Los Angeles to get lied to and beaten up. Chandler is his worst enemy. Little of his pain is redemptive. The novels he narrates neglect human particularity, complexity, and unpredictability; nor do they uncover hidden reverses of hope and talent. And despite all Chandler's disclaimers against the alleged artificiality of English literary detection, the society portrayed in the Marlowe books is extremely truncated, lacking teachers, ministers, parents of small or growing children, and members of the industrial middle class. Sayers' advertising agencies and Christie's rural villages offer a much thicker and meatier cross-section of people than can be found in Chandler. Even Marlowe's outstanding quality, his language, was never spoken by male adults in North America.

Although one of the best-written essays on modern crime fiction, "The Simple Art of Murder" makes misleading statements about Chandler's art. The "element of uplift" he found lacking in the parochial English mystery emerges more clearly from a Christie or a Sayers novel than from one of his own. In the cozy English mystery, the apprehension of the murderer restores the harmony that the murderer disrupted. Brigid Brophy has explained how "the quality of redemption" Chandler saw as belonging to all art celebrates the order that prevailed before the murder. Arguing from premises first set forth in Auden's "Guilty Vicarage" (1948), Brophy shows how the detective's reconstruction of the crime and his naming of the criminal certifies the innocence of the innocent: "The psychological purpose of the story is summed up in ... acquittal. The detective myth exists not to provoke or endorse guilt but to dissipate it. The solution promises the general absolution."[13] By contrast, the removal of the criminal in hardboiled American fiction reaffirms nothing. The city of dreadful night is still dreadful. Marlowe himself feels drawn into the general nastiness at the end of *The Big Sleep*, during which he had comforted and protected a stricken family as well as he could. Neither justice nor order is reinstated. How could they be, not having been there to begin with? Life is a battlefield. Eddie Mars calls Marlowe "soldier" several times; the butler of General Sternwood, a retired soldier, credits Marlowe with having "the soldier's eye," a quality also attributed to the ex-IRA officer, Rusty Regan. Hitler's War plays a part in both "No Crime in the Mountains" (*Detective Story,* September 1941) and *The Lady in the Lake*. Finally, Marlowe gets a big lead from a para-military organization run by a retired army colonel in *The Long Goodbye*.

Because all military operations create casualties, each battle is best fought with a poker face. Victory in one skirmish may be followed by defeat in the next, which could erupt at any time. Murderers in "Pickup on Noon Street" (*Detective Fiction Weekly*, 30 May 1936) are still at large after the story ends; nor has an earnest search for them been mounted by the police. The flawless case John Dalmas, the detective, builds in "Bay City Blues" against a policeman can't serve justice because the police, a closed, self-regulating unit, won't act on it. Nor would the law have convicted Helen Grayle or Eileen Wade. No satisfaction can crown the detective's reconstruction of the crime when the reconstruction stops no criminal. And very little redemption can occur if the sleuth can't see, first, that his heart has motivated him and, next, that his efforts have helped the innocent. The novel in which Marlowe serves his client most imaginatively, *The Big Sleep*, also ends on a note as bleak and bitter as any in the canon.

II

This note was intended. Chandler wrote his strong disturbing books in a prose marked by excellence and care. He also saw himself primarily as a stylist, calling style (in a 7 March 1947 letter) "the most valuable investment a writer can make with his time." This stance never wavered; he always believed in the primacy of style in fiction. In a letter to his publisher, Alfred A. Knopf, written at the start of his novelistic career, 19 February 1939, he announced his intention to win dramatic excitement from "a very vivid and pungent style"; he told his Hollywood agent, H.N. Swanson (22 September 1954), "There are a hundred clever plot architects for every writer who can do you a paragraph of prose with a touch of magic to it"; finally, in a 25 May 1957 letter, he claimed, "Any man who can write a page of living prose adds something to our life." The consistency of attitude reflected in these statements constitutes a position paper. Style *did* matter more to Chandler than did any other aspect of writing. For once, his artistic practice squared with his critical preachments. Whatever redemption exists in his work grows out of his clear, open, rhythmical style. Now style to Chandler meant the interplay of cadence, harmonics and tone. Few writers of his day selected and arranged words so carefully. His sense of rhythm and balance helped him build sentences firmly; the flash of imagery and metaphor brightened them. His ear-pleasing cadences have their own shape, swing and balance. Clear and graceful, his prose is also fastidiously chiselled in both its spare, chill moments and its grander flourishes. Ten straight sentences in the seventh and eighth paragraphs of "Trouble is My Business" begin either with the pronoun subject I, or, twice, usher in the I-subject with a one-syllable word. Yet Chandler avoids monotony by varying both sentence rhythm and length, placing phrasal and clausal modifiers of different lengths in different parts of the sentences. He controls *all* parts of speech well. The neat management of concrete details by means of highly active verbs creates a bright lyricism in *The Lady in the Lake*. Generally viewed as a city writer, he hasn't received the credit he deserves for creating tactile values from his descriptions of natural scenery:

A bluejay squawked on a branch and a squirrel scolded at me and beat one paw angrily on the pine cone it was holding. A scarlet-topped woodpecker stopped probing in the dark long enough to look at me with one beady eye and then dodge behind the tree trunk to look at me with the other one.

Live, hopping verbs also build excitement in "Try the Girl." Notice how the link verbs in the first and last main clauses of the following paragraph mediate the wildness between them.

We weren't near to the sedan, but I wanted his attention. I got it. He slammed me over the head and grabbed the wheel and yanked the brake on.

We ground to a stop. I shook my head woozily. By the time I came out of it he was angry with me again, in his corner.

Chandler knew other ways to slow the movement of a rhetorical unit. The prepositions and the heavy closing beat of the following sentence from "The Lady in the Lake" convey the distance dividing a man who has just discovered a corpse, presumably's his wife's, and the helplessness to relieve the man's stress felt by the detective alongside him: "His voice seemed to come to me from a long way off, over a hill, through a thick growth of trees."

As the passage suggests, point of view in Chandler fends off the dead hand of externality. His first-person narrations don't usually criticize, interpret, or analyze. Yet they go beyond bald factual reporting, selecting details which impart color, meaning, and emotional response as they describe. The terse final sentence of a section of "Finger Man" delivers this inclusiveness as early as 1934: "I took my cramped fingers from the top of the railing, and a lot of people broke for the bar." Rather than saying that a $10,000 spin of a roulette wheel unnerved Marlowe, Chandler shows the physical counterparts of the unnerving; Marlowe was gripping the sides of the table so hard that his fingers cramped. (The parallelism employed in the second half of the compound sentence shows the other bystanders to have shared his agitation.) Most of Chandler's descriptions of violence will use the same technique: "Courtway lifted his gun and his finger whitened on the trigger and the gun roared," says the narrator-detective in "Guns at Cyrano's." Rather than saying that Courtney shot somebody, Chandler has translated the shooting into a sequence of physical events, recording his narrator's exact visual and auditory impressions of the shooting. This impressionism brightens the novels. Marlowe recounts his discovery of the first corpse in *The Little Sister* in the same way somebody chancing upon a corpse in real life would react to *his* find. At no time does he say that the dead man was stabbed to death: "A square yellow wooden handle was attached to the back of Lester B. Clausen's neck," the passage begins. Not until three sentences later is it revealed that the handle jutting from Clausen's occipital bulge belongs to an ice pick.

Other features distinguish Chandler's style. Durham has noted Chandler's ability to match characters like Anne Riordan of *Farewell, My Lovely*, Mrs. Murdock of *The High Window,* and Marlowe himself to homes expressive of their personalities.[14] There are also the descriptions of Marlowe glissading out of consciousness and into a shaft of blackness after getting knocked out; given the frequency with which blackjacks crash down on skulls in

Chandler's southern California, the poetic force generated by such moments occurs in nearly every book. A further source of verbal distinction inheres in Chandler's ability to write with authority and verve on many subjects. Though he criticized English fiction for leaning too heavily upon specialized knowledge, he, too, was curious about little-known processes and practices. Technical details of ballistics, weapon assembly, book collecting, jade, rare coins, botany, and toxicology lend sinew to his plots. But, to his credit, he didn't use his inside lore to solve a case, as did his counterparts in England, like F.W. Crofts, with his knowledge of railways, and Dorothy L. Sayers, whose interest in bell-ringing saturates *The Nine Tailors.*

Chandler's voice operates at different timbres, inflections and speeds. In its more exuberant moments, it takes the form of the simile both in narration and dialogue. Simile preponderates over metaphor in Chandler as a figure of speech because the novels themselves are metaphors of the urban nightmare. Lambert's belief that "the authentic Chandler overtone"[15] comes from combining the casual with the strange applies to Chandler's carefully developed similes. The similes can fuse, along with the banal and the exotic, data from altogether different realms of activity, as in "This car sticks out like spats at an Iowa picnic," from "Mandarin's Jade." The ability to fuse far-flung elements artistically creates, in Lambert's view, that "throwaway exactness"[16] which makes Chandler's prose memorable. Writing more waggishly than Lambert, Clive James finds this exactness offensive: "He was always prone to overcooking a simile," says James, remarking further:

At their best, Chandler's similes click into place with ... perfect appositeness. He can make you laugh, he gets it so right—which perhaps means that he gets it *too* right. What we recognize as wit is always a self-conscious performance.[17]

Striking Chandler's similes are. But they must stand on the effect they produce on the reader, i.e., whether they draw him/her into the narrative or jerk his/her attention away. Let us look at his two most famous, or notorious, similes. The fourth paragraph of *Farewell, My Lovely* ends with a simile concocted to dramatize the incongruity between the gaudily garbed Irish-American giant, Moose Malloy, and the run-down neighborhood where his errand has taken him: "Even on Central Avenue, not the quietest dressed street in the world, he looked about as inconspicuous as a tarantula on a slice of angel food." The outrageousness of the simile enhances, rather than breaks, the developing mood. First, Chandler's flexing of his rhetorical muscles confirms his credentials as a word man. The simile wins him our trust; anyone capable of such a rhetorical flourish deserves our attention. Nearly immediately, he has set the tone of the action and served notice that we must play the game by his stylistic rules. His rhythmic, graphic description of Moose earlier in the paragraph already demonstrated that the game would be worth playing. Conveying, in its humor, the detachment needed to tell a story of urban violence, the simile has done its work, riveting rather than distracting us because it precedes the plot. As Conrad was fond of doing, Chandler started *Farewell, My Lovely* with a bold image rather than with an idea or an issue. His elaborate verbal wit can't deflect our attention from an action that has not yet declared itself. Furthermore, in view of the association of danger and large hairy spiders in the popular imagination, Moose's being likened to a tarantula prefigures the deaths he will later cause.

The simile used in *The Big Sleep* to describe the thronging vegetation in the greenhouse where Marlowe and General Sternwood meet makes an even stronger impact than the one comparing Moose to a tarantula: "The plants filled the place, a forest of them, with nasty meaty leaves and stalks like the newly washed fingers of dead men." Impressive enough in its own, this dazzling combination, which prefigures the key word of the novel's next-to-last paragraph, namely, nastiness, gains more power when seen in context with two similes which follow it closely.

The next paragraph, mostly a description of the General, ends with another vegetation simile: "A few locks of dry white hair clung to his scalp, like flowers fighting for life on a bare rock." This telling figure combines the General's tenacity with the heavy odds he must fight simply to survive. He displays his tenacity within a minute. Fierce and tired, implacable and broken, he remembers his fondness for brandy: "I used to like mine with champagne. The champagne as cold as Valley Forge and about a third of a glass of brandy beneath." The reference to Valley Forge sharpens the zest for life the dying old warrior expresses in his simile. The self-disclaimer he makes minutes later, again couched as a simile, doesn't lessen the sympathy he has won from Marlowe and the reader: "I seem to exist largely on heat, like a newborn spider." Throughout the sequence, his gnarled, enfeebled old age has exuded both the banefulness of the spider and the helplessness of the newborn. Chandler's reminding us of these qualities brings to the fore the General's will to survive. The classic meeting of General Guy Sternwood and Philip Marlowe is one of the best scenes Chandler ever wrote, and the graphic, perturbing similes infused into the scene enhance its power.

Perhaps Chandler's most original contribution to figurative prose stems from a yet nameless formation. Like litotes, the formation states the opposite of what it means, but much more extravagantly and often in the form of a simile. Its extravagance pushes it into the realm of hyperbole, or overstatement. Yet it also denies any wild claim it makes. *Farewell, My Lovely* uses this figure of speech more often than does any other Chandler work. Here it is describing Moose Malloy three paragraphs into the book: "He was a big man but not more than six feet five inches tall and not wider than a beer truck." By using parallel phrasing to describe Moose's height and width, Chandler forges a bond his denial can't dispel; Moose's width does remind one of a beer truck. Regardless of its name, the qualified hyperbole, hyperbolic litotes, or hyperbole with a stinger in its tail barely modulates the outrageousness it sets forth. The simile, from *Farewell, My Lovely*, "The green stone in his stickpin was not quite as large as an apple," records Marlowe's amazement over the largeness of the stone. When the detective says, later in the novel, "I didn't jump more than a foot," he's saying that he was shocked. Perhaps Chandler first used the device in "Killer in the Rain" (*Black Mask*, January 1935), in the anonymous narrator's description of his client's wallet as "not quite as big as a bale of hay." These funny, yet jarring formations appear less often in Chandler's later writing and, when they do occur, reflect a simpler play of verbal wit. Compare Marlowe's reaction to the Grayle mansion to the one prompted by the Potter estate in *The Long Goodbye*: "The house itself was not so much," says Marlowe in *Farewell, My Lovely*; "It was smaller than Buckingham Palace ... and probably had fewer windows than the Chrysler Building." This archness relaxes in *The Long Goodbye*, where Harlan Potter, a man with a hundred million dollars, receives Marlowe in "a dim room that couldn't have been less than seventy feet long."

If the hyperbolic litotes in Chandler's hands is mannered, it is also funny, ironical and expressive of the highly wrought, impacted phrasing he adopted to convey the pressures exerted by the modern city. Some of his other rhetoric is less apt. In "Try the Girl," he mixes metaphors when he says, "KLBL was on the western fringe of that part of the city that melts into Beverly Hills"; fringes don't melt. The detective in "Mandarin's Jade" says that he "unshipped" his fountain pen flashlight. His referring, two pages later, to "my own little flash" conveys his knowledge that his flashlight is too small an object to be "unshipped." Such stylistic miscues come early in

Chandler's career, appearing, mostly, in his short stories. When he "cannibalized" the stories to turn them into novels, he removed them. He also said in his introduction to the short-story omnibus *The Simple Art of Murder*, reprinted in *The Midnight Raymond Chandler* (1971), "There are no 'classics' of crime and detection." Mystery fiction was an exciting genre to him, with its prizes open to all. On the basis of the pains he took with his remarkable prose, he wanted to snatch one or two for himself.

Chapter Three

A Common Yet Unusual Man

THE WORD CHOICE, observational powers and transformational play of mind defining Chandler's novels all take root in his narrator-detective, six-foot-one, 190-lb. Philip Marlowe. The novels are framed within Marlowe's ability to perceive, imagine, and associate. They record only the impressions, ideas, and imaginings of Marlowe. What do these data gain in being presented from his standpoint? Using a first-person narrator in a work of fiction can create solid gains in intimacy, immediacy, and often, irony. On the other hand, in the case of an actionist narrator like Marlowe, the device forfeits moral perspective; all exists in a shrill, unshadowed present. Selfhood pre-exists detection in Chandler; the cases Marlowe investigates rarely ripen him or those he meets as a crime-stopper. Speir has discussed the limitations Chandler imposed on himself by omitting an expanding moral consciousness from works unfolding in a society without history or moral guidelines: "Marlowe is finally too stylized a creation to permit growth and development. It is not a problem of which Chandler was unaware."[1]

The partnership of Chandler and Marlowe rankled from the start. Marlowe's stance as a cool, tough stoic of wide and varied experience sorts ill with Chandler's serious artistic intentions. Politics, the way we structure our shared life, gets reduced to a smash-and-grab raid. The hard, brilliant finish of the novels both robs the novels of texture and destroys the idea that they stemmed from the unconscious. The Marlowe books lack echoes and recesses. That Marlowe's professional integrity and personal honor ignore social issues also hobbles them. Marlowe cares little about the squalor of poverty, the senselessness of accident and the tyranny of pain. Chandler's fresh, figured style both serves a rigid, largely prohibitive morality and gives a foreshortened picture. Besides omitting any plea for social justice, the novels ignore the marvelous and the tragic infusing daily life. Marlowe's preoccupation with the straightforward impulses of duty, honor, and integrity sometimes make the novels look naive and simplistic. When Leslie Murdock accuses Marlowe of not liking him in *The High Window*, the response he gets, "It's a silly subject . . . . And damned unimportant. To both of us," draws too obviously upon the stereotype of the tough, capable detective. Certainly a private eye needn't like a client any more than a dentist needs to like a patient or a teacher, a student. But, like any other seller of his services, he must also sell himself. Marlowe's sometimes truculent disregard of diplomacy undermines the confidence a detective must plant in the hearts of clients and witnesses before extracting the truth.

What shackles him as a detective also dwarfs him as a narrator. Ross Macdonald has argued that Marlowe's voice is "too rigidly stylized" to create a Dickensian fullness, a Jamesian precision, or a Conradian depth: "Marlowe's voice is limited by his role as the hardboiled hero. He must speak within his limits as a character, and these limits are quite narrowly conceived."[2] Such is the strength of Chandler's powers of impersonation that Marlowe's limits look self-imposed. When the detective claims, in high dudgeon, to be facing reality squarely, he's usually posing before a mirror. He will risk his license for a client and flout the law for a friend. To buy time for clients who will later betray him, he delays reporting suspected murderers to the police in *Farewell, My Lovely, The High Window*, and *The Little Sister*. In *The Long Goodbye* he drives Terry Lennox to Mexico on the condition that Lennox keep silent about his reasons for making the trip; Marlowe knows that Lennox's wife is dead; were Lennox to connect the death to the Mexico trip, Marlowe would have to arrest him.

This hairsplitting refusal to mix detection and sentiment questions the relationship between truth-finding and justice. From what Marlowe knows of pampered, sluttish Sylvia, information about her death, however incriminating to his friend, wouldn't promote justice. Lennox isn't only incriminated but also guilty in his friend's mind. Doesn't Marlowe's demand for Lennox's silence hinge on his having already condemned him without hearing a scrap of evidence? Also implicit in his pinchbeck generosity is the conviction, shared by Chandler, that Sylvia deserved to die for being rich, divorced several times, and sexually loose. Such an attitude reflects the "angry puritan morality" marring Chandler's novels according to Ross Macdonald.[3] Other episodes in *The Long Goodbye* reveal Marlowe subverting his private morality by riding it too hard. Only the most arrant snobbery can explain his refusal to discuss his trip to Mexico with the police; he wants the luxury of being beaten up without having, technically anyway, broken the law. This elitist attitude toward both crime and the police persists. His reconstruction of the crime infers Eileen Wade's guilt. But he will not share his findings with the police. It suffices that his solution to the crime satisfies *him;* crime needn't be punished. The operation of the law, he claims, is the court's business, not his. And the lawyers and police assigned to the Wade case have blundered so badly that they have no right to ask for justice. (In "Mandarin's Jade," too, the detective confronted the culprit with her guilt, not to vindicate the law, but to serve warning that he wouldn't play the sucker.)

I

The subtlety and ambiguity E.M. Beekman finds in Marlowe clashes with the cynicism reflected in the detective's attitude toward justice and the law: "In Chandler's novels," says Beekman, "Marlowe is the only figure with warmth and compassion, but there is a constant infiltration of the autumnal moods of weariness and futility."[4] Not only does Marlowe waver between idealism and cynicism and between direct statement and irony; those he likes best (all of whom are men) possess the same ambivalence. The inertia created by sickness and age tugs against a zest for life in General Sternwood. Moose Malloy has the malignancy and instinctive wisdom of the primitive. Red Norgaard mixes gentleness and tough talk. Though lost and degraded, Terry Lennox has retained the firm but gentle offhandedness of the British public school man. All four men, in addition, are either marking time or hiding from themselves. (Into this category should be added Mona Mars, who, with her cropped hair, also fuses elements of the male and female.) Like them, and like Chandler, too, Marlowe performs praiseworthy deeds which his drive to concealment makes him devalue.

Honest, brave, and loyal, he prefers helping or protecting somebody to the making of money. Noble impulses like these embarrass him, though. In fact, he's so nonplussed by gentleness that, when it surfaces in him, it often makes him growl evasively about the follies and vices of mankind. Although he refers to Shakespeare, Pepys, Browning, Flaubert, Anatole France, Hemingway and T.S. Eliot, he won't discuss literature. He even discourages literary discussion. When Vivian Sternwood Regan mentions Proust, he pretends never to have heard of him. Always, he prefers to keep people at bay rather than sharing insights with them on commonly held subjects. Both before (*The Long Goodbye*) and after ("The Poodle Springs Story") his marriage to Linda Loring, he communicates with her by means of half-truth, sarcasm, and irony. Verbal fencing is both his favorite defense against real communication and his classic dodge from himself. In *Farewell, My Lovely*, he wisecracks so often that people find his conversation pointless and frustrating. Jerry Palmer has explained why he maintains such a well-stocked arsenal of word bullets:

It is an attempt to assert oneself verbally rather than an attempt at communication, more a way of keeping people at a distance than of getting close to them, a kind of verbal fencing, tough and wary simultaneously.[5]

Palmer is right about Marlowe's passion for privacy. The sometimes heartless objectivity of Marlowe's narrations hides the heart within; Marlowe is rarely as detached as he pretends. He will record the physical decrepitude of General Sternwood in cold, photographic detail. Yet the simile concluding his description, "A few locks of dry white hair clung to his scalp, like wild flowers fighting for life on a bare rock," denotes a strong inward response. His risking his neck for the General shows that he cares more about people than about posing. *Playback* also reveals him concealing an emotional commitment, but on a smaller scale. He chides somebody for throwing a cigarette out of a car window: "You don't do that in the California hills," he scolds, alighting from the car to stamp out the glowing butt, "not even out of season." But he can't protect the environment without feigning indifference toward it. Minutes before delivering his reprimand, he had confided to the readers, "The view was magnificent. I looked at it for all of three seconds."

The insecurity that prompts him to dismiss, ridicule, or find fault lest he come under attack himself declares itself in different ways. Already noted has been his including himself in the squalor suffusing greater L.A. at the end of *The Big Sleep*. Better to wallop yourself than to let another person do it; you can pick the time and place. But you also damage your self-esteem and direct any worries about sin and guilt into masochistic channels. Brave, loyal Marlowe's "I was part of the nastiness now" discredits the sacrifices he made on behalf of the Sternwoods. A person who discounts and maligns himself will treat others accordingly; cruelty suffered leads to cruelty inflicted; the world darkens. Despite his shaky self-image, Marlowe feels morally superior to almost everyone he meets. His sexual morals are higher; he does his job more honestly; he can also detect crime more quickly. Yet all this brings him little peace. He's forever showing off—his toughness, his piquant language and his ability to resist both bent money and beautiful women. Of Terry Lennox, who perhaps claims his friendship longer than anybody else in the canon, he remarks inwardly, "I liked him better drunk, down and out, hungry and beaten . . . . Or did I? Maybe I just liked being top man." The control he feels compelled to gain in his private relationships means that he's offering others not friendship but condescension. A less pathetic General Sternwood might not have inspired so many of his best energies.

Yet his character is fluid. Although he'd never admit it, his investigations humble and enrich him. The detection that brings him no lasting friendship does offer other compensations. He isn't too callous to leave a case sadder and wiser, or even to learn his lesson well. The lesson, though, can aggravate his worst fears. He lacks the reserves of self-trust to face with cheer and confidence a world that keeps resisting him. Changes occurring in his life during the twenty-five years between 1934, the publication date of "Finger Man," and 1959, when "The Pencil" appeared, show him mellowing reluctantly. Though making plain his adaptability, the process has also tamed his blood. At a weary moment in *Farewell, My Lovely*, he says, "I needed a lot of life insurance . . . . I needed a vacation, I needed a home in the country. What I had was a coat, a hat, and a gun." He nearly gets his wish, trading mobility and danger for the middle-class security he always scoffed at but wanted. In *The Long Goodbye* he has left the throbbing city to live not in the country but in a suburb; in *Playback* he buys a blue chip insurance policy by becoming engaged to a millionaire's daughter; "The Poodle Springs Story" shows him returning from his honeymoon with her.

His various moves during his crabwise pilgrimage to security betray either Chandler's carelessness or bad memory. In "Finger Man," he rents an office in the Condor Building and lives in a Hollywood apartment house called the Merritt Plaza. His treacherous client, Miss Glenn, lives in the Hobart Arms, on the 800 block of South Minter. In *The Big Sleep*, Marlowe is cocooned in the Hobart Arms, his quiet domestic routine of Mozart and chess clashing with Miss Glenn's description of the building as "a place where you don't have to answer questions at the desk." Marlowe would have little reason to move to such a shady place. Not only would his conservative habits alienate him from his neighbors; the place also has negative associations in that a friend died there at the hands of one of the building's tenants. The anonymous detective of "Killer in the Rain" (1935) lives in the Berglund Apartments, as does

John Dalmas in "Mandarin's Jade" (1937), and Marlowe in "Red Wind" (1938).

By *The High Window* (1942), Marlowe's movements have stabilized. He works out of the Cahuenga Building on Hollywood Boulevard near Ivar, where he has been at least two years. He has also moved to the Bristol Apartments, in Hollywood, which he will like well enough to remain in through *The Little Sister* and 1949. But if his stay at the Bristol contents him, it also creates some problems for the reader. When he pawns the Brasher Doubloon in *The High Window*, he surprises the Santa Monica pawnbroker by giving the Bristol as his address. This mild shock implies that someone living in such a good neighborhood shouldn't need to borrow $15. His expensive life style continues to belie his allegedly low income. In *Playback* (1958), he is asked, "How can you afford an expensive car like this? You don't make much money, do you?" Much money? He doesn't seem to make *any* money. In a letter of 21 February 1959, Chandler said of him, "He is destined to be poor"; he describes himself in *The High Window* as knowing everything except how to make a decent living; in *The Big Sleep* he tells a rich casino owner not to interfere with his, Marlowe's, business because the pay's too small. He's speaking the truth. In this book and elsewhere, he is forever trying to return, or refusing to spend, the fees he earns. He also discourages would-be clients from hiring him; Chapter 21 of *The Long Goodbye* shows him sending three prospective clients from his office without asking any of them for a consultation fee. How *did* he pay for his Oldsmobile? And how *can* he afford to live in a high-rent district? Any answer to these questions will discredit Chandler, suggesting that he isn't playing fair with the reader. Either Marlowe has a private income which Chandler is keeping dark or the recorded adventures in his casebook aren't representative. This latter possibility implies that Marlowe foregoes money to work on challenging cases; that these cases are rare, since he has to live; and, finally, that in describing him in such atypical circumstances, Chandler never shows, because he doesn't understand, what a detective's life is like.

In any case, Marlowe followed the migratory pattern that ruled 1950s America; as has been said, he partook of the White Flight, moving from his city apartment to a suburban home. In *Playback* and "The Pencil," he's living in the same furnished house on Yucca Avenue in Laurel Canyon where he had moved some time between 1949 and 1953. His change in residence suggests a change in outlook. Having left the crowded city, he may be trying to substitute personal for job-connected relationships; the detective wants to achieve full growth as a man. This redirection of energy occurs most notably in *The Long Goodbye*, where he lights an extra cigarette, pours an extra cup of coffee, and orders an extra gimlet to honor his absent friend, Terry Lennox. Unfortunately this delicacy isn't sustained. He last sees Lennox in his office in the city, headquarters of the crusading self he had tried to outgrow, and not in the companionable suburbs. The sound of Lennox's receding footsteps leave him feeling disgust—for Lennox, for himself and for the city of dreadful night he can't flee. In "The Poodle Springs Story" he has moved even further from Hollywood, to Palm Springs. Whether a failure to adjust to his new life in the desert would have catapulted him to the city can't be known. Chandler did say, though, that Marlowe never should marry, and the Marlowe of "The Poodle Springs Story" isn't only married but also both living in a home and driving a Cadillac paid for by his wife's millions.

Besides installing the detective in alien surroundings, Chandler also shows his uneasiness with Marlowe's marriage by restoring Anne Riordan of *Farewell, My Lovely* in "The Pencil." Her restoration shows her importance to Marlowe. A sign of her affinity to him comes in her father's having been fired from the Bay City Police for insubordination, an infraction which also cost Marlowe *his* job with the police. Her waiting to tell Marlowe of her father's dismissal from the force until the third time they meet indicates her poise and patience at their first meeting, which occurs at the site of Lindsay Marriott's death in Purissima Canyon. Their second private meeting takes place when Marlowe turns up unexpectedly at her Bay City home after breaking out of Dr. Sonderborg's mental asylum. Her intelligence, compassion and generosity in this scene he repays with nastiness. According to Speir, "the scene calls attention to Marlowe's deep-seated alienation and his difficulty in trusting anyone."[6]

His conduct during the sequence is contemptible. In the first place the danger he exposes her to by going to her home shows his selfishness, as he admits: "I had no business coming here. If they [his former captors] knew as much about me as I suspected, they might come here looking. That would be a mess." His scruples don't stop him from drinking Anne's liquor and eating the food she cooks and serves him any more than they stopped him from ringing her doorbell. But his having disclosed, in coming to Anne, a spontaneous need for another person has upset him; he insults her while rejecting her offer to sleep in a spare bedroom.

Denial is his only gift to this mother figure, who, although his junior by five or ten years, has made him the maternal offerings of food and shelter. This generosity is not her first affront to his compulsion to be in charge. While driving him back to the city from Purissima Canyon, she tried twice to prolong their time together. Each time she was rebuffed. Yet she has retained good cheer. Just before dropping him off, she gives him her address. Seventeen chapters and several weeks later, after being turned down again, she again renews her faith in him, driving him back to Hollywood rather than taking him to a taxi stand, as he had asked. In turn, he has been acting as if he'd rather face death than spend one moment more than is necessary with her. He obeyed a compulsion by going to Anne; one just as blind pulls him from her side. The relief of being out of her company outpaces the threat awaiting him at his apartment, where his former captors would most surely go after discovering his escape. Luckily, no harm comes to him. The last paragraph of the chapter, "I undressed and went to bed. I had nightmares .... But in the morning I was a well man again," distills his reactions to the events of the previous evening—dismay over waking in a locked room and relief to be away from that other potential trap, Anne.

What makes her so threatening is the temptation she poses. Her greeting to him, when he appears unannounced under her porchlight, "My God .... You look like Hamlet's father!" shows that, like Marlowe and Chandler both, she identifies eroticism with the parent of the opposite sex. The father she has on her mind isn't Hamlet's, but her own. Marlowe represents the risen spirit of her father, another honest cop sacrificed to his principles. What she means to Marlowe has already been spelled out. His comment after enjoying her eggs, toast, coffee, and brandy, "A fellow could settle down here .... Move right in. Everything set for him," calls attention to her ability to fill a void in his life. But his very next words, "No butter .... That makes it tough," depict the speed with which his defenses snap back into place. Though spoken as a joke, these words reveal his stubbornness, his taste for privilege and his alienation from the middle class. Marlowe belongs on the fringes of society, either in his shabby office or in the mansions of the Sternwoods, the Grayles or the Wades. He probably also belongs unattached. Even after moving to suburban Laurel Canyon, he maintains his preference for fleeting relationships. The only people appearing in more than one Marlowe novel are the policeman Bernie Ohls, the lawyer Sewell Endicott, and Linda Loring, who, as a voice heard on the phone in the last chapter of *Playback*, seems like an afterthought. Where all this leaves Anne Riordan is where she doesn't want to be left—alone in the wings. Marlowe needs her but not in the way she deserves to be needed. Her value for him consists of providing support; the knight needs to be restored and refreshed before returning to the lists.

The distance he preserves between himself and her, the woman with whom he has more in common than any other we see him with, also preserves her image. And it is her image, rather than her flesh-and-blood reality, that counts most with him. He never grants her free-standing reality. Just as he has relegated her to the wings, rather than giving her the star billing she craves, he holds her at a distance for the sake of his fantasy ideal. Ironically, a less able, intelligent and attractive woman of her background would have fared better with him. More ideal than flesh she is; her age in the 1959 story, a chaste twenty-eight, hasn't changed from what it was in the 1940 novel. Only her virginity has grown more burdensome. But her hopes must languish because for Marlowe the actualization of the dream kills the dream; to remove the goddess from the pedestal is to introduce her into the drab prose of reality, where her sheen will tarnish. Besides, having sex with Anne would obligate Marlowe in ways he lacks both the time and temperament for. An ideal can be dealt with more conveniently than a person; it doesn't demand the same investment in time, energy, and patience. Marlowe knows that Anne deserves a fully committed love. Yet he also knows that he can't afford love's outgoings. Given his self-protectiveness, one can see why she was left out of the 1975 film version of *Farewell, My Lovely* directed by Dick Richards and starring Robert Mitchum as Marlowe.

II

Marlowe combines faults and virtues in realistic proportions. As his tie with Anne reveals, he can react as both a churl and a knight. This modern Everyman feels as comfortable in a mansion as in a poolroom; social mobility, a major trait of Everyman, permits him to question anyone and to look at evidence unearthed anywhere at least once. He's linked to his society both actively and passively in that his activities reflect the microcosms of family, business, and politics as Chandler understood them. Often in his movements over the social map, he will discover freshly murdered bodies (which may be subsequently removed). The stubbornness with which violence clings to him darkens Chandler's portrayal of him as a thinker of evil thoughts which sometimes become deeds. This modern Everyman also plucks denial and cruelty from noble motives. Ponder sees self-knowledge as the goal of the knightly quest in Chandler: "In the detective's search for himself, the detective defines himself in a code contrived to reconcile opposites."[7] Marlowe also finds that the code distorts and depletes, as his fending off of Anne Riordan proves; tenderness and intimacy scare him. Few private eyes set themselves standards as high as Marlowe's; few are as sad, confused, or lonely. Alienated and one-dimensional, he is the most private of private eyes. In *The High Window* he mentions receiving a postcard from Santa Rosa, in northern California, where he spent four days working on a case the previous year. Chandler also calls Santa Rosa Marlowe's birthplace (in a letter written 19 April 1951). Marlowe's staying in a hotel in the town of his birth suggests either that all his friends and family have scattered or that they wouldn't have asked him to their homes had they not all moved or died. Either reading of his trip to Santa Rosa— where he went for business and not for fun—brands this man who lives alone and never mentions the past as an outsider. An outsider he remains. Hammett's Continental Op served a large firm; Archie Goodwin does Nero Wolfe's legwork; Lew Archer works with the police and sometimes co-opts detectives out of town. But Marlowe operates alone. In fact, whenever another person teams with the Chandler detective on a case, that person will die and/or emerge as the culprit.

This steady isolation takes its toll. No bureaucrat, Marlowe takes charge of his life and accepts the responsibilities of his choices; R.W. Flint called him in 1947 "the American middle-class existentialist; the People's Existentialist."[8] But he can't serve the public and fulfill himself simultaneously. Perhaps he yields to the surrounding nastiness because the steps he takes to avert calamity often produce calamity. As uneasy as he is about being warm and gentle, he cares about others. Having no family, he releases his bottled-up anxieties in acts of kindness to strangers. He calls for an ambulance for a wounded crook in "Finger Man," after the crook had tried to hurt him. Nor has the shoddiness and brutality of the city calcified his heart. In "I'll Be Waiting" and "The King in Yellow," two kindly hotel detectives, alter egos of Marlowe, make sure that sleeping women have enough warmth and air before leaving their rooms; Marlowe displays similar compassion toward a sleeping woman in *Playback*. Everybody deserves the detective's pains because everybody matters; three people love the depraved Carmen Sternwood in *The Big Sleep*. But the detective fidgets and even bolts when people start mattering too much. Both his and his author's fear of entrapment by women find expression in rings, symbolic of female sexuality and marriage. In Chapter 27 of *The Big*

Sleep, Marlowe is foiled by two rings—the inner tube the garage mechanic Art Huck imprisons him inside (called "a perfect ringer" by Marlowe) and the solid cylinder of coins gangster Lash Canino makes a fist around before knocking Marlowe out. Fear of capture by the female remains an issue, as Marlowe wakes up from Canino's haymaker in the presence of Mona Mars, whom he only opens his heart to after she reveals herself as Eddie's wife and thus no threat to his, Marlowe's, freedom. In addition to restraining him, the encircling female will also soil him. Chandler concludes his description of the squalid Fulwider Building in Chapter 26 of *The Big Sleep* by mentioning "a pouched ring of pale rubber." In *The High Window*, Marlowe hides a counterfeit coin supposedly minted in 1787 but symbolizing, in its falseness, the hollowness of American tradition, in a tobacco pouch. That the tobacco pouch is his and that he wore rubber-heeled shoes the day he went to the Fulwider Building, where he found the pouched rubber ring, reveals his ongoing fear of women. It's no wonder that he has chosen a line of work which discourages others from getting close to him.

Detection puts him into people's lives intimately and dramatically while offering the promise of escape. He leaves the criminal milieux he investigates as suddenly as he had entered them; once finished with a case, he presumably moves on to a new one. The haste with which he departs a social circle can mystify the circle's members. In *The High Window*, a man whose family he has helped bids him an unbelieving goodbye: "You are going—just like that? I haven't thanked you. A man I hardly know, taking risks for me—I don't know what to say." Marlowe commits himself briefly but fully. He has no close friends, owing to his erratic work schedule, the rough company he keeps, and the care he must take to avoid serving special interests. If word ever got around that he could be manipulated, his effectiveness as an investigator would suffer. "Just don't get too complicated, Eddie. When a guy gets too complicated, he's unhappy. And when he's unhappy—his luck runs out," says one shady figure to another in *The Blue Dahlia*. His words also apply to Marlowe. Knowing that his strength and his effectiveness both lie in simplicity, he rules his life by a stern and simple morality. He forgoes friendship, and he won't accept payment unless he feels he deserves it, which means he must put in many hours, drive many miles and come close to being killed in the line of duty: "I've got a five-thousand-dollar bill in my safe but I'll never spend a nickel of it. Because there was something wrong with the way I got it," he says in *The Long Goodbye*. Yet his moral integrity can mislead, puzzle, or anger him. Noble expectations go smash and the Victorian morality he has always relied on proves stale and untrustworthy.

Marlowe is the typical American loner hero, sensual, cynical, and childish. His occasional clowning bespeaks the sensitivity and insecurity of the misfit, just as his bravery and loyalty confirm his high principles. He isn't materialistic in that he wants neither money nor goods (even though, as Linda's husband, he gets both). Nor does he crave exotic food, foreign travel, or the more contemporary ideals of sharing and participating; not for him such goals as developing a caring relationship or redeeming his unfulfilled potential. His rejection of urban America to create an America of the mind would have made sense at Brook Farm, Walden Pond, or any number of frontier homesteads. He has cultivated a fussy, exaggerated morality to correct an exaggeration in the opposite direction. Setting himself high professional standards, he reserves the right to obey his conscience even when it clashes with powerful vested interests, like the police. In *The High Window*, he defies both a police lieutenant and his own rich client, both of whom order him off the case. His search for a better justice recalls Huck Finn's decision to flee what passes for civilization in favor of the territory ahead. The American literary hero won't settle for something less than he can imagine.

But urban sprawl has denied him the space to create a new world. Now that the frontier has closed, he must build *ex nihilo*. As Grella has said, "The private eye observes a moral wasteland and, with no 'territory' to flee to (unlike Huck Finn), he retreats into himself."[9] Being himself is his own luxury in a world stained by crime. Honesty and integrity are all he has to know himself by. He wears his badge of distinction proudly, believing that an honest detective can't make money and accepting the sacrifice. In *The Long Goodbye* he turns down a drink from a woman he believes a killer (thus supporting the argument that although he drinks heavily and drinks alone, he's no alcoholic). To keep moral distance between himself and the gambler-blackmailer Eddie Mars of *The Big Sleep* he rejects Mars as a client. The shabby, dusty office he goes to in nearly every one of his novels stands as proof that he hasn't been corrupted. Often he will go to his office after an unnerving episode. Such moments restore his spirits. Take away his honesty and you pick him clean. Only his scruples divide him from the gaudy, the shoddy, and the vicious. Determined to give good value, he offers to return the fee he had collected from General Sternwood because the job he did for the General fell short of his professional standards. His moral puritanism has blinded him to his own merits. The cover-up crime in the novel—the disposal of Rusty Regan's corpse—costs more in heartache and money than did the original one, Regan's gunning-down. Only Marlowe's ability to resist the temptations of sex and money ends this exploitation. His refusal of loose money in both "Red Wind" and *The Little Sister* also gives him bargaining power. In a society in which money confers worth, a person who sneers at money is unpredictable; he has removed the accepted common denominator for any transaction. In *Playback*, where his reluctance to take money makes his client call him "a queer sort of detective," he even demands to know why he was overpaid.

His integrity enriches his professional standards. By de-emphasizing sex and money, he has become more aware of existence as a whole. He rejects the sexual overtures of the Sternwood sisters in order to give them something more lasting and beneficial. Other examples of his integrity come to mind. He won't accept payment twice for doing the same job, even if his labors help someone other than his client. Nor can he be bought by a higher bidder off a case he has agreed to investigate. As is seen in his destruction of the negatives showing Carmen Sternwood naked, he also practices discretion (he'll destroy incriminating photos in *The High Window* and *The Little Sister*, as well). He doesn't trade secrets with the police; he buries them. And even though his professional integrity sometimes alienates, it also contains room for a leavening of humor. Marlowe will laugh at himself both to defuse danger and to avoid taking himself too seriously. Feeling his wrists jerked behind him and a knee slammed into his back, he scoffs at his pain: "A knee like a cornerstone went into my back. He bent me. I can be bent. I'm not the City Hall. He bent me." This lightheartedness is good therapy. His search for an unfallen world commensurate with his moral standards would end in the barrens of megalomania and paranoia without it. The objectivity implied by his humor has also taught him to accept realities other than his own. No crusader, he explains the truth of Horace Bright's death to Merle Davis in *The High Window* as fully and as accurately as he can; he also drives her to her family in Kansas. If he can't convince her that she has been brainwashed for the past ten years, he has done his best.

But these moments of moral clarity don't come often enough to quiet his fears about being drawn into the cultural collapse surrounding him. Hardboiled fiction always calls attention to the loneliness of the private eye. In Hammett's *Dain Curse* (1929) and Ross Macdonald's *Moving Target* (1949), the culprit is the detective's friend. In Ross Macdonald's *The Galton Case* (1959) and

Chandler's *Farewell, My Lovely, The High Window,* and *The Little Sister,* he/she is the detective's client. "Killer in the Rain" ends with the detective saying, "I felt tired and old and not much use to anybody." His exhaustion can foster moral elitism. A hubris of the imagination sometimes makes Marlowe cling to principles he has pushed beyond realistic limits. He's a moral absolutist in a world of relative values; all too sadly, he proves that riding a morality longer than is feasible carries stiff penalties. By flouting common sense, he subverts both his integrity and himself. "The smart thing for me to do was to take another drink and forget the whole mess," he tells the reader in *The Big Sleep.* His train of thought continues, "That being the obviously smart thing to do, I called Eddie Mars and told him I was coming down to Las Olindas that evening to talk to him. That was how smart I was." One drawback of pushing limits beyond the bounds of common sense is isolation; nobody wants to join you on the cold, arid edge. As has been seen, Don Quixote recoils from the sight of himself in the mirror. Like him, Marlowe also sees facts as the enemies of truth. Also like western literature's most famous knight, he delays as long as possible his confrontation with the Knight of the Mirrors. But the self must be faced. He can't escape from his own feelings; nor can he keep hiding behind a pose or a job. When self-confrontation occurs for him, usually at the edge of a bed in a lonely room, a glass of whisky in his hand, his life looks as pathetic as Don Quixote's did to *him* trembling before the Knight of the Mirrors.

The Long Goodbye finds Marlowe trying to moderate his extremism by opening himself more to people. His attempt fails. When he's not sunk in self-pity, he's showing off to himself. A riptide of egocentricity, he absorbs terrific punishment to vindicate his snobbish ideas about the way the law should work. His snobbery infects all. In the final scene, he can't resist drawing the letter against Terry Lennox, whose suffering at the hands of German doctors in a wartime prison camp surpassed by far his own knocks in a local jail. Marlowe lacks both the compassion and the imagination to see the difference. His relish in condemning Lennox to his face has ended a relationship consisting largely of absences. Marlowe is no more capable of meeting the daily demands of close friendship than were the wan recluses of Chandler's early poetry. Having relished seeing Lennox again, he recites the bitter farewell speech he had rehearsed so many times in his mind. He could impress us more by cultivating his own merits than by impugning those of others. Lennox's dignified departure after Marlowe delivers his homily leaves the detective empty, alone, and afraid. He has neither come significantly close to another person nor shored up his shaky self-esteem. He has little hope of reaching either goal before his death.

Harold Orel's calling Marlowe "a cockeyed and careless investigator [who] succeeds where the police fail"[10] is only marginally true. To begin with, he would disclaim credit for besting the police. He fares forth into the mean streets to dig up information. Without complaining, he does his own legwork, gets dirty, lied to, and thrashed because his ambition in life is to be a good detective. By contrast, the police, especially those of Bay City, are blackmailers, bully boys, and suborners of witnesses. They want to collect graft, take bribes, and get promoted. Sharing little of Marlowe's zeal to stop crime, they investigate carelessly, pay informers, plant evidence and beat up suspects. Detection enables Marlowe to act out feelings and to test values he slights elsewhere. The cockeyed carelessness Orel mentions is a calculated strategy both to keep other people at bay and to ward off the moment of self-recognition symbolized in Cervantes by the Knight of the Mirrors. Only Marlowe's energy and professionalism give the illusion that his work fulfills him. He loves the romance of detection—the legwork, the long hours, the interviews with suspects, witnesses, and policemen. Thorough and conscientious, he tracks all leads, even unpromising ones. His methodical search of a hotel room in which he finds a corpse in *The Little Sister* recalls the slow haste of Sam Spade; the parallel phrasing, showing how each item he inspects gets his full attention, underscores his professional care:

I searched the bathroom carefully. I moved the top of the toilet tank and drained it .... I peered down the overflow pipe .... I searched the bureau .... I unhooked the window screens and felt under the sills outside. I picked the Gideon Bible off the floor and leafed through it again. I examined the backs of three pictures and studied the edge of the carpet .... I stood on a chair, looked into the bowl of the light fixture .... I looked the bed over.

Sometimes the vulnerable man will supplant the tough seasoned pro. Although he won't sleep with Vivian Regan, he does enjoy kissing her; a witness he is questioning and ogling at the same time in *The Little Sister* tells him, "I wish you'd make up your mind whether you are giving me the third degree or making love to me." His heart keeps surfacing. He will show fear by rolling a cigarette between his fingers. In the second paragraph of his debut, "Finger Man," he performs the nervous gesture while hearing from the local D.A. that his life is in danger. Viewing the corpse of a man he had spoken to the day before provokes the same emotional symptom in

Chapter 8, as does the discovery, in Chapter 10, that he's being framed to take the blame for a murder he didn't commit. The gesture also conveys his nervousness in "Trouble is My Business" and "Red Wind," when he's plucking up the courage to kiss a pretty woman.

The more his feelings are suppressed, the more stubbornly they erupt, sometimes with surprising results. A fear of death both underlies his choice of work and accounts for his apparent contempt for danger. Being a detective helps him act out the guilt he feels for surviving the rest of his immediate family. He feels exposed, the Marlowe to die next, having no older kin who will presumably predecease and thus screen him from the grave. The bipolar tension between his fear of death and a death wish explains in part the sharp, aggressive manner that both increases his exposure to and helps him survive danger. The knowledge that the previous detective assigned to a case in "Trouble Is My Business" died in the line of service doesn't deter him; if trouble is his business, he must accept it as part of a normal day's work. He will also intensify or bring on trouble by trading insults with anybody. His habit of needling people stems more from design than from instinct. By making others lose their composure, he can extract information more readily than otherwise; a flustered witness will blurt out more than one under control will. Speir has described the benefit gleaned by Marlowe's witty backchat: "Wit in the face of adversity is one of Marlowe's distinguishing characteristics, a technique which often serves to throw his foes off stride, just enough for him to retaliate."[11]

Some of these foes are powerful. In *The Big Sleep* he defies Eddie Mars, who has him covered with a Luger and whose henchmen are just steps away. The novel's next chapter finds him accusing Joe Brody of murder while Brody's pistol is pointing at him. Time after time, he'll invite beatings by intensifying pressure instigated by someone else. He insults a police captain in *The Long Goodbye* in front of junior officers whose respect the captain needs to do his job. He insults the captain, moreover, while sitting with his hands cuffed behind his back. Such behavior is outrageous. Reversing all ideas about personal safety and survival, his eccentricity confuses the captain long enough ("he sat there perfectly still and let me say it") for the Police Commissioner to demand his release on the telephone. Perversity can lead to wisdom. The tactic of riding with the flow of energy to apply pressure from a position of weakness can defeat an opponent at least once. Its originality and courage make good practical sense. A brilliant shock tactic, it only appears to heighten danger. First, it removes pressure from Marlowe. By holding ground, he wards off the contempt that would automatically follow from his groveling. By forcing the issue, he makes his opponent consider violence as an option before the opponent is ready. The tactic, like all others, sometimes backfires. To stop the psychic consultant Jules Amthor from controlling their interview in *Farewell, My Lovely*, Marlowe affects slang and wisecracks. His wit earns him a blackjacking and arrest at Dr. Sonderborg's, where he's drugged and held for two days. Yet even this suffering reaps gains, buying him enough time both to solve the case and help reform Bay City's corrupt police force. Upon the drug-dealing Dr. Lester Vukanich of *The Long Goodbye*, he scores more lightly but more quickly. He lets the pompous physician know he has penetrated his facade by speaking ungrammatically. Answering one affectation with another, he mocks Dr. Vukanich's cultured airs while carrying forward the doctor's intention to prove his superiority, but in terms insulting to the doctor. Again, he carries the day by going with the flow of energy established by someone else but by imposing his own momentum.

His refusal to show that he has been impressed with money, rank, and power goes beyond his abuse of doctors. With Sheridan Ballou, the influential Hollywood screen agent in *The Little Sister*, he is just as tough and aggressive. His final insult consists of gulping Ballou's vintage Armagnac brandy rather than sipping it reverently. He will also steal the advantage from the bullying Derace Kingsley of *The Lady in the Lake*, even though their interview takes place on the executive's home ground, his office. Marlowe stands up to Kingsley, smoking without asking for permission and answering sarcasm with sarcasm. To Kingsley's, "I don't like your manner," he replies, "That's all right .... I'm not selling it." His self-control has worked for him. He knows that he's offering Kingsley a service he needs—the skill and understanding of a good detective. He can afford to let him bluster. But his ability to handle people goes beyond gaining the upper hand. The respect he accords eighty-year-old Henry Clarendon IV in *Playback* conveys tact, timing, and delicacy. Even with Kingsley, he tempers his aggressiveness as the interview goes forward; better a cooperative client than a hostile one. Having established the mutual trust and esteem needed for a good working relationship, he waives Kingsley's offer of a retainer (something he did not do with Mrs. Murdock of *The High Window*).

Marlowe's clarity and effectiveness both increase as he moves away from himself—his losses, frustrations, and sorrows. Many readers agree that the American fictional detective, like his forebear, the frontiersman, distinguishes himself in action but embarrasses himself in thought. The actionist Marlowe stumbles most badly in the area of feeling. The brilliant strategies he improvises don't serve any master plan geared to promote his well-being. This man without deep emotional ties may lack the inner reluctance of Sam Spade and the compassion of Lew Archer. But he's just as modern a detective hero as these two men, in spite of himself. He sees his prepackaged ideas about right and wrong and about appearance and reality go smash in nearly every case he takes. No other series detective takes more physical battering than he. His ability to soldier on, sometimes with self-irony, in the face of pain, much of which, admittedly, is self-imposed, has also made him one of modern fiction's most readable, likable detectives.

Chapter Four

The Mind and Art of the Short Stories

CHANDLER'S SHORT STORIES resemble his novels in their reliance upon nightclubs, casinos, cheap hotels, and mansions owned by big-time hoodlums. Other resemblances follow. As is implied by the name of the detective in "Spanish Blood" (*Black Mask*, November 1935), Sam Delaguerra, meaning Of the War, life emerges once more as a battlefield peopled by headstrong individuals careless of the means they adopt to reach their goals. Their unscrupulousless mines the battlefield with dangers. Blackmail resurfaces as a common criminal motive; the detective, who is usually knocked out at least once, will often wake up from a blackjacking in the presence of a murder victim; time and again, he will confront the culprit with his guilt while looking down the bore of the culprit's handgun. As in the novels, casualties run high on this civilian battlefield. Many die, and few of their survivors get what they want. Those who want publicity, like the ageing actor in "Pickup on Noon Street," pay too great a price for it by calling upon the services of the mob. A missing persons case will generate sour ironies. General Dade Winslow of "The Curtain" hires a detective to find a man already dead for weeks. The motif recurs in "The Lady in the Lake" with a sinister twist, as the detective's client killed the missing person himself a month before hiring the detective to look for her. In "Trouble Is My Business," a gambler discusses the importance of keeping alive a debtor who, unknown to him, has been killed and then stuffed into a closet in the next room. The detective, here and elsewhere, earns little money or satisfaction for his efforts on this corpse-strewn battleground. "I felt tired and old and not much use to anybody," reads the last sentence of "Killer in the Rain." Having fought in a war that crosses generations, infects homes, and wrecks families, he feels also numb and soiled.

The title "Trouble Is My Business" captures an actionism and mannish arrogance that sometimes cheapens the stories. Masculine

90

posing asserts itself in the car the Chandler detective-hero drives. John Dalmas' Packard roadster in "Smart-Aleck Kill," Marlowe's 1925 Marmon touring car in "Finger Man," Sam Delaguerra's Cadillac convertible in "Spanish Blood," and the Chrysler sedan driven by the anonymous narrator-sleuth of "Killer in the Rain" all reveal a fetish for power and size. Delaguerra and the Marlowe of "Smart-Aleck Kill" show that the Chandler detective will put up with age in a car to get size and power. Chandler, who enjoyed driving his car fast, sees a big car with a strong engine as a man's due, regardless of the disrepair of the man's bank balance. Like the financially squeezed English gentry who never considered firing their servants to relieve pressure, the Chandler sleuth accepts his car as part of his stock-in-trade as a he-man.

But he isn't always driving fast or talking tough. Often in the short fiction, men will display a delicacy of feeling that installs them in the role of interceder or protector usually assigned to women in western literature. Delaguerra shields Belle Marr's feelings by hiding her husband's guilt from her. Grasping unstated truths, other men beside the detective display tenderness. In "Guns at Cyrano's," a prizefighter confesses to a murder performed by the woman he loves. The tender-tough giants with prison records who cleared an artistic path for Moose Malloy of *Farewell, My Lovely* also rate compassion over profit and gain. The first of these bruisers, Tony Dravec of "Killer in the Rain" (1935), will pound or choke a man with his steelworker's hands. But he's gentle, hesitant, and unsure of himself while discussing the woman he loves. He also cares enough about her to ask for help when he finds her drifting into trouble. Big Steve Skalla of "Try the Girl" not only takes the blame for a crime enacted by his beloved. Conveying Chandler's finely tuned appreciation of the depth and purity love can attain, he also accepts the penalties of caring. His chivalry backfires when the widow of his beloved's murder victim overhears him confessing to the crime. Not knowing his confession to be a lie, she avenges her husband's death by shooting Skalla to death. His last words convey an instinctive wisdom missing in his more sophisticated counterparts: "Leave her alone. Maybe she loved the guy." The primitive Skalla is close to the animal sources of truth. Having been misled himself, he knows how love misleads and destroys. His rising above vengeance makes the survival of the others in the story look cheap and small. General Dade Winslow's tender loving concern for his missing son-in-law, Dudley O'Mara, in "The Curtain," shows love based on comradeship ennobling a man. Women, too, face the dangers of love in the short fiction, although, mostly, because

Chandler didn't understand women as well as men, these dangers are asserted rather than dramatized. The third paragraph of "Goldfish" puts Kathy Horne's vulnerability to her scapegrace husband in the same category as Moose Malloy's love for Velma:

> She ... had once been a policewoman and had lost her job when she married a cheap little check bouncer named Johnny Horne, to reform him. She hadn't reformed him, but she was waiting for him to come out so she could try again.

Although this loyalty could produce narrative excitement, Kathy and her husband never appear together. In fact, "Goldfish" ends before Johnny's prison release. Accordingly, the lover for whom the heroine of "Red Wind" would have sacrificed everything died years before the time of the recorded action. Chandler didn't dramatize this magnanimity because he doubted it. The suspicion and fear of women reflected in the novels recurs in the stories, whose brevity might have tempted a writer more adventurous than Chandler to refresh or expand his moral outlook.

The Marlowe of the short fiction also resembles the battle-weary knight of the novels. In "Red Wind," he refers to his "long practice in doing the wrong thing." The story introduces a plotting variation that, rather than changing, solidifies his personality and style. Lacking a client, he helps a distressed woman because, he claims, he likes the sound of her voice. When the gentle-speaking woman helps him overcome an armed attacker, he offers to serve and honor her with the fervor of Don Quixote. In his euphoria, he has forgotten that the woman exposed him to danger. It is almost as if he had been waiting for her to materialize. He isn't exaggerating when he tells her, "That buys me .... Anything I have is yours—now and forever." He doesn't overrate the importance of the help she gives him so much as seize the chance to repay it with interest. His response to her the rest of the way exceeds the stimulus she has provided, too. His mannered farewell to her at the end, his last chance to move her with his chivalry, wavers between stoicism and self-pity, as if he were setting before her his full range of emotional responses to improve her opinion of him. "If anybody bothers you ... let me know," he tells her just before walking away from her without looking back.

Kindness comes more easily to him away from an attractive woman, who might read it as a token of commitment; the prospect of being romantically obligated terrifies him. Holding no grudges, he pours a drink of scotch in "The Pencil" for a thug, now disarmed, who just threatened to shoot him. Later in the story, he applies a tourniquet to the bleeding hand of another hostile gunman. Chandler's detectives may help their enemies more than they do their friends, before whom, in order to keep up the he-man image, they must beat back feeling. When John Dalmas comforts a wounded friend in "Smart-Aleck Kill," he sounds like a movie cowboy consoling his sick horse: "Take it easy, old timer . . . . Easy, boy ... easy." The feeling the detective-hero expresses most spontaneously, amid friends as well as foes, is defiance, especially of the rich and powerful. When a gangster who has come to his office in "The Pencil" points a pistol at him and orders him to put his hands up, Marlowe refuses to comply; he won't be told what to do on his own turf. At times, he's so contrary that he'll ignore other inclinations for the satisfaction of defying someone in power. Harriet Huntress' adoring references to his brown eyes in "Trouble Is My Business" fail to stir him. He only starts dating Harriet after gambler Marty Estel tells him to stay away. He shouldn't have bothered. He and Harriet have little in common, as the story's last sentence makes clear: "I was glad when she left—even though she didn't bother to tell me goodbye." He only took her out twice before she left town. Had Marty Estel not ordered him to leave her alone, he'd probably not have wasted both her time and his own by asking her out to begin with.

Through it all, his crime-stopping technique remains strong. He follows trails conscientiously, even if they take him to northern Washington ("Goldfish") or Flagstaff, Arizona ("The Pencil"). He uses his knowledge of the law to protect himself, with both lawmen and outlaws. In "Goldfish," he reminds an ex-convict covering him with a Colt .45 that the possession of a firearm, for him, constitutes a felony. His stand-in, Ted Carmady, helps himself in "The Man Who Liked Dogs" by reminding the director of a mental home that a policeman can't act as a complaining witness in a mental case (as Marlowe will do in *Farewell, My Lovely*). Carmady stops a foe again, however briefly, in "Try the Girl," by saying that arrests can only be made by someone holding an official, not a special, badge. Reacting quickly also helps Marlowe. When the heroine of "Red Wind" jabs her automatic into the ribs of a man holding him at gunpoint, the detective, spotting his chance for freedom and safety, stops the man with a swift volley of punches and kicks.

But what has he salvaged? Sadness touches all his enterprises, none of which fulfills or gladdens him. Chandler's naming the heroine's dead lover in "Red Wind" Stan Phillips and an early murder victim in *The High Window* George Anson Phillips lowers the cloud cover around his detective. The fog belt thickens. As has been seen, "The Pencil" shows Marlowe spurning the chance to pierce the mists; nor would he (or Chandler) have been able to sustain the patter that flickers over his marriage in "The Poodle Springs Story." The Marlowe of the short fiction mirrors the self-evasive knight who both steers and stumbles through the novels.

I

Recurring elements, some tired and some fresh, also carry Chandler's signature. Four straight stories published in 1937-38 name a color in their titles—"Mandarin's Jade," "Red Wind," "The King in Yellow" and "Bay City Blues." Like *Farewell, My Lovely* after them, "Goldfish," "Mandarin's Jade," "Red Wind" and "Pearls Are a Nuisance" all center on a jewel theft; Mr. Jeeter of "Trouble Is My Business" prefigures Marlowe's irascible, ageing millionaire clients in *The Big Sleep* and *The High Window*; in "Trouble" and "Pencil" Marlowe is warned off a case shortly after accepting it, as he will be in *Farewell, My Lovely* and *The High Window*. Many of the stories share structural similarities with the novels, as well. As *The Big Sleep* will do in its opening paragraph, "Blackmailers Don't Shoot," "Spanish Blood" (*Black Mask*, November 1935), "The King in Yellow," and "Trouble" all begin with a closely detailed description of a person. A story opening Chandler uses more often comes in his showing his detective, a week or more away from his last case, having his idleness broken by a visitor or a phone call. "I wasn't doing any work, just catching up on my foot-dangling," says a lounging Marlowe at the outset of "Goldfish." The John Dalmas story, "Mandarin's Jade," opens similarly: "I was smoking my pipe and making faces at the back of my name on the glass part of the office door.... There hadn't been any business for a week." In this story, as in "Mandarin's Jade" before it and "The Lady in the Lake" after it, he gets work from a homicide detective named Violets M'Gee, so named because of the violet cachous he uses as breath fresheners. Whether M'Gee visits Dalmas in person or telephones him, he is chiefly a device to get the detective detecting. Like the nameless Old Man, director of the Continental Detective Agency in Hammett's Continental Op Stories, he drops out after putting the sleuth to work; having instigated narrative movement, he needn't re-enter.

The Chandler detective is a Sherlockian blend of indolence and high-speed action (a hotel manager in "No Crime in the Mountains" is waggishly named Mr. Holmes). Even prolix, bookish-sounding

Walter Gage of "Pearls Are a Nuisance" is loafing his morning away until a phone call sets him moving. The story's opening sentence, with its superfluous first five words, shows that he needs an editor as badly as a prod: "It is quite true that I wasn't doing anything that morning except looking at a blank sheet of paper in my typewriter and thinking about writing a letter." Creations of a writer who believed that good literary detection consists of exciting scenes, Gage and his fellow investigators in the Chandler canon display great energy once given the chance. A plot device used in "Nevada Gas," "Guns at Cyrano's" and "The Man Who Liked Dogs" to keep the detective hopping is the reversal. A new gun will enter a room in which someone is being covered; the entry of the new gun, a foe of the gun in control, shifts the balance of power immediately. Unfortunately, such narrative excitement makes for weak resolutions; nonstop movement blocks the formation of either values or relationships capable of dissolving tension plausibly. Relying upon sensation and violence, Chandler will often bring his criminals together in the last or next-to-last chapter of a short story. Evildoers shoot it out in the closing pages of "Smart-Aleck Kill," "Guns at Cyrano's," "Pickup on Noon Street," and "Bay City Blues." In "Blackmailers Don't Shoot," three sets of gangsters save Chandler trouble by disposing of one another. Regrettably, these exterminations exclude the detective. Were the detective to control them, defeating the culprits with a divide-and-conquer strategy, Chandler could claim some credit for deft plotting. But the shootouts usually occur in a gangster's lair, where the detective has been taken at gunpoint. Lacking the ingenuity of a Sam Spade, the Chandler detective will get swept into the mayhem rather than controlling it by setting crooks against one another.

A plotting device just as hackneyed but more artfully deployed than the blood-and-cordite resolution is the nightclub setting. MacShane has shown how the cabaret both serves as a microcosm of society and captures the topsy-turvy morality of southern California, where images count more than the indwelling reality, where play has supplanted work, and where depravity, rather than virtue, provides the normal standard of behavior:

As heir to the speakeasy of Prohibition, the nightclub is a natural arena for Chandler's dramas. It is a place where night is turned into day and where people reveal the undersides of their nature. People from all levels of society mingle there.[1]

The most wicked of nighttime activities, and the one which trades most heavily upon the dark side of humanity, is gambling. The power acquired by gamblers like Marty Estel of "Trouble Is My Business" describes this darkness as more natural than perverse. It surfaces effortlessly and, lacking civilized controls, drifts into the web of an Estel, who exploits it ruthlessly. Gambling debilitates; Gerald Jeeter gets murdered while several thousand dollars in debt to Estel; in "Finger Man" someone leaving a casino in the company of a big winner at roulette dies within hours. Adopting a conservative stance, Chandler scorns gambling as a surrender of choice to chance. It offers the surface glamor of adventure and the false promise of quick, easy money, pseudovalues which sort well with Hollywood's fetish for illusion. Gambling is despair because it ignores the few aids culture has marshaled to fight off inertia. "There were no windows and it was very warm, from the fire," Chandler says of the central office of the Club Egypt in "Nevada Gas," making this red hot center of gambling a symbol of hell. Fittingly, a man gets killed in the ovenlike office minutes after he enters.

The casino and the cabaret are two settings Chandler's contemporary readers would have recognized from the gangster films of the day. From the start of his career as a pulp fiction writer, Chandler used settings, attitudes, and character types familiar to the movie-going public as a way of winning them as readers. Because *Black Mask* aimed at a readership less educated and refined than that of the slick magazines of the day, it had to rely more heavily upon visual imagery, believed Chandler. Thus his first published story, "Blackmailers Don't Shoot" (1933), includes many black-and-white images to give its cinema-going readers something familiar to break down their resistance. A friend of gangster movies who saw in a magazine story elements that pleased him on a screen would be encouraged to keep reading. The most basic of these elements is the black-and-white pictorial mode of the pre-technicolor film. Chandler deserves praise both for using this mode to join the fictional film to literary detection and for shading in his own chiaroscuro so well in a first story. In ways, "Blackmailers Don't Shoot" is a tone poem of black, white and gray. The dimness in which most of the action unfolds imparts a pearly glow to the stark motives of the characters. Rhonda Farr, the movie actress afraid that her contract may not be renewed, enters as a black-and-white apparition, wearing all black except a white collar and wig. The pale-hued, black-eyed gambler she claims to have sent some incriminating letters first appears in a black car while wearing a white scarf and gloves.

In "Guns at Cyrano's," much of which also takes place in dim hotel corridors and nightclubs, the black-white interplay is equally stark. A prizefighter who wears black and silver trunks in the ring matches black trousers and shirt with a white coat and tie to go to Cyrano's, where the story's central action occurs. The scene uses black and white imagery to build a mood of portent. Just before a man carrying a black .45 automatic is shot to death by a smaller white-handled pistol, a stage act takes place in which four black men wearing white headdresses, loincloths, and sandals come on stage carrying a white mummy case. The white woman who comes out of the case and sheds her white shroud puts forth an image of resurrection that the plot will reject, just as the whitish rain that falls most of the way denies the renewal and refreshment it seems to promise. These reversals join form and content with a sophistication rarely attempted in pulp fiction. What is more, Chandler reminds us of it later in the story by introducing both an albino and a black-eyed man with "white hair . . . so thick and fine that no single hair was visible in it."

Such deft touches come, alas, rarely. Chandler's creativity was tuned more to the novel than to short fiction, as he admitted in both a March 1948 letter to John Hersey and his introductory note, written in 1959, to "The Pencil." Lacking "the short story mind," he says full-length books are his "natural element." Preceded by such adverse publicity, Chandler's short work has won few friends. One foe, Jon Tuska, calls the stories "hopelessly dated."[2] His disclaimer can be contested. The stories are no more dated than the novels; further, what one reader finds offensively outmoded may please another with its period charm. Most of Chandler's stories do fail artistically, but because of poor plotting, derivativeness, the substitution of stock materials for originality, and an excess of gangster cant. Chandler's people in the short stories use as much slang as those of James Hadley Chase, whom Chandler disparages in his letters for the same failing. Two examples from "Goldfish" will show that Chandler had no right to criticize any writer for using underworld slang. An ex-jailbird fearing recognition by another tells Marlowe, "I'll stay under cover. He's too stir-wise for me. I smell of the bucket." Later, at the second ex-con's home, Marlowe is told by an armed enemy, "Hoist the mitts while I get your iron. Up, mister."

Derivativeness mars the stories because of Chandler's heavy, sometimes shameless, borrowing from some of the popular mystery writers of his day. The later stories are more original. Whereas Marlowe will admit to being frightened, saying in "Red Wind," when facing an angry gunman, "I wasn't scared. I was paralyzed," Mallory of "Blackmailers Don't Shoot" always tries to make his work look easy, like Sayers' airily casual Lord Peter, S.S. Van Dine's Philo Vance, and the early Ellery Queen. This breeziness distinguishes many other characters, too. The people in Chandler's short stories will affect nonchalance or boredom while discussing crucial matters or preparing to strike out violently. Indolence usually denotes purpose in Chandler's stories; people are most dangerous when they look slack and weary. Mallory's first response to a policeman pointing a gun at him is to stare at the policeman "emptily."

The strongest influence on early Chandler is Hammett. Like Sam Spade of *The Maltese Falcon* and Ned Beaumont of *The Glass Key*, Mallory keeps us wondering if he's a crook, as his client claims, or a man of virtue. His face will harden and soften, bend into a grimace or relax, like those of Spade and Beaumont, depending on the pressure being exerted on him. A clearer borrowing from *The Glass Key* comes in "Finger Man" and "Spanish Blood," where the outcome of a murder trial bids to influence a coming election. Then there is the breezy greeting that Chandler's detectives have picked up from Beaumont. " 'Lo, Lou," says Marlowe to a friend in "Finger Man," and Ted Carmady of "Guns at Cyrano's" greets an elevator operator by saying, " 'Lo, Albert." Hammett pervades "Guns at Cyrano's." The story's crooked senator recalls Senator Ralph Henry of *The Glass Key*, and the prizefight which the favorite has agreed to lose but then crosses his gambler-backers by winning refers to *Red Harvest*. The story presents other problems besides those caused by these loud echoes. It includes people called Carmady, Conant, Courtway, and Cyrano, whose name recurs in the title. Although Chandler may have intended the story as an exploration-critique of his father and thus of himself, the numerous C-named characters hinder the investigation.

Nor are these people the only textual imponderables in the short stories. Chapter Nine of "Blackmailers Don't Shoot" contains the following paragraph:

Mardonne's hand came up from the desk with a blued revolver in it. A bullet splashed into the floor at Mallory's feet. Mardonne lurched drunkenly, threw the gun away like something red hot. His hands groped high in the air. He looked scared stiff.

From whose revolver did the bullet come? What happens after the round explodes implies that Mallory squeezed it off. But why would he fire at his own feet if he wanted to scare Mardonne? And why should he succeed? Certainly any fragments dislodged by the round, including those from the round itself, would endanger Mallory more than Mardonne, who has a desk between himself and the explosion. Just as perplexing, but in a different way, is the failure of both Chandler and his editors to correct the mistaken reference to Westwood Village as "Westward Village" in the opening sentence of Chapter 3. But the most egregious proofreading error in the canon comes from Chapter 9 of "Smart-Aleck Kill," where Chandler erroneously calls Dalmas, whose name appears in the previous paragraph, Mallory. The error has never been corrected—by Chandler; by the editors of *Black Mask*, where the story first appeared in 1934; by Houghton Mifflin, who reprinted it in hardcover in 1950; or by Ballantine Books, who included it in the 1972 paperback omnibus *Pickup on Noon Street*.

The only story in which Mallory appears, "Blackmailers Don't Shoot," marks a promising, though not outstanding debut for Chandler as a writer of hardboiled fiction. Chandler, who often overrated his work, disparaged the story to Paul Brooks, president of Houghton Mifflin, in a letter written on 19 July 1949: "Take the story called 'Blackmailers Don't Shoot,' the first I ever wrote. It took me five months to write this thing, it has enough action for five stories and the whole thing is a goddam pose." Mallory's posturing has already been mentioned. Even when he's not frowning or scowling for the reader's benefit, he exudes self-consciousness. Coming from Chandler's birthplace, Chicago, he combines sensitivity and resolve, breeding and power. Yet Chandler lets him stumble into the gutter shortly after distinguishing himself from the southern Californians he moves among. As he did later with Marlowe, the Chandler of 1933 couldn't yet portray strength as an internal quality. Thus Mallory calls one gangster a "dirty little wop" and another "fat boy," smirching his well-bred image; the sadism he displays with a third puts him closer to Mickey Spillane's Mike Hammer than to Marlowe:

Mallory took an unopened pint bottle of rye off the mantel and tore the metal strip from the cap with his teeth. He pushed Costello's head far back, poured some whiskey into his open mouth, slapped his face hard.

Such violence and cruelty, perpetrated by others beside Mallory, pepper the story, the first six chapters of which take place at night. Yet the plotting is less conventional and less influenced by *Black Mask* aesthetics than Durham believes.[3] No whodunit, "Blackmailers Don't Shoot" slights the process of detection.

Mallory, the detective, seems more crooked than the criminals he encounters while looking for some letters written by his client, Rhonda Farr. On the credit side, the interest created by the story hinges neither on crime nor on the violence crime engenders but upon criminal motives. Also, Rhonda Farr's desire to boost her flagging career as a Hollywood star takes the investigation over a broad social canvas. The richly varied action moves from a nightclub to a large, well-kept estate and then to a rundown shack before peaking in an apartment house in the city.

Lending the search unity is reversal. Mallory's first words, "The letters will cost you ten grand, Miss Farr," appear to identify the Chicagoan as the blackmailer of the story's title. The impression is quickly reinforced, as he is called a blackmailer by Miss Farr and then arrested as a blackmail suspect. But reversals soon come into play, changing our minds, drawing us into the fast-paced action and sharpening our attention. Like the female clients of *The Little Sister* and *Playback*, Miss Farr rejects the detective's help after clamoring for it. The letters she had wanted to recover she tells Mallory to forget. Others add their share to the pattern of reversal. A policeman who manhandled Mallory with sadistic relish befriends him. Such sudden shifts justify the question asked by Mallory in Chapter 3, "Who's kidnapped?" Within a minute of the time he asks the question, Mallory goes from being a kidnapping victim to the rescuer of another kidnappee. His last interview with Miss Farr, in Chapter 7, introduces another surprise, as he turns down her offer of payment, an act of knightly implausibility that leads to others.

As Chandler told Paul Brooks in his July 1949 letter, the story is congested—with entrances, exits, scenes, and characters. A new character, in fact, seems to enter the story in each of its ten chapters. As has been seen, Chandler gets rid of many of them by having them shoot each other to death in pairs. Mallory also breaks faith with a client, an act of unprofessional misconduct to which Marlowe would never sink. Three chapters from the end, he reveals that he was originally hired by the recipient of the Rhonda Farr letters but that he shifted loyalties because "The girl got to me with a better bid." Yet what could this bid consist of? And what does it say about Mallory as a judge of character? He calls Rhonda Farr "a nasty little rat," claims he dislikes her, and, in a gesture of contempt, kisses her hard on the mouth. She deserves his scorn, having caused four deaths in order to win herself publicity.

The prose in which the story is couched also shows that Chandler didn't have the tools of his trade in hand. His description in the first paragraph of Mallory's hair as "ever so faintly touched with gray, as by an almost diffident hand," is too literary; much more simple, direct and inventive is his calling another character's hair "the color of the inside of a sardine can." The story needs more of this unaffected sharpness. Mallory's words in his first exchange with Miss Farr, "You're good," make him sound like Sam Spade talking to Brigid O'Shaughnessy. Chandler is still groping two chapters later in his adverb-laden description of a living room: "It was a very new room, very bright, very full of cigarette smoke." Furthermore, the story's title is a misnomer. The air Mallory breathes stinks of cordite fumes and hot lead; nearly everyone in the story carries and fires guns, mostly to help resolve the action. Last of all, the proposition, blackmailers don't shoot, says nothing about Mallory, who fires a pistol with deadly accuracy and who doesn't practice blackmail. Logically, the work is a shambles.

The flaws weakening it recur throughout Chandler's short fiction, betraying his lack of development as a short-story writer. His next piece for *Black Mask*, "Smart-Aleck Kill," finds the detective, John Dalmas, telling a witness, "I'll tell you what's wrong with your story .... There's not enough fear in it." Chandler said, while introducing his 1950 Houghton Mifflin short story omnibus, *The Simple Art of Murder*, that pulp fiction generated a "smell of fear" that made it memorable. The excitement bred by "Smart-Aleck Kill" runs to waste because, as in "Blackmailers Don't Shoot" before it, it disregards the total effect. The story's bad ending testifies to its slipshod construction. A statement made by a police captain at the end, "Hell with the loose ends," doesn't make the gimcrack plotting any less embarrassing to Chandler. "Smart-Aleck Kill" resolves itself with materials different from those used to form its plot. The culprit, a political boss, is killed offstage by his wife, who never appears in the action. Though Councilman Sutro might have escaped conviction for murdering a film director, he falls before the primitive justice of an angry wife. Nobody can object to the idea of a wife's discovering her husband's infidelity and then killing him for it. But the treatment of the idea can be quarrelled with, especially when it's nonexistent. Chandler should have saved the idea for a novel, where it could get the expansiveness it deserves. Instead he ruined "Smart-Aleck Kill," a tense dramatic narrative, by smuggling it in at the end. He was right to condemn the story to Paul Brooks in his July 1949 letter as "pure pastiche."

In the same letter, he calls his next story, "Finger Man," "The first ... I felt at home with." This ease and confidence isn't felt by the reader. The story starts badly, introducing too much material in its opening pages to create forward flow. In 1934, Chandler didn't know that rhythm in a work of fiction depends upon selection and arrangement. Overcrowding remains a problem in "Finger Man," the development of character blocked by an excess of mayhem and murder. The detective's final judgment of the crime, "It was too elaborate, took in too many people," also applies to the story, which has plenty of action but little drama. Instead of moving his detective to center stage for the denouement, Chandler resolves the plot by having two gangsters die of bullet wounds while a third lies wounded. So useless is the detective that the last-chapter reconstruction is done by a crooked gambler just before his death. Other stories of the 1934-35 period also suffer from bad planning. "The Man Who Liked Dogs" starts badly and never comes right. In addition, Chandler misleads the reader in that the title figure isn't the main character. Nor does the dog, a German shepherd named Voss, play much of a part.

"The Curtain," published the same year, 1936, controls the reader's responses somewhat better. But it, too, bulges with materials. The story's family drama—a missing person loved by his father-in-law but hated by his stepson—splinters the frame of the story. As he did in "Smart-Aleck Kill," Chandler tried to squeeze a novel-size subject into a short story. Although the search for the missing person prompts some fine insights, it never attains full artistic growth. The sentence from Chapter 5, "He stood stiffly as a scorched tree, his face as white as snow," typfies the story, which also fuses the stale and the striking. Chandler sustains originality slightly better in another 1936 work, "Pickup on Noon Street," the only work from his hand that contains as many black characters as white. The solid, well-realized settings include a fashionable Hollywood apartment, an all-night diner, and a brothel in the black section of town. Yet the silly names of the characters, like Token Ware and Trimmer Waltz, distract our attention, while a breakneck tempo again prevents the formation of both feeling and character. Things also happen unaccountably. A prostitute who walks the streets of Central Avenue (where *Farewell, My Lovely* will open) provides the second of three black corpses in the story. She dies before her role in the story becomes clear. The most plausible explanation for her murder is that Chandler punished her for street-hustling. This explanation is less far fetched than it sounds, even though it makes Chandler look prudish. The adulterous Helen Carpenter of *The Blue Dahlia* also offended him; she, too, took a bullet in the heart.

The moral intrusiveness that marred "Pickup on Noon Street" turns into a zest for violence in "Bay City Blues." Chandler's closely detailed accounts of bruised, battered human flesh, especially during his description of Al DeSpain's sadistic pounding, kicking, baiting, and torso-bending of Moss "Big Chin" Lorenz, displays a fascination and near-pornographic accuracy. This vividness is undermined by poor plotting. Characters die for no reason, and the solution of the crime depends on luck. Rather than creating his own opportunities, the detective recognizes the villains from photographs belonging to the murderee. These defects don't sink the story, though, a sign of which is Chandler's having been able to rework and recombine some of its materials in *The Lady in the Lake*.

A 1938 story that warrants closer attention than "Bay City Blues" is "Red Wind," Tuska's favorite among Chandler's short fiction.[4] The story opens with power and originality. Applying the general to the particular while fanning the reader with hot desert swirls created by the Santa Ana, the first paragraph endows the wind with a disarming playfulness:

There was a desert wind blowing that night. It was one of those hot dry Santa Anas that come down through the mountain passes and curl your hair and make your nerves jump and your skin itch. On nights like that every booze party ends in a fight. Meek little wives feel the edge of the carving knife and study their husbands' necks. Anything can happen. You can even get a full glass of beer at a cocktail lounge.

The wry joke concluding the paragraph, while lacking the sharp immediacy of the references to the wind's effect upon hair, nerves and skin, reminds us, together with the pronoun "You," that the hot wind can change direction and blow misfortune our way. The capricious Santa Ana burns and howls through the first six chapters of the seven-chapter story, blackening flora and rattling both nerves and windows. Flinging dust everywhere, it makes teeth gritty and spoils complexions. Those laced by it feel that they're in hell. It's a red wind because, addling the mind and wrecking social reserves, it whips up a bloodthirst. That primordial drive, treachery, moves to the fore in its wake, making the story one of wrath and revenge. The treachery is contagious. While one man is betraying his wife with another woman, a second dies because he once testified against some underworld cronies; then Marlowe is betrayed by a police lieutenant to whom he had turned over a murderer.

These primitive emotions are well crafted. The elements of mystery and adventure declare themselves early. Marlowe witnesses a murder when a stranger who enters a bar and describes a woman he has been waiting for to the bartender gets shot by a gunman feigning drunkenness on a corner barstool. He carries no identification, and his killer, whom nobody recognizes, leaves the bar and drives away before he can be stopped. More pieces come into the puzzle. In Chapter 2, Marlowe meets a woman wearing clothes matching those described by the murder victim in the bar. Invoking a motif from "Mandarin's Jade," "Pearls Are a Nuisance" and *Farewell, My Lovely,* the woman asks Marlowe to recover some stolen pearls. The pearl theft and the proposed buyback enrich an investigation that includes an unsolved murder, a woman in distress, a heroic rescue, a good cop, a brutal cop, and a hot, noisy wind that wrecks people's appearance and judgment. The wind seems to have already blown different forms of mischief into L.A. The distressed woman has a husband with a Russian mistress he had met in Shanghai and a helper, who dies during the story, from Uruguay. The contrast between this internationalism and the native-bred Santa Ana that howls and gusts throughout creates a sense of pressure. But the narrative frame holds solid against the outward-driving pressure until the last scene. Here, Marlowe, standing by himself on Malibu's seafront, throws some simulated pearls one by one into the surf. Though a romantic cliche, his self-pitying behavior releases the accumulated tensions slowly enough to let us feel their force as they dissipate. This force, it needs saying, has developed away from nightclubs, gamblers and crooked politicians. Avoiding stock characters and settings helped the Chandler of "Red Wind" write with verve, concentration and conviction.

The strong opening paragraph of "Trouble Is My Business," published a year after "Red Wind," in 1939, promises the excitement and power of the earlier story:

Anna Halsey was about two hundred and forty pounds of middle-aged putty-faced woman in a black tailor-made suit. Her eyes were shiny black shoe buttons, her cheeks were soft as suet and about the same color .... She said: "I need a man."

Neither the innuendo in the last sentence nor the character making it will figure in the following action. Marlowe's fraught reaction to the policeman Sebold, to the "fat and erotic" building detective, Hawkins, and to George Hasterman, the Jeeters' handsome chauffeur, gives homosexuality more prominence in the story than heterosexuality. Nor is Anna Halsey the story's only outside operative; there is also John D. Arbogast, an obese handwriting expert who dies early. These grotesques play no more part in the action than do two hired guns called Skin and Beef, or the Lavon brothers from St. Louis—a gunman with a nose so white that Marlowe calls him Waxnose and "a little terrierlike punk with bristly reddish hair ... watery blank eyes, and bat ears" who acts so impulsively that the firing pin has been removed from his pistol. Chandler's failure to exploit the dramatic value of his materials shows faintheartedness. Though he perceives the materials clearly, he hasn't shaped them artistically. Skin, Beef, and the Lavons play such minor roles that they don't deserve the descriptive flourishes extended them. Speir calls the story "typical of the genre and evidence that Chandler could ... be content with tried and true formulas."[5] Formulaic "Trouble" is. But it pays more heavily for settling for stereotypes than Speir lets on. Lacking a controlling center, the story suffers from inconclusiveness and congestion. Harriet Huntress' elaborate revenge plot against her father's persecutor, for instance, needs ampler treatment than it gets.

The Dartmouth graduate, George Hasterman, a man of breeding and culture working beneath his capabilities as a chauffeur, also calls for a steadier look than the admiring glances Marlowe shoots his way. As often happens in a Chandler tale, "Trouble" contains enough material for a novel. This baggage brings about a resolution both implausible and dull. Standing in a millionaire's living room, as Agatha Christie's Hercule Poirot has so often done, Marlowe takes nearly 2000 words to establish a murder motive. His reconstruction is as unconvincing as it is longwinded. According to him, the millionaire Jeeter murdered his adopted son in order to inherit his money. His laborious explanation overlooks several important points—that Jeeter already has enough money; that, as a widower or divorce, he'd prize a son more than money even if had much less of it than he has; finally, that he'd have to pay his confederate, the chauffeur George, as much money as he'd get from Gerald's will. A mature man nearing the close of a successful business career like Jeeter should have devised a more effective strategy to add to his bankroll. In addition, his hunger for Gerald's estate and his refusal to give Harriet Huntress a cent not to marry Gerald betray an all-or-nothing mentality that clashes with his success in business. Marlowe's final statement on Jeeter in the denouement, as the greedy old man sinks to the floor in shock, "Let him fall.... Down is where he belongs," reflects Chandler's own wish to forget his failure to motivate Jeeter plausibly and thus redeem a shaky story with a sturdy finale.

Chandler's last story, "The Pencil," also violates plausibility, its solution resting upon the ability of Anne Riordan to spot two hired contract killers arriving at Los Angeles International Airport from either New York, San Francisco, or San Diego; even Marlowe mentions the great distance between airport buildings: "You can get callouses walking from TWA to American." Although he ignores the number of daily arrivals in L.A. from these cities, something he does say refers to the flimsiness of the plot. When asked why the syndicate sent a decoy to L.A. before flying in the two lifetakers, he answers feebly, "I couldn't really say. Unless the big boys feel so safe they're developing a sense of humor. And unless this Larsen

guy that went to the gas chamber was bigger than he seemed to be."
But who is Larsen? (And why isn't Chandler writing in complete
sentences?) Invoking a character who never appears and who is
only mentioned once, two pages from the end, the already weak
finale of "The Pencil" cries out for rewriting. The date of the story,
1959, explains some of this embarrassment. Chandler wrote "The
Pencil" against his creative inclinations, as he admits in his
introductory note. He also wrote it in his last year, when he was
tired, confused and alcoholic. What is more, Marlowe has no place in
the social scene of 1959, publication date of Bellow's *Henderson the
Rain King*, Kerouac's *Dr. Sax*, Updike's *The Poorhouse Fair* and
Roth's *Goodbye, Columbus*. References in the story to Series E
Bonds, Senator Kefauver and beatniks also clash with the spirit of
Chandler's L.A. Marlowe belongs in the Los Angeles of 1933-53. The
1978 United Artists remake of *The Big Sleep*, starring Robert
Mitchum, failed because it tried to transplant Marlowe to London. A
Marlowe in Europe is as incongruous as a black Marlowe or a
Marlowe detecting in 1970 L.A., which is where the 1973 version of
The Long Goodbye, with Elliott Gould as Marlowe, dropped him.
Few literary figures are rooted so firmly in their milieu. Neglecting
this truth, Chandler built "The Pencil" upon a false premise. His
miscue also helped bring about a sad end to his career as a short
story writer.

II

As Chandler showed in "The Bronze Door," "A Couple of
Writers" and "English Summer," his nonrepresentative works
sometimes contain pleasant surprises. Two such stories, both of
which unfold late at night in hotels and feature hotel detectives, are
"I'll Be Waiting" and "The King in Yellow." Of the twenty stories
Chandler published between 1933-39, "I'll Be Waiting" is the only
one to appear in a slick, as opposed to pulp, magazine specializing in
hardboiled fiction. In a March 1957 letter to crime novelist William
Gault, he recalls feeling caged by the decorousness demanded by
The Saturday Evening Post, where the story ran in October 1939:

It was too studied, too careful. I just don't take to that sort of writing. The
story was all right, but I could have written it much better my own way,
without trying to be smooth and polished, because that is not my talent.

His talent was more flexible and broadly based than he knew,
hobbled, as he was, by an alleged disdain for literary performance.
"It was a much better short story than he was willing to admit," said
Durham of "I'll Be Waiting," "for he had an aversion to slick
magazines."[6]

The story centers on Tony Reseck, a Polish-American hotel

detective described as "a short, pale, paunchy middle-aged man with long, delicate fingers." His artistic-looking hands and his admiration for Mozart give this squat, rumpled detective an ambivalence that justifies his moral delicacy. Chandler would often temper the toughness of his detectives with such details. The internal complexity of Pete Anglich, the battlescarred nark of "Pickup On Noon Street," shows in the tension generated between his cold eyes and gentle mouth. Marlowe's fondness for Mozart and chess also proves that a detective can have refined tastes. Another trait of Marlowe, his conservative life style, distinguishes Tony Reseck. In the third paragraph of the story, he is fretting because his nightly routine of listening to the radio by himself has been broken by redhaired Eve Cressy. Eve, who hasn't left the Windermere Hotel since checking in five days before, worries Reseck for other reasons. He learns that she has been waiting to join her husband, who is scheduled to be released from jail very soon. But he also learns that some mobsters want to punish Johnny Ralls for having crossed them before being convicted. What Reseck does with his knowledge is more than "a curious piece of experimentation that mimics the romantic exploits of a knight rescuing a tower-bound lady," as Speir claims.[7]

First, the rescue Speir refers to takes the story out of the realm of adventure and turns it, instead, into a psychological morality tale. As the title implies, the norm of the story is waiting, the stresses that waiting imposes and the things people do to fill in the waiting hours. Chandler connects waiting to death. Reseck worries about Eve Cressy because a previous occupant of her room committed suicide by jumping from the balcony; Johnny Ralls, the awaited husband-felon who has been waiting to get out of jail, kills an enemy waiting for him near the hotel; Reseck awaits death at the end for having engineered Ralls' escape, contrary to the mob's warnings. Eve's words, "Waiting is the hardest kind of work," have a *Godot*-like ring that pulsates through the story, which, one might point out to Chandler's credit, preceded Samuel Beckett's 1952 play by thirteen years. The story's mood is one of quiet, smoldering desperation. Starting at one a.m. on a cold, damp night, it features discards full of regret for missed chances. Yet the story doesn't drift aimlessly, having unity of both time and place to sharpen its emotional issues. Unfortunately, Chandler didn't resolve the issues with the same care. To protect Eve from flying bullets, Reseck convinces Ralls to leave the hotel without her, even without speaking to her. But his protectiveness fosters deprivation and pain. Left out of the decision-making, Eve keeps waiting patiently without getting an explanation or a reprieve. Although Reseck looks at her "as if he were looking at an altar," he doesn't want her for himself; the very quality that has won his love, her faithfulness, has also put her out of reach. Besides, he knows that he'll soon be chewed up by the mob for defying them. The most he can ask for is to sit in his radio room listening to soft music while watching over a beloved from whom he withholds the most important truth of her life—that her husband won't return to her. The ending of "I'll Be Waiting" causes deep regret. Had Chandler gone with the flow of his creative energies, he might have finished with a stroke sensitive enough not only to improve the story but also to give him the self-confidence to branch out from the hardboiled formula.

Some of the tenderness ennobling "I'll Be Waiting" gets into "The King in Yellow," a longer and, in ways, more complex story. When King Leopardi's trombone wakes up the eighth floor of L.A.'s Carlton Hotel, house dick Steve Grayce goes upstairs to restore silence. His request that Leopardi stop playing is met with a loud trombone blast and thump on the head. Neither brutal nor vengeful, Grayce responds by cuffing the abusive King openhandedly. Only after Leopardi fires a pistol at him does Grayce put him out of the hotel. But he learns within minutes of Leopardi's departure that, no mere drunken nuisance, the musician has been feeling great stress. In the wastebasket of his vacated room lies the explanation for his wildness—a note advising him to pay $10,000 or expect to die. Chandler's hotel stories look ahead to more recent drama. Grayce's response to his discovery of the note invokes Harold Pinter's *Birthday Party* (1960) just as the tension of "I'll Be Waiting" anticipates *Waiting for Godot*: "This is a quiet place. So I can't figure anybody coming here to put the bite on him." Grayce must find the answer himself. Having been fired by the hotel manager for ejecting Leopardi, he can't count on anybody; even Leopardi rejects his apology and offer of friendship.

Meanwhile the extortion case has raised some new questions. Why was Leopardi put on one of the middle floors, where transients stay, rather than in the tower suite? And what role in the extortion plot, if any, has Halsey "Jumbo" Walters, owner of both the Carlton and the nightclub where Leopardi was hired to play? This second question is slighted, once again Chandler having weighted a story with more data than it can resolve. Walters stays out of the action too long to convey Chandler's beliefs about the oppressiveness of power. Coming in only briefly at the end to speak on the telephone with a benign Irish lilt, he should have been left out. Chandler can also be indicted for cluttering his story with cliches, Grayce muttering to himself for the reader's benefit inanities like, "Steve, I think you got another job," "Hunch. Play it up, Stevie," and "Bunk .... Wasting your time, Stevie."

Other elements imply Chandler's discomfort with the third-person narration in which the story is couched. As has been said, "The King in Yellow" contains more characters and scenes than it can assimilate. So crowded is the story that the solution to the mystery relies upon off-stage action, Grayce doing his most important detection while out of view. As in "I'll Be Waiting," Chandler's failure either to cut or expand undramatized materials causes regret. The late-night hotel setting inspired some of this insomniac's best energies, though he might not have known it. Even the noise, scene shifting, and murder-clogged plot of "The King in Yellow" can't destroy the mood of repression and isolation the story carried forward from "I'll Be Waiting."

Chandler's inability to judge his artistic strengths creates fewer problems in "The Lady in the Lake" and "No Crime in the Mountains," two nonrepresentative works in which the detective leaves greater Los Angeles for the Sierra Madres, where he will meet a slow, affable constable who figures largely in the investigation. Jim Tinchfield brightens "The Lady in the Lake" because he represents a breakthrough in character portrayal with his lack of sarcasm, competitiveness, and zest for violence, those distinguishing marks of most of Chandler's city cops of the 1938-40 period. Like the two hotel-based works, "The Lady in the Lake" and "No Crime" suffer from technical problems. But the two years between them encouraged Chandler to follow his creative lights rather than lapsing into the false security of formula writing. On its own "The Lady in the Lake" is fairly routine, most of its merits having been reworked to undergird Chandler's 1943 novel. The story contains some excellent prose. The detective Dalmas' first glimpse of Little Fawn Lake, for instance, with its clearly etched details and mingling of sense experiences, will remind readers of the joy felt by the Joads during their first look at a California fruit valley in *The Grapes of Wrath*, a book published the same year (1939) as Chandler's story:

Suddenly below me was a small oval lake that lay deep in trees and rocks and wild grass, like a drop of dew caught in a furled leaf. At the near end there was a yellow concrete dam .... Near that stood a small cabin of native wood covered with rough bark. It had two sheet-metal chimneys and smoke lisped from one of them. Somewhere an axe thudded.

Along with this sharp clarity of line, the story times its revelations well, acquiring drive from Chandler's yoking the mystery of Julia Melton's disappearance to the problem of identifying a female body that has been decomposing under water for a month. But the momentum created by this deft dovetailing is slowed by problems in motivation. After finding the dead body of the man believed to have run off with Julia Melton, Dalmas unaccountably removes fingerprints from various surfaces and disposes of some lipstick-tipped cigarette butts. He can't explain his attempt to help the unidentified murder suspect. The reason he gives, "Damned if I know. I guess I took a dislike to him," i.e., the murder victim, robs one of his biggest undertakings of plausibility. Another "unaccountable intuition" of the sort he derided in "The Simple Art of Murder," his recalling seeing a woman's handbag near the murderee, sends him back to the Chevy Chase death house some days later, where he conveniently brings the two culprits to boot.

"No Crime" avoids greater L.A. once it reaches the mountains and emerges stronger for it. The story's title, which is spoken in conversation, proves ironical. Its noisy, overcrowded bars, traffic jams, shooting galleries, and blatting outboard motors have already spoiled idyllic Puma Lake. Anything can happen there. This depredation is foreshadowed when John Evans, in his only bow as a Chandler detective, gets a letter containing a $100 check and a request to come to Puma Point. One of the first things that happens to him upon arrival is the discovery of his client Fred Lacey's bullet-scorched body. From Lacey's wife comes another mystery, presumably unrelated to the shooting death. Some days before, Lacey had stuffed $500 from his gambling profits into the toe of one of her shoes. Not knowing about the gift, she gave the shoe to a maid at the hotel where she and her husband were staying to be repaired. Her discovery of what she did sent her straightaway to the shoemaker. To her surprise, the shoe still held the $500, but in counterfeit bills. Evans teases this information out of her while bluffing, piecing together material, and encouraging her to keep talking. His timing creates a useful precedent. Other examples of solid detection come in the ability both to identify a set of automobile tires from the marks the tires leave and to pick out the fresher set in a pair of overlaying ruts.

The crimestoppers will have to use all the skills they can muster, for, besides catching the counterfeiters, they'll also have to dismantle a kidnapping plot, a drug operation, a jewel heist, and, for the only time in Chandler, a spy ring. The energies put forth in the manysided investigation discredit Speir's verdict that "No Crime" is "a tired story, almost a cliché."[8] Chandler's seating the action in a vacation resort in high season gives the counterfeiting subplot special prominence; counterfeit bills become very hard to trace when circulated in heavy volume among a transient population. The search for the counterfeiters ends in a deserted mine, where some surprising reversals reminiscent of Agatha Christie keep the action hot. The full moon ending the story's first half implies that the malefactors will mix with the vacationers to work their mischief undetected. The implication is made good in the exciting, well-built second half. Through it all, Chandler has knit his motifs skillfully. The counterfeit money threatens national security because foreign spies have been passing it to downgrade our economy. Chandler's treatment of them reflects our public's attitude toward Nazis and Germans in September 1941. The Japanese is small, wears glasses, and hisses when he talks; he'll also mouthe improbabilities like, "Ha, ha. Very funny man. Some boob I guess yes." His Nazi aide is just as stereotyped with a fiendish intelligence undermined by a pathological tilt of mind that destroys him at the brink of success.

Their two friends from the hotel, Anna Hoffman and Gertrude Smith, or Schmidt, reveal a different perversity. As Christopher Isherwood did in *Goodbye to Berlin* (1939) and Ross Macdonald would do in *The Dark Tunnel* (1944), Chandler joins fascism to sexual abnormality. Gertrude and Anna live in a remote cabin allegedly because, working at night, they need quiet during the daylight hours in order to sleep. Yet Anna's mannishness and the tenderness of her exchanges with Gertrude imply sexual motives. Sexuality also sharpens the warning served by the finale, in which the two women and the Japanese, Charlie, escape with some suitcases of counterfeit bills. Though often guilty of mangling his denouements and of ending his stories inconclusively, Chandler invites neither charge in "No Crime." The story couldn't have ended differently, since, in September 1941, when it came out, the United States wasn't at war with either Germany or Japan. Thus Gertrude, Anna and Charlie threaten America's welfare by being at large but without serving, technically anyway, governments hostile to ours. Chandler's skill in dramatizing these two realities without slackening dramatic tension deserves praise.

But the story's finest achievement is local sheriff Jim Barron. A large, easygoing rustic like Jim Tinchfield of "The Lady in the Lake," he gets more attention than his prototype and, for it, emerges as a brilliant impersonation of gingham affability. His slow, smiling manner, enhanced by an up-country drawl, disguises a clever ruse he concocts to trick the spies. He always conceals his knowledge of both crime and criminal motives behind his folksy exterior. The care Chandler took with him pays big dividends even if it nearly reduces John Evans to a point of view, or device. The story's structure conveys both Barron's mounting prominence and Chandler's dislike of team detection. Evans stirs up trouble in the first half, appearing at Puma Point at an awkward time for the spies, discovering Lacey's death, and asking questions pertaining to it. Barron, who enters the action in Chapter 6 of the fourteen-chapter work, quiets the trouble. Perhaps Chandler turned the investigation over to him because, in a time of impending war, he, with his roots in the mountain outdoors, represented American values better than the city shamus, Evans. (Intriguingly, when he wrote his Marlowe-narrated *Lady in the Lake*, Chandler renamed his fatherly sheriff and restored him to the secondary role held by Jim Tinchfield.) With an eye to winning Barron reader sympathy, Chandler has him credit Evans for providing important help, and he later has Barron break the sad news of her husband's death to Mrs. Lacey. Barron also scolds Evans for smoking in a restricted area. But Evans has little *to* do besides stand around and smoke until the end, when he explains the spies' strategy to them. This restoration of Evans to center stage shows a care for artistic form rare in Chandler. His recognition of the need to smoothe the novel's texture reflects the craftsmanship that tempers the story's exuberance throughout. But "No Crime" is his last story before "The Pencil," which came out twenty years later. Though he probably acted wisely to drop short fiction for the novel, where his failings as a constructionist would be less apparent, his abandoning the form after such breakthroughs in setting, subject and character makes us wonder where he would have taken it had he persisted longer.

Perhaps he wouldn't have taken it anywhere new or exciting. An earlier story with promise that was followed by routine efforts is "Spanish Blood" (1935). Like most of his best work in the genre, the story veers from the Chandler mode in being a third-person narration, in having as its hero a police lieutenant rather than a private eye, and in incorporating a last-minute plot twist. As his counterparts do in "Smart-Aleck Kill" and "Mandarin's Jade," the hero rightly accuses an attractive widow of murdering her husband.

But then, following the husband's wish to spare her the trauma of a murder trial, he doesn't arrest her. Belle Marr's not turning herself over to the police or killing herself marks a major advance for Chandler, in that it shows him withholding both judgment and punishment from a murderess, which he won't do in *Farewell, My Lovely, The Lady in the Lake* and *The Long Goodbye*. His moral charity brings hope to a city ridden by violence. Durham's statement, "The seven murders in 'Spanish Blood' may have been excessive for one short story, but they weren't excessive for Los Angeles,"[9] captures an important truth. Lt. Sam Delaguerra's name, meaning Of the War, it bears repeating, underscores Chandler's belief that life is warfare. In a story that moves between social levels, Chandler's decision to make Delaguerra his central intelligence implies that crime is the lifeline joining people. Chandler backs his implication by describing the mendacity of politicians, judges, and the police commissioner, i.e., public officials pledged to protect society. His descriptions include telling accounts of betrayals, fistfights, and gunplay. And he deepens these descriptions by making the home and family as well as public service a battlefield where fatalities occur.

This resonance doesn't save the story. Ironically, two men who promise to figure largely in an upcoming election both die before the recorded action begins. Chandler pads the sting of this irony by cheating. Though Delaguerra recognizes a dead man he finds near a mountain woodshed in Chapter 4, he waits till Chapter 12 before sharing his recognition with the reader. The story suffers in general from this kind of misdirection. Most of the action deals with urban politics and crime, both of which are run by men. The resolution features a woman, whose crime isn't public but domestic. This last-chapter wrenching of focus shows Chandler disregarding the difference between fooling and cheating the reader; a story should be resolved along the same lines of force where it grew; otherwise, it slights the issues it raises. Finally, Delaguerra's Spanish ancestry has no bearing on the case or its solution other than to call into question the truth of his recollection of Belle and Donny Marr: "We went to school together. We used to be buddies. We carried the same torch for the same girl. He won, but we stayed good friends, all three of us." To assume that a Chicano could attend the same school as an Anglo in 1910-20 Los Angeles is to ignore not only social but also religious dynamics, since the Chicano would probably register in an all-boys' parochial school. He might not even know enough English to compete in a predominantly Anglo school. Though Delaguerra's Spanish blood could explain his courtliness in freeing Belle Marr while hiding from her the knowledge that Donny killed a man, it serves no thematic end. Chandler made Delaguerra a Spanish-American for the same reason he made several underworld figures in both "Pickup on Noon Street" and "Mandarin's Jade" black. He wanted to flex his artistic muscles. Such activity promotes growth. On the other hand, its proper place is the writer's notebook, not the published story. Chandler should have seen that Delaguerra's Spanish blood didn't help the story and then deleted it. He hasn't confronted the materials directly.

No such miscue mars "Goldfish," Chandler's best short work. Avoiding bars, gamblers, blackmailers, and political bosses, the story owes more to Chandler's imagination than to popular fictional stereotypes. The strong, clear writing shows him warming to this freedom. Striking images abound. Besides his previously quoted recreation of tropical fish swimming in a tank, there is also an engrossing passage devoted to the feet of an ex-convict that two grifters burn with an electric iron to learn the whereabouts of some stolen pearls. The story line declares itself early and clearly: Marlowe must get to the pearls before Peeler Mardo's torturers do. No whodunit, "Goldfish" features a piggyback chase. Marlowe and his rivals both want to reach their common goal first. Yet both must also mislead, sidetrack, or eliminate the competition before bounding ahead. The pursuit varies in other ways as well. Chandler relaxes narrative tempo for a chapter by sending Marlowe to an L.A. insurance office before building to the roaring climax in Washington state. He also keeps Kathy Horne, who tells Marlowe about the Leander pearls, in L.A. while killing off the adventurer called Sunset, who only joins the hunt in Olympia, Washington. Despite the speed and violence created by this story of greed, Chandler has also left room for the indirect and the unsaid. His mercenaries won't let impetuosity spoil their chances for gain. What is more, Marlowe, showing an artist's understanding of shadow and subtle detail, won't underrate them. Sunset's deadpan response to one of Marlowe's wild guesses tells the detective that his guess was right. Subtext of this sort colors the scene. Aware of the power of wordless communication, he keeps his weaponless gunhand in view while looking into the muzzle of Sunset's piece. Sunset's role in the work, though short, explains how the plot keeps rebuilding itself, Chandler introducing lively characters and scenes in proper sequence both to tighten and brighten the narrative. The various climaxes slot smoothly into place. Marlowe arrives at the thief Wally Sype's before his rivals to give Sype time to consider his offer of $10,000 for the pearls, to create an exciting finale, and to lend meaning to the excitement by prefiguring it with Marlowe's prophecy that, despite his legal reprieve, Sype will always be stalked by other thieves.

Marlowe's ability to laugh at himself freshens the tone and keeps the action from peaking too early. Chapter Five, in which Marlowe first meets the murderous Carol Donovan, begins on such a note: "So far I had only made four mistakes," he says, ironically just before getting ready to make a fifth, drinking doped whiskey served by Carol Donovan's lawyer-partner. He'll need all the clarity and humor he can muster to deal, not only with Carol but also with Mrs. Sype. "Goldfish" contains two treacherous women, who differ enough from each other in age, looks, and style to spell out Chandler's warning without any overlapping of function. Besides the ruthless Carol, who has the presence of mind and steadiness of hand to shoot a man through her handbag while the man has her covered, the story includes Hattie Sype. Mrs. Sype reveals, perhaps more vividly than any other figure in the canon, that Chandler both understood and valued tenderness and intimacy. She also extends his practice of denying noble impulses to female characters. "She had a handsome face, quiet, firm-looking," Marlowe notes of her upon first meeting. The quiet, simple dignity with which she responds to her husband's death during the melee following Carol Donovan's arrival moves both Marlowe and the reader: "Will you help me carry him to the bed?" she asks; "I don't like him here with these people." Chandler can charm as well as grip. Her devotion makes Marlowe's retributiveness look cheap—until she exposes her greed. When Marlowe refuses to give her the Leander pearls, after she gives herself away with an uncharacteristic lapse in style, she spits in his face and slams into the house.

The morality put forth by her and her husband's overthrow creates another surprise. To Sype's statement that all he wants is peace, Marlowe answers: "That's the one thing you can never have—until you give in." The peace the pearl thief of yore covets must take root in honesty. The impulse must come from within and not from any official pardon; Sype must want honesty enough to give up the fruits of his *dis*honesty. His greed makes his death inevitable. Because he views the peace that keeps eluding him arbitrarily rather than as a part of a redemptive process, he can only attain it in death. The potent, insightful finale of "Goldfish" fuses morality and art more convincingly than does any other Chandler title.

But the work remains an oddity in the canon. Whatever Chandler learned from writing it, he quickly forgot. Too few of his stories rise to the excitement that pervades "Goldfish." Certainly the three stories that followed it into print, sluggish in movement and stereotyped in both mood and situation, show that it promoted little immediate growth. And "Red Wind," which followed these three misfires ("The Curtain," "Try the Girl," and "Mandarin's Jade") outshone the nine stories which followed *it*. But we should remember that parts of "Red Wind's" three disappointing predecessors reappeared, with modifications, in two of Chandler's most admired novels, *The Big Sleep* and *Farewell, My Lovely*. And since he has been remembered as a novelist, these misfires and others like it can't be despised. Though his short story art falls short of Conan Doyle's or Hammett's, Chandler never claimed much for it; his letters show him insisting, at different points in his career, that he felt more at home in the novel than in the short story. Yet, aside from having crafted at least one outstanding story, he had both the taste and the editorial skill to fuse, adapt, and expand some of his most promising short-story material. For an overview of his artistic and editorial strengths, let us turn to Julian Symons. The astuteness of his summary makes it fitting that Symons, who has written both widely and well on Chandler, should have the last word on the subject of Chandler's short stories:

The basic defect of the stories is that the length to which they were written did not fit Chandler's talent .... The novels gave more space for the development of situations and the creation of an environment. One of

Chandler's great merits was his capacity to fix a scene memorably. He sometimes did this in a phrase, but he could do it even better in a paragraph or a page. The stories did not give him time to create anything of this kind.[10]

Chapter Five

No Game for Knights

BASED ON THE *BLACK MASK* stories, "Killer in the Rain" (January 1935) and "The Curtain" (September 1936), *The Big Sleep* is a novel of damp, overheated emotions (Chapter Two unfolds in the "thick, wet, steamy" air of a greenhouse) written with dry clarity. Dilys Powell believes it "the best of the Chandler books," and Rabinovitz, following suit, terms it an "extraordinary novel."[1] Much of the merit found by these readers stems from what Ruehlmann calls the "internal pattern of antiromantic elements" unifying the action.[2] The unseasonal mid-October rains which follow Marlowe and which are foreshadowed in the book's first paragraph portend disaster. Together with the hapless knight represented in the stained-glass panel in the next paragraph, the rains usher in the wrongness that reverses nearly all of Marlowe's ideas about knightly conduct. For one thing, the rains help give the impression that the action is taking place in a jungle or a swamp rather than in a city. The soggy veils they create limit our vision and stop us from getting a foothold. Relations among the Sternwoods are as unnatural as this out-of-season occurrence; as has been seen, no Sternwood ever appears in the same chapter with, let alone in the company of, another. The novel's first corpse, too, materializes in a home more oriental than western. Ferguson has shown how the murder victim embodies an aspect of the confusion Chandler has been building: "The name Arthur Gwynn Geiger, by echoing the names of Arthur and Guinevere, suggests a sexual confusion resulting from the perversion of romantic ideals, particularly appropriate since Geiger is a bi-sexual peddler of pornography."[3]

Geiger's one-eyedness conveys his cheap, flattened outlook. And nature seems to celebrate his death, as if it removed the nastiness and muddle coursing through the book's first eight chapters; Chapter 9, which opens the morning after the death, begins, "The next morning was bright, clear, and sunny." But the cheer vanishes quickly. The rain starts up again, and with it disorder and negation set in. Marlowe is to learn that a wide gap divides the ideal from the real and that the short hop separating the quester from his quest holds surprises. The missing person Marlowe is hired to find lies dead within view of his client's property; Porter says rightly that *The Big Sleep* (1939) "takes the ironic form of the unnecessary journey."[4] A major development in the irony comes before we're ready for it; in the first chapter, Carmen Sternwood pretends to faint so that Marlowe can catch her. His discovering later that she murdered the man he was hired to find means that he literally caught her, the murderer, before taking the missing persons case. This irony squares with the moral and ideological distortions pervading the murder. Carmen lusted for her sister Vivian's husband and then killed him for denying her sexually. As has been said, the word she uses to express erotic desire is "cute." She calls Marlowe cute at first meeting. When she goes to his apartment and climbs into his bed naked, she declares her availability by calling herself cute. So depraved is she that even Geiger looks cute to her as a corpse. If the drowning death of the young man who loved her, her father's chauffeur, Owen Taylor, prompts a sea change in her, the change only takes place after the novel ends, when we can't witness it.

I -   *Color coding*
        evil = green

The novel offers little cause for hope. Marlowe's legendary meeting in Chapter 2 with General Guy Sternwood in the greenhouse puts forth nastiness as a norm, not an aberration. The nastiness goes beyond the Sternwood milieu and its rites. The plants filling the greenhouse have "nasty meaty leaves and stalks"; the General calls his orchids "nasty things" because "their flesh is too much like the flesh of men." The equation of human flesh, or meat, and the green-thronged jungle recurs in Chapter 10, where Marlowe hails a cab to follow a suspicious person. The cabdriver's reply to Marlowe's saying that he's a private eye on a tail job, "My meat, Jack," harks to the moral chaos invoked by the floral riot of Chapter 2. The recurrence of green as a function of destructive primitive emotions bespeaks a disgust with the human body that matches the novel's grim view of the body politic. Just moments before leaving Geiger's bookstore, Marlowe had noticed the eyes of the salesclerk giving off a "faint greenish glitter" while "her fingers clawed her palm." Vivian Regan will wear a green velvet dress to the Cypress Club the night she wins $30,000 at roulette. At the start of the scene in which her sister Carmen tries to kill Marlowe, Carmen appears framed by a green expanse consisting of trees, gardens, and grass terraces. Green is Carmen's color, showing that the absence of civilized restraints can corrupt growth and abundance. She wears a green woolen dress and jade earrings to Geiger's house the night she is drugged and photographed naked, which is also the night Geiger is shot to death. Chandler modifies his symbolic equation of erotic green and death during Carmen's next visit to Geiger's, when she comes wearing a green-and-white checked coat, "her face gnawed white by nerves." Her next appearance, which shows her waiting naked for Marlowe in his bed, ends with her leaving the detective's apartment with a green hat on her head and a green handbag under her arm. Though Marlowe tears angrily at the sheets she had been lying between, he can't expunge nastiness; Carmen's residue remains. The next chapter, which starts right after he tears the bed apart, opens, "It was raining again the next morning, a slanting gray rain like a swung curtain of crystal beads."

The nastiness has entrenched itself. So total is Chandler's pessimism that he dresses Mona Mars, Marlowe's dream girl, in green and white for her only meeting with the detective. Her two-tone garb, her silver wig and her appearing first to Marlowe during a rainstorm all foreshadow the first question she asks him: "What did you expect ... orchids?" In view of its context—Marlowe's hands and feet are bound—this reference to General Sternwood's disclaimer against orchids posits a degraded world. Color symbolism continues to spell out moral chaos. Though Carmen's colors are white and green, her name connects her with red, the color her green-clad sister plays while winning $30,000 at the Cypress Club. Vivian's eyes and knuckles also blanched in Chapter 3 when, displaying herself sexually amid the white trappings of her sitting room, she threatened to throw a Buick at Marlowe for defying her. (The Sternwoods' chauffeur will soon die in a Buick.) Her provoking Marlowe sexually sharpens the parallel between her favorite haunt, the Cypress Club, and the death in the next chapter. Here, Marlowe tricks a frightened customer of Geiger's into disposing of a book in a row of Italian cypresses; suitably, rain begins falling at the same time. Chandler carries his thesis forward with a Joycean attentiveness. The smell of cold sea in Chapter 21, which unfolds at the Cypress Club, and the surrounding fog, which is so thick that Vivian and her would-be robber look like "two figures blended in the fog ... part of the fog," deepen the degradation. The thief's blending visually with his intended mark implies a moral similarity that stays to the fore.

Chandler's unregenerate, unredeemed world adjoins the cold-smelling sea which humanity struggled out of long ago but which, in its nearness, also describes our failure to evolve. The traditional association of cypresses with cemeteries, or gardens of death, joins gambling to the primordial calamity which has already featured sexuality and the colors red, green and white. This calamity reverberates. General Sternwood's statement in Chapter 2 that no member of his family has "any more moral sense than a cat" and his family's West Hollywood residence on Alta Brea Crescent makes the evil Marlowe fails to crush as basic as ABC. It has rooted itself at the Sternwoods. The very means by which human life is sustained, sexuality and business, have become poisoned there. Carmen is both a nymphomaniac and a model for pornographic photos. A source of the Sternwood millions survives as a huddle of greasy oil sumps and wells rusting, falling apart, and stinking from disuse. Chandler's making this decay and grossness the site of Carmen's murder of sexual revenge against Rusty Regan shows the public and the private and also the primitive and the contemporary meshing tightly.

Important on its own, this desolation also matters because of the test it poses to Marlowe. The test is opportune, the cocksure tone of the book's opening paragraph exposing his need for moral education. Chandler's mentioning twice the stained-glass panel above the Sternwoods' main hallway entrance (in the book's second paragraph and in Chapter 30) reminds us that Marlowe, no knightly rescuer, needs to have *his* ropes cut by Mona Mars in order to survive. The ending of the book's second paragraph, describing his smirking response to the knight's failure to free the tree-bound lady, conveys his unreadiness: "I stood there and thought that if I lived in the house, I would sooner or later have to climb up there and help him. He didn't seem to be really trying." Pridefully, he has envisioned himself both living in the Sternwood home and improving upon a work of art. Though his age, thirty-three, is ideal for a fictional sleuth, permitting the acquisition of street sense without a corresponding loss in physical prowess, he lacks seasoning. He also lacks the magnanimity for the role his age and job seem to qualify him for—that of martyred redeemer. At her wickedest moments, Carmen appears to him old and wasted. The defunct derricks, reeking oil drums, and stagnant sumps that whet her murderousness also exude the decrepitude of age. Throughout, he connects age to corruption and death. His first reaction to General Sternwood is that he is "an old and obviously dying man," and all future descriptions of the General stress the ghoulishness caused by ageing. Although he helps the General, Marlowe rejects him instinctively, most certainly because of his age and possibly because he owns the mansion Marlowe wants for himself.

Another character the detective midjudges is Mona Mars. In order to dupe the police into believing that she ran away with Regan and thus allow Eddie to blackmail Vivian, who had asked him to dispose of Regan's corpse, Mona has buried herself in Realito, some forty miles from Los Angeles; the world is so topsy-turvy that a wife can best love her husband by living away from him. The selfless, unquestioning love Silver-Wig extends to Eddie Mars vexes Marlowe, whose head swims with romantic stereotypes. She won't leave Realito with the detective because of her tie to Mars. The tie is stronger than he can imagine, posing truths about sexual love he has never asked: sometimes the damsel's fetters are invisible; sometimes, what looks like a fetter proclaims the damsel's freedom and courage. Practicing a moral double remove beyond Marlowe's imaginative range, Mona loves her jailer-husband despite his dark deeds. Her cutting off her hair to help foil the police expresses her wifely loyalty so clearly that Marlowe shouldn't have disparaged Mars to her. Even if she had believed his attacks, she'd never have given the detective the satisfaction of knowing. By marrying Mars, she committed herself to him, and she takes the commitment as seriously as Marlowe takes *his* professional obligation. He learns later that the cover-up crime, disposing of Regan's corpse, has cost more in money and heartache than the original one, Carmen's shooting Regan dead. He also dismantles the costly blackmail operation by resisting the temptation of money. Thus he overcomes great odds to solve problems and to quiet suffering. Yet because he can't commit his heart to another, he finds life a burden rather than a privilege; his days are an ordeal to fight through.

His invocation of Silver-Wig in the book's last paragraph reminds him that her husband, though the cause of most of the suffering he has witnessed the past week, has gone unpunished. It also shows that the special quality recommending Silver-Wig to the detective, her loyalty, has also put her beyond his reach. But need he feel ransacked and depleted? He has judged himself too harshly. His being "part of the nastiness" constitutes a recognition that should have occurred years before. Rather than muttering about his entrapment in nastiness, he might have resolved to take his place alongside other fallible, flawed people in their attempt to ease pain.

Such efforts thwart an Eddie Mars. MacShane is right to call *Big Sleep* "a comedy of human futility."[5] Much of this futility rays outward from Marlowe, the voice, mind, and heart of the novel; the ease with which the detective defers to the nastiness inhibits justice and helps defeat the innocent. In the last chapter, he achieves his finest moment. He makes Vivian promise to get Carmen the psychiatric help she needs; he won't arrest Carmen if she goes to a mental hospital; neither Hammett's Spade nor P.D. James' Adam Dalgliesh would free a killer. What's more, Marlowe's act of moral charity occurs ten years before the appearance in print of Ross Macdonald's Lew Archer in *The Moving Target* (1949) and some twenty years before Archer renounced his hardboiled pose in favor of his celebrated compassion. But Marlowe can't withhold judgment against himself, especially when it steers him to the sidelines, where he can indulge his self-pity. He knows that moaning about his knocks and aches is easier than trying to heal them. And though he also knows that he'll continue to serve wholeness, he must first give vent to his woes. He loves to dramatize himself, perhaps as a way of protecting his individuality in the urban sprawl. Ironically, his posturing recoils on him, turning him into just one more loser perched on a barstool. He needs his double Scotch. He has worn himself out for nothing.

More objectivity would have helped him foresee the futility of playing the crusader in urban America. Although he knows that the Sternwood-Regan case is no game for knights, he keeps looking at it through a romantic haze. The rats behind the wainscoting he twice mentions refer to a hidden or disguised evil he has failed to stamp out. A remark made by Walter Wells about *Farewell, My Lovely* applies to Marlowe's misplaced idealism in *Big Sleep*: "In Marlowe's world, innocence does not exist at the beginning; hence there is none to restore."[6] The novel's outstanding example of perverted innocence is Carmen. The king-size dollops in her character of stupidity, lust, and infantile malice make Carmen a real threat. Her giggling, thumb-sucking, and incontinence in times of stress gauge the difference between innocence and infantilism. Her father describes the futility of asking her to explain her conduct when he says, "If I did, she would suck her thumb and look coy." Coyness allows her to crawl underneath the wreckage she has caused and leave it for others to repair or remove. (Does Marlowe's running practice of calling women "girls" reflect the same irresponsibility? If women are girls, then he's just a boy and not a mature man.) An attribute of her simplistic morality is revenge, a childish emotion practiced by dolts like herself and Carol Lundgren, Geiger's postadolescent male lover. Carmen killed Rusty Regan for both supplanting her in her father's heart and rejecting her body. She wants to kill Marlowe for the same reasons. What's more, she wants the murder to occur in the same site—the oil wells, now ugly from age and disuse, that helped make her family rich. But Marlowe has outsmarted her. Although she believes she has lured him to a spot where she can kill him safely, he has tricked her into re-enacting the Regan murder. In her simple-mindedness, she can't resist his offer to take target practice near the abandoned oil wells. She doesn't know that, far from having gone undetected, the Regan murder has already bled her family. This ignorance is self-replicating. The false security actuated by her repetition compulsion has blinded her to the truth that Marlowe's gun contains only blanks. Marlowe has protected himself because he knows revenge to be an amoral destructive force. Regan didn't deserve to die; neither did Joe Brody, the grifter Carol Lundgren shot because he mistakenly believed him Geiger's killer.

Lundgren's identifying mark is his ubiquitous leather jacket, which Chandler calls a "jerkin" in both dialogue and narration. The deadpan acceptance of this archaism on the part of the characters who speak it or hear it sharpens its effectiveness; the outlandish always gains impact by being contrasted with nonchalance. Carmen's identifying marks reflect the same authorial skill. Besides suggesting abnormality, her thin, narrowing thumbs turn the mind to Harry Jones, the shady dealer who wears dated clothing and, at a lean five feet three, "would hardly weigh as much as a butcher's thumb." Large, stylishly groomed Eddie Mars, who engineers Jones' death, has thumbs with manicured, polished nails, and he likes to keep them outside his jacket pockets, while his other fingers nestle within. What this rich, powerful gambler shares with the runt Harry Jones and skinny, psychotic Carmen is vulnerabilty. Like them, he's threatened. Despite his advantages, he could be crushed like an insect under a casual thumb. As the giggling Carmen proves, much of the evil perpetrated in the novel stems from the casual and gratuitous; the promise of fun takes people to the Cypress Club, where they often pile up huge debts. Privation has already touched Mars. That his wife used to sing in nightclubs deepens the void caused by her absence; as crooked as he is, he must have perceived in her the excellence that seized Marlowe. His life lacks harmony with her away. But Mona is languishing in the back country because Mars sent her there. Fittingly, Harry Jones' woman, Agnes Lozelle, also leaves town. Because they have snubbed civilized controls, most of the people in *The Big Sleep* foment violence; Carmen and Eddie Mars, both of whose thumbs attract notice, meet in an atmosphere of violence in Chapters 13 and 15. If the thumb is a phallic sign, then, as was shown by the impulses raying out from General Sternwood's erotically green plants, it bears close watching else it point to deprivation and defeat.

A motif that also reverberates over a broad range is that of the color white. Ordinarily a symbol of purity and innocence, in the moral devastation ruling *The Big Sleep* it represents infantilism. A series of brisk, highly inventive images, centering on the pale face of

Carmen, conveys the wreckage caused by the failure to learn from experience. The process occurs in the "scraped bone look" that seizes Carmen in moments of passion, making her froth at the mouth and twisting her into an ugly, ageing animal; the blessings of youth run to waste unless monitored by restraint. The more closely one looks at her, the more one feels the menace of her amorality. Her giggling mouth contains a whitish tongue and small, sharp teeth "white as fresh orange pith," as if their whiteness bespoke an alien, perhaps sinister quality. But, as her father's remark about the hereditary Sternwood amorality shows, Carmen represents but a phase in an ongoing family drama. The point is made poetically. The few surviving hairs on the whitebrowed General's head are white, and the part in Vivian's black hair blazes whitely. The upstairs sitting room of the Sternwood mansion where Vivian receives Marlowe in Chapters 3 and 32 is also done in tones of white. Reflecting the physical and emotional disorders plaguing the family, the room, though richly appointed, bespeaks chaos. Nothing coordinates in this tasteless, expensively adorned salon. The carpet looks out of place, and the various hues and textures flatten rather than enhance each other. The paragraph describing this flaccidity, it needs saying, fuses different varieties of the same shade, rather than contrasting opposite shades, which would have been easier. The gaping bigness of the room also describes the process by which, without the mediating device of good taste, more dwindles to less:

The room was too big, the ceiling was too high, the doors were too tall, and the white carpet that went from wall to wall looked like a fresh fall of snow at Lake Arrowhead. There were full-length mirrors and crystal doodads all over the place. The ivory furniture had chromium on it, and the enormous ivory drapes lay tumbled on the white carpet a yard from the windows. The white made the ivory look dirty and the ivory made the white look bled out.

The character associated with the vapid outsize sitting room, Vivian, reveals herself a slave to appetite, with her addiction to gambling, her having had three husbands, and the blatancy of her sexual overtures to Marlowe. It is germane that her eyes whiten as Marlowe inflames her in Chapter 3 and that she talks of being bled white by Eddie Mars in Chapter 32. Another aspect of her blind animal craving for Marlowe comes in Chapter 23 in his car, when she begins making sexual advances to him by turning away from him. Then, as Carmen did in Chapter 2, also to let him know that she wanted him sexually, she falls backward into his arms. Her calling him both a killer and a beast in this scene, along with the harshness of her hair, defines the rankness of her lust. Less than an hour before, she had said at the roulette table, "One more play ....

Everything I have on the red. I like red. It's the color of blood." Blood still snaps and sparkles before her inner eye. She has been set glowing by the violence in Marlowe, not the gentleness, decency, or professional integrity, those qualities that help him serve her father so well. She may have also been stirred by the violence in the IRA brigade commander Rusty Regan, who, like Marlowe, had what the family butler calls "the soldier's eye." Were this the case, he bored and finally alienated her when his Irish geniality surfaced. Yet she's no ogress. She wouldn't let Eddie Mars blackmail her unless she were protecting her father from the news of Regan's death. And she does promise both to get Carmen psychiatric care and to spare her father word of her madness. Vivian also prizes sexual love even though she and Carmen can't afford its outgoings themselves. To the statement that Owen Taylor, the chauffeur, wanted to marry Carmen, she answers, "Perhaps it wouldn't have been a bad idea .... He was in love with her. We don't find much of that in our circle."

Her recognition never improves her sexual morals. One reason Marlowe prizes Mona Mars is because, unlike Vivian, who finds him demonic, she values the kindly and the gentle in him. Appealing to his better self, she assures him that she doesn't find him dangerous. She also trusts her instincts enough to declare her love for Eddie; he didn't have to assign a guard to her during her spell of house arrest in Realito. Marlowe's conduct with her shows that he doesn't understand love—its depths or how it works. By asking her to leave Realito with him after she cuts his ropes, he's demanding more than she can give. Her freeing him, he knows, constitutes a betrayal of the husband she loves. He grows angry at himself for repaying her kindness so shabbily. Though his slandering of Mars proves counterproductive, he can't stop his mouth. Yet she does kiss him goodbye, and she helps him kill her husband's henchman, Lash Canino. These loving acts baffle him because the moral ambiguity informing them clashes with the absolutism of his knightly code. His anger rises whenever he thinks of her because he suspects that he deserves her more than Mars does.

His behavior here and elsewhere in *The Big Sleep* sets the model for his responses in future works; unlike Ellery Queen and Ross Macdonald's Lew Archer, he remains fairly uniform in personality, attitude, and style over his career. He also attracts women. Mona Mars wouldn't have outraged her principles unless she felt compelled; Carmen's compulsion to sleep with him, seizing her at first sight, persists throughout the book; although he walks out on Vivian after defying her in Chapter 3, she comes to his office to apologize in Chapter 11. His integrity wins the day for him elsewhere too. Firmly but politely he refuses to tell the D.A. all he knows about Owen Taylor's murder; his client, he reasons correctly, is legally entitled to his silence. Having a firm sense of himself enables him to hold a style with different sorts of people. He responds graciously to Vivian's apology; he pries the naked snapshots of Carmen from Joe Brody without paying for them, even though he states most of his case with Brody's revolver trained on him; by making Harry Jones feel important, he coaxes more information out of the little man than he had intended to give. Accordingly, within the same span in *Farewell, My Lovely*, he has speech with the prissy, Anglicized lounge lizard Lindsay Marriot, the roughly hewn Lt. Nulty, and the smooth, hip-talking black manager of the Sans Souci Hotel. Later in the novel, he resists avenging himself on a Bay City cop who had previously manhandled him. His restraint serves him as well as his social mobility. By treating the policeman better than both men know he deserves, Marlowe wins his trust. He also gains interviews with reluctant witnesses and suspects by convincing them that he can help them. Chapter Twenty-Six of *The Little Sister* brings back this ability to win people to his side. Dolores Gonzales gives him useful information because he has persuaded her that they have a common cause.

His ability to handle people comes largely from his rating feelings as high as facts. Because he respects the intelligence of a salesclerk in Chapter 5 of *The Big Sleep*, he won't bully or trick her into giving him the information he has come for—a description of Arthur Gwynn Geiger. He counters her growing resistance by telling her that the sheriff's badge he just showed her is worth a ten-cent cigar. His judgment of the clerk proves correct. Appreciating his irony and self-mockery, she tells him what he wants to know. He doesn't save his discretion for women. Ever mindful of shielding General Sternwood from pain, he keeps quiet about taking Carmen home from Geiger's the night of the pornographer's death. He even forbids the butler to call him a cab. "I'm not here. You're just seeing things," he replies to the butler's offer, preferring to walk more than a half hour to his car rather than making his presence at his client's known to a cabdriver. The grantee of his delicacy needn't be rich. An ageing elevator man in *The High Window* helps him because he treated the elevator man civilly. Marlowe's good will has occasioned poetic justice. The detective spoke decently to Mr. Grandy not because he wanted something in return. Such selfishness would have recoiled upon him. By not setting out to use people, he wins their confidence and their help. The imagination is served.

A person capable of moral delicacy will perforce prize it in others. "It wasn't your money you cared about .... You really liked Regan," he tells General Sternwood the last time he sees him. He admires the General both for caring more about people than money and for going beyond the blood tie in search of love. In the posthumously published (1976) essay, "Farewell, My Hollywood," Chandler calls integrity "an act of courage and defiance performed at the risk of losing your job, and for no personal gain but the desire to do that job a little better than they wanted you to do it."[7] Marlowe was fired for insubordination by the L.A. Police when he kept investigating cases his superiors had shut down. Tenderness like that shown by General Sternwood prime this integrity. Not only does Marlowe put all his skill, training, and experience at the General's disposal; he also offers to return the money paid to him when he learns that some of his methods have riled the General.

Rabinovitz anchors his description of *The Big Sleep* as an anti-detective novel in the bleakness that takes over at the end:

The novel ends not with the soothing conservative affirmation of order but with something more politically unsettling: loose ends, a detective who fails, and a pervasive sense of individual despair, social chaos, and the triumph of evil.[8]

Though basically sound, Rabinovitz's description is overstated. Marlowe enters the Sternwood case with high professional standards, which he never relaxes. He continues investigating after Geiger's death, even though his assignment ended officially at this point. While protecting himself and his client, he plays it straight with the police. He also saves his client money by refusing to pay Joe Brody for the pictures of Carmen, and he reports to the General regularly. Above all, he shields him from pain. The General might be dying; he may also repel Marlowe physically. Regardless, the detective overcomes great danger (in two straight scenes, guns are pointed at him at close range) to make sure that the General's thin hold on life doesn't slip.

He also finds the missing person, nearly becoming his double by following him to his murder site together with his murderer. Yet he accepts this danger so warmly that he defuses it. The Sternwood case lacks the pleasing finality of classic literary detection. Marlowe's meddling helped kill Joe Brody; Eddie Mars (who was accidentally shot to death at the end of the 1946 Warner Brothers film of *The Big Sleep*) remains as firmly entrenched in his power and his villainy as ever; the detective's efforts produce little that is constructive besides sending Carmen to a psychiatric home, where she has belonged all along. The novel's structure conveys this inconclusiveness. The first puzzle given Marlowe is the last one he decodes. Carmen's throwing herself into his arms in Chapter 1 describes the inside-out, upside-down world which Marlowe has entered. He has the courage to view murder as a crime and not an unpleasantness that can't be judged because of the social and psychological tensions underlying it. Thus he has to restrain himself from arresting Carmen, just as he overcame his sexual instincts by not sleeping with Vivian. Credit him with half a victory. His crusader's complex has duped him into underrating himself. If Mars is still prospering at the end of the book, his success isn't Marlowe's fault. Marlowe wasn't hired to stamp out crime. He's only responsible for protecting his client and his family, a tough crew to watch over, with their headstrong ways. By destroying the plateholder and the negatives from Geiger's house, by stopping a would-be thief from stealing Vivian's $30,000, and by both naming and prescribing for Rusty Regan's killer, he protects them very well indeed.

II

Deft interweaving of the narrative strands comprising *The Big Sleep* makes his first novel better integrated than any other by Chandler. Figures like Harry Jones, Joe Brody, Lash Canino, and Eddie Mars show Chandler distinguishing between degrees of criminal guilt rather than resorting to the facile blanket censure that cheapens some of his other work. He attends closely to artistic form in other ways, Chapter 21 summarizing the major elements of the case for the reader and thus freeing the fast-moving final third of the action of weighty background data. Narrative sequence in these closing scenes reflects the same careful planning. Both Vivian and Carmen offer Marlowe sex, but because Carmen's proposition is more outrageous it follows her elder sister's. Carmen's audacity in prying her way into Marlowe's apartment and then waiting for him naked in his bed also motivate the detective's moral outburst, which ends Chapter 24, and the renewal of the rain at the start of Chapter 25. But Chandler knew how to retard as well as speed a story. The chapters in the book's second half are longer on average than the ones in the first half. As the action moves ahead, Chandler both fleshes out the data he had foreshadowed in the early going and includes progressively more commentary by Marlowe on developments exploding around and within him. Chandler speaks of the raindrops that fall in Chapter 25 as "tapping icily" at his face. Mona Mars' farewell kiss to him, given later that day, brings the same chill. To show Marlowe happy in love as a result of the

Sternwood case would have violated artistic propriety. Besides, Mona Mars' white-collared green dress, her silver wig, and her cigarette lighter of green leather implicate her in the same disorder that dimmed the wits of Carmen, whom Chandler associates with green and white throughout.

Such dovetailings, as impressive as they are, can't hide the structural blemishes marring *The Big Sleep*. Chandler referred to one of these in a February 1954 letter while discussing technical problems inhering in the first-person detective tale:

The first person story is assumed to tell all but it doesn't. There is always a point at which the hero stops taking the reader into his confidence. There is the solution which turns on a recondite piece of knowledge .... There is the solution which depends on something not disclosed to the reader until almost the end.[9]

In *The Big Sleep*, the naming of the killer stems, not from recondite knowledge, but from reasoning done by the detective off stage and only revealed to us later. While out of the reader's view, Marlowe reasons that Carmen shot Regan by the derelict oil wells and then fills his gun with blanks to trick her into repeating the crime on him. His offstage calculations annoy us more than do similar ones by Agatha Christie's Hercule Poirot because the narrator in the Poirot stories isn't the detective. Another comparison, and one more damaging to *The Big Sleep*, involves Marlowe and Ross Macdonald's Lew Archer. A brilliant reasoning performance like *The Chill* (1964) shows that solid detection can occur in a sleuth-narrated mystery without the reader's feeling deceived.

But *The Chill* was Macdonald's sixteenth novel, while *The Big Sleep* was Chandler's first. To expect Chandler to attain the structural mastery found in a mature work by an immaculate craftsman like Ross Macdonald would be unfair. One could object more legitimately to the thin, spare, untextured quality of *The Big Sleep*. Often praised for its poetic realization of setting, the novel is poor in social resonance. Chandler's Los Angeles lacks both the material spectacle of life and the evocative power of Conan Doyle's London or Simenon's Paris. Some of Chandler's scenic recreations are as flat as his panoramic ones. His tendency to explain life in terms of ugliness and corruption can blind him to intimate details of social behavior. As sharply drawn as he is, General Sternwood doesn't carry his concept of family beyond the blood tie as dramatically as his prototype did in "The Curtain," where the dying old soldier's hidden tenderness gets more attention, proportionately. On the basis of evidence found elsewhere in the canon, we may assume that Chandler limited General Sternwood's appearances to remove any competition with Marlowe for our sympathies.

Errors of commission more than errors of omission cloud the novel's bitter clarity. One such blot comes in Chapter 26 during a sequence that, astonishingly, Dennis Porter has singled out for praise (his wrongheadedness shows in his claim that Lash Canino remains anonymous through the sequence, even though he's named four or five times).[10] Porter admires the scene in the squalid office building in which Marlowe overhears Canino taunting and then poisoning Harry Jones. According to Porter, Chandler's leisurely development of the scene builds a suspense that couldn't have occurred otherwise: "The scene embodies a remarkable lesson of how not to make something happen too quickly," Porter claims.[11] He's wrong. The longer Chandler lets Marlowe eavesdrop, the more the scene betrays its implausibility. A detective should create his own breakthroughs rather than being permitted by his author to listen in on conversations that coincide with his appearance nearby. Chandler embarrasses Marlowe again by having him stand idly by while Canino poisons Jones. The reason for Marlowe's idleness declares itself later: having borne witness to the poisoning, Marlowe can shoot Canino dead with impunity during their gunfight in Realito. The reason, unfortunately, can't offset Marlowe's having done nothing to stop a murder. Presumably skilled in picking up nuances and innuendoes, he should have inferred Canino's butchery from his words and then averted it. Finally, Porter miscues by praising the dialogue in the poisoning scene: "The actual dialogue," says Porter, "consists largely of a few fixed phrases of Canino's normally employed to expresss conviviality but sadistically ironic in the context."[12] Porter has forgotten the irony lacing Marlowe's words to Agnes Lozelle, Jones' girlfriend, who later phones the office where Jones is lying dead. Marlowe's irony, a private joke between Chandler and the reader, mocks Agnes just as Canino's had mocked Jones. Although Marlowe's mockery doesn't lead to murder, it nonetheless sets up a parallel between the detective and the hired thug which sorts ill with the fatal shootout in Realito only hours later.

That the blunders marring the poisoning sequence at the Fulwider Building follow a brilliant description of the building's sordid ground floor and stairwell recalls other interiors brought to vivid life by Chandler's braided whip language, like the Sternwoods' upstairs sitting room and the red-adorned gambling room of Eddie Mars' Cypress Club; the novel's rendering of southern California takes root in descriptions of interiors rather than of streets, crowds, and building architecture. *The Big Sleep* contains much more good writing than bad. As if he wants to prove that nothing can faze him, a policeman describes Owen Taylor's drowning with elaborate casualness: "Yeah .... A nice new Buick sedan all messed up with sand and sea water .... Oh, I almost forgot. There's a guy inside it." But the idle afterthought has uses besides describing a policeman's attempt to look tough. Chapter Six ends with the following one-sentence paragraph: "Neither of the two people in the room [Carmen and Geiger] paid any attention to the way I came in, although only one of them was dead." Chandler's reporting the book's first death in a subordinate clause undercuts its importance. But by conveying the information at the end of a right-branching sentence, he also arranges that the word "dead" ends the sentence, the paragraph and the chapter. Impact has been recouped with a dividend. Verbal brilliance permeates *The Big Sleep*. Besides noting the final sentence of Chapter 6, one can cite several other passages in the book that have been admired—Marlowe's parodic posturing in the first paragraph, the stained-glass panel in the next, the legendary greenhouse meeting of Marlowe and General Sternwood, Carmen's face tightening to scraped bone around a hissing, frothing mouth as she shoots Marlowe five times without stopping him. The reader shares Carmen's consternation in this scene because he/she has found much more before it in *The Big Sleep* to praise than to damn. The book deserves its place as a classic of hardboiled literary detection.

Chapter Six

Wrong Place, Wrong Game, Wrong Players

USING MATERIALS FROM *the Black Mask* stories, "The Man Who Liked Dogs" (March 1936), "Try the Girl" (January 1937), and "Mandarin's Jade" (November 1937), *Farewell, My Lovely* tests a proposition put by Edward Margolies at Chandler's animating core: "how the rich and socially powerful use and manipulate others less strong than they, as if their humanity meant nothing."[1] This exploitation is more impersonal, more effective, and thus more frightening than it was in *The Big Sleep*. Whereas Eddie Mars, the cause of most of the distress in *The Big Sleep*, appeared several times, the powerful Lewin Lockridge Grayle and Laird Brunette show their faces but once. Nor do they exude menace. The nervously apologetic Grayle mixes Marlowe a drink at his wife's request, and Brunette agrees to deliver a message for the sleuth. Yet the damage they cause cuts deeply; Wells has praised Chandler's 1940 novel for its many compelling images of dissolution, breakdown, and defilement.[2] These images are thematic. *Farewell* extends its vision of depravity from L.A's crowded inner city to the openness of the outlying canyons and seafronts and also from small, rundown bungalows to exclusive suburban mansions. And most of the depravity it records is traceable to Brunette or Grayle.

The elegant facades of these local czars help focus other sharp contrasts in the book. Helen Grayle, the former Velma Valento, embodies the difference between seem and be, the most important of these contrasts and the book's unifying principle. The grail, chalice, or sacred female vessel promising salvation and renewal turns out to be poisoned; Helen was a prostitute as well as a cabaret singer before her marriage. In the supreme example of treachery in all of Chandler, she ends Moose Malloy's eight years of waiting for her by shrilling, "Get away from me, you son of a bitch," her only words to him in the novel, and then shooting him five times. The high idealism of his quest has been mocked and smirched by the foulness of the quest's object.

132

Several contrasts of lesser note lead up to the one in which Moose's hopes explode along with his life. Lieutenant Nulty of the Los Angeles Police Department spells out the venality of the law. He automatically assumes that Marlowe was bribed to set Moose Malloy free after the big man killed the manager of Florian's, the nightclub where Velma sang eight years before. Nulty also describes Moose's being at large to complicity. He shrinks from the Malloy case; solving it will bring him no recognition while exposing him to risk: "Another shine killing," he complains out of a sense of injured merit; "That's what I rate after eighteen years in this man's police department. No pix, no space, not even four lines in the want-ad section." Nulty's opposite number, the sensitive homicide officer, Lt. Carl Randall, investigates the case earnestly. Whereas Nulty invited Marlowe to look for the missing Moose, Randall discourages the detective. His skills as an investigator imply that he can handle the case alone. A murder investigation, he also claims, belongs exclusively to the law. Yet rather than dismissing Marlowe rudely, he welcomes the help Marlowe gave him. In Chapter 12, the two men analyze the case thoughtfully. Neither tries to show up the other; even when they disagree, they speak politely, never shouting, interrupting, or cracking wise. They prove that detectives can act like gentlemen while working. Testing different explanations, they will modify or build upon each other's ideas without trying to demolish them. But no camaraderie develops between the men. Even though Marlowe admires Randall, he lies to him (to protect Anne Riordan); Randall also withholds information from Marlowe, orders him off the scene and makes clear his disgust when Marlowe reports Moose's murder. If detection isn't a job for rogues, it offers little besides loneliness and danger.

A subtler and richer contrast than the one between these two crime-stoppers, or the one between the basically honest LAPD and the corrupt police force of Bay City, pits Marlowe against the murder victims, Lindsay Marriott and Moose Malloy. Like that involving Marlowe and Randall, the contrast gains force from taking root in similarity. As several critics have said, Marlowe re-enacts some of the major experiences of the victims whose murders he investigates. He retraced the footsteps of Rusty Regan to the Sternwoods' derelict oil wells accompanied by deadly Carmen in *The Big Sleep*. In *The Long Goodbye*, he will generate sexual heat with Eileen Wade, another murderess, as he does with Helen Grayle in *Farewell*. Though neither encounter ends in intercourse, he should feel more lucky than deprived. Eileen kills her husband, and Helen kills Mariott and Moose, both of whom she probably had sex with. Her sickly looking husband she has turned into a living death. After marrying her out of town under a false name, he sold the radio station where she once sang to shield her from any former business colleagues of his who might remember her from her days on the game. He now lacks purpose, having been reduced to mixing drinks for her guests and spying on her. Moose and Marriott protect her, too, Mariott by refusing to identify her to Marlowe as the owner of the stolen jade necklace he has agreed to buy back and Moose by suppressing his knowledge that she betrayed him to the police eight years before. Marlowe, who is about the same size as Marriott, drives his car and wears his raincoat to the lonely gorge the night he is blackjacked and Marriott is killed.

The comparisons yoking Marlowe to Moose are still more dramatic. Once again, Helen is the connecting principle, with murder providing the means of connection. Moose enters the novel looking for Helen, whom he knew as Velma, and kills a man some fifteen minutes later within Marlowe's hearing. At the end, he is shot dead in Marlowe's apartment. The five slugs he takes in the body from Helen's automatic recalls both the five blanks Carmen Sternwood fired at Marlowe and the identity between Moose's initials and those of Mona Mars, who touches the detective's heart as deeply as any woman in the canon. A last similarity also stems from the past: Moose spent eight years in the state prison of Oregon, which is also the state where Marlowe attended college (said Chandler in an April 1951 letter).[3] Although Marlowe piques Moose with his sharp tongue, he likes him and always speaks well of him. He differs from both the big primitive and the decadent gigolo Marriott in resisting Helen's body. His powers of resistance impress us. Yes, only the chance intrusion of her husband cools his lust when he and she are kissing heavily on her living room sofa. But this act of grace isn't wasted on him; he uses it to snap Helen's spell and restore self-control. He won't make the same mistake twice. Though he talks to Helen on the phone, he never appears alone with her again. His ability to resist her confirms his coping power. Whether his resistance of Anne Riordan in the same novel cheapens his survival puzzles Chandler as much as it does him.

I

Allowing for small variations, *Farewell, My Lovely* fits the pattern of the archetypal Chandler narrative as set forth by Jameson in 1970: "Chandler's stories are first and foremost descriptions of searches, in which murder is involved, and which sometimes ends with the murder of the person being sought for."[4] The missing-person story line takes more turns than the one in *The*

Big Sleep; *Farewell* has two missing persons, as Moose vanishes during his search for Velma. It also probes motives more deeply and practices a darker irony. Marlowe tells a witness that Moose has come to L.A. "looking for the fink that turned him in eight years ago." Does he know more than Moose was willing to admit? Moose had only mentioned finding Velma, whom he spoke of dotingly. Yet within minutes after leaving the witness, Marlowe also tells Lt. Nulty that Moose may know the traitor who sold him to the police. His logic implies that, like Oedipus centuries before him, Moose is following unconscious impulses to force the revelation that will break him. His search for Velma's missing jade necklace makes up the novel's main plot line. The exposure of the jade necklace as a fake punningly identifies its supposed owner, Velma, as a jade, or whore (that other sexual vagrant, Carmen Sternwood, wore jade earrings while posing naked for the camera). Moose's discovery of her can only crush hearts.

Among the novel's contrasts between seem and be, none imposes more than that pointed by Helen's beauty and her villainy. Besides souring Marlowe's view of able, attractive Anne Riordan, it also conveys the wrongness pervading the action; between-wars southern California pulsates with dread. As in *The Big Sleep*, the weather causes discomfort and distress. Marlowe notes in Chapter 17, "The last day of March and hot enough for summer." The freakish heat restores Moose to L.A., destroying the security of Velma and bringing out her deadliness; Jessie Florian's monthly maintenance check stops coming, and then Jessie, widow of the former owner of the nightclub where Velma sang, dies. Moose's demanding service in Florian's, now an all-black bar, prefigures several other violations of social or professional protocol which end in grief. In exploiting people they should be protecting, the Bay City Police cause more crime than they stop (the model of Bay City, Santa Monica, has risen socially since the time of the novel, as has the sullen Brighton of Graham Greene's 1938 *Brighton Rock*). Healers don't heal: the psychic consultant, Jules Amthor, is a fraud, while Dr. Sonderborg uses his mental hospital both to hide fugitive criminals and to front for a drug ring.

The heat of early spring melts decencies, civilized graces and traditional expectations everywhere. Helen Grayle (i.e., Velma) violates the marriage bond; despite his Chamber of Commerce facade, John Wax of Bay City violates the office of police chief; Lindsay Marriott proves a deceitful client in his failure, which later kills him, to confide in Marlowe when he hires the detective to buy back Helen's jade necklace. Showing in another way how the heat has wilted the renewal and redemption associated with Easter, Anne gets nothing in return for the patience and compassion she extends Marlowe throughout the action. Her last words in the novel, spoken to him, "I'd like to be kissed, damn you!" crown a discussion of the events leading to Helen's slaughter of Moose. Chandler never says whether Marlowe kisses Anne. But his ending the chapter right after she voices her wish and his cutting in the next chapter, the book's last, three months ahead in time, imply that any kiss she and Marlowe shared at the end of Chapter 40 prompted few, if any, encores. Though the topic of conversation in Chapter 41 is still the Helen Grayle-Moose Malloy case, Marlowe is now discussing it with Lt. Randall, not with Anne, who isn't mentioned.

Suitably, the person dominating Marlowe's last-chapter reconstruction with Randall is Helen, who also occupies his last recorded thought in the book. She is the book's most dynamic force. Moose, who comes straight to L.A. from prison to look for her, errs in calling her "Little Velma." Velma/Helen is big enough to look after herself. She changes her name as often as she changes her hair color; she blackjacks Marlowe hard enough to knock him out and Marriott hard enough to inflict death; after killing Moose, she flees undetected to Baltimore, where she supports herself as a nightclub singer. Perhaps she wanted to relive the past decade, which culminated in her marriage to a millionaire. She knows how to get what she wants. Resourceful, dazzling and tough, she has bewitched men as different as the gorilla Moose, the Anglicized Marriott, and the sickly, ageing media executive Grayle, who gave up everything for her and now condones her indiscretions. Chandler mistreats her by making her a marijuana addict. She needs no such stimulations. Her indiscretions she takes no trouble to hide. After deciding that she'd like to have sex with Marlowe, she shoos her husband out of the room. She rewards Moose's years of loyalty, patience, and love by killing him; her need to repel him outpaces his need to be with her. Her shooting him in the body focusses her triumph. She views men as slabs of meat in a butcher's shop; men only interest her physically. Now that sickness and age have wasted her husband, he barely exists for her. When she agrees to come to Marlowe's apartment, presumably for sex, she tells him, "You have a lovely build, mister." Nor is Moose the only person she shoots in the body. She also kills the Baltimore detective who spots her with three body shots, and she commits suicide by shooting herself in the heart—twice, against all probability. Obviously, she'd have also shot Marriott in the torso rather than clubbing him to death had not the noise of snapping bullets ruled out firearms.

Although she tantalizes and captivates men, including perhaps the Baltimore detective who absentmindedly held her coat for her before taking her to the station house, she lives narrowly and meanly. All her relationships with men are based on sex; she uses sex as both an instrument of survival and a weapon; sex is what she offers men, and, along with some expensive trimmings, all she knows. Her death entails a recognition of the deadness of her heart. Having divided sex from feeling has saddened her, rousing motives of guilt and contrition. She craves punishment. Perhaps Marlowe undersold her by claiming that she shot the Baltimore cop because she didn't know she could have escaped conviction for the Malloy death. Her association with big-time bandits like her husband and Laird Brunette has shown her the shoddiness of man's law. The rough justice she exacts upon herself reflects Chandler's belief that a promiscuous woman forfeits happiness and fulfillment. Helen prefers suicide to indulgence, exploitation, and treachery. But by stopping the heart she had long since denied, she's also acting out her author's notorious sexual puritanism rather than the drama she has been directing.

This intrusion, though bad art, testifies to her power. She is vitality. Had Chandler not stopped her, it's doubtful that anyone else could have done so. The dark power radiating from her beauty crushes all. At first meeting, she asks Marlowe about his job, tells him he's "a very good-looking man," and explains that she's assessing him—all in Anne Riordan's presence. She acts quickly on her assessment. Within moments she maneuvers Anne out of the sitting room, just as she had done Grayle. Her husband's frailty bespeaks his vulnerability to her. Nor can Moose's great bulk help him withstand the lethal effect of the bullets she pumps into his compliant body; the ease with which her bullets enter his big frame signals his acceptance of her worst: "She shot him five times in the stomach," says Marlowe; "The bullets made no more sound than fingers going into a glove." Judging from the sexual inroads she makes on Marlowe during their first meeting, she could enslave him fatally, too. She makes trendy observations in polished cadences; calculatingly, she brushes his fingers with hers while handing him a drink. Then the tempo of the seduction picks up. To look at her watch, she draws back the sleeve of her blouse far beyond the wrist; she displays her legs at different angles; complaining about the heat, she lowers her dress from the neck. When Marlowe responds to these enticements by moving next to her, she brazenly accuses him of working fast. He hasn't touched her yet. He only kisses her several minutes later, when he is asked to. Her calling him old fashioned, in fact, registers her annoyance that he isn't working fast enough.

Despite her charms, she exudes unreality. First seen by the reader as two photographs, she leaves the action as a corpse. Purissima Canyon, the place where she first materializes, under cover of darkness, defines her menace. Unreal, she threatens to make men copies of herself. She subtracted from Moose's reality by sending him to jail, following her usual practice of operating out of her victim's view. Her unreality is contagious. Besides diminishing Moose, she has gotten her husband to retire and then play the cuckold. At Purissima Canyon, the Latin origins of whose name imply a limit or an extreme, she works much more quickly, knocking out Marlowe after killing Marriott. The context for this menace, as always with her, is sexual. Like the high window of Chandler's next novel, Purissima Canyon overturns the promise connected with its sexual symbolism to provide a passage to death. This wild, wet, bramble-fringed gap, sometimes called a hollow, gorge, or cleft, adjoins the sea, symbol of the universal female. Marlowe's penetration of the gap is also described in sexual terms: "Below was darkness and a vague far-off sea sound .... The road ended in a shallow bowl entirely surrounded by brush. It was empty." As has been seen, immersion in the dark, moist, hidden riches of sex undoes him. Within moments of observing, "I seemed to have that hollow entirely to myself," he is sapped. Helen, the loathly lady, has perverted sex by supplanting thrills with disappointment and pain. The climax of sex with her, symbolic or real, always brings letdown. Her power to dazzle and destroy, amply borne out by her scroll of victims, shows also in her knocking Marlowe out from inside a car, where she'd have needed perfect balance and accuracy to make up for the lack of swinging room. This modern *belle dame sans merci* uses every opportunity to smash men. The friendliness of the car's dark interior, her natural bent for betrayal, and the canyon setting make the adjustment easy for her. She's on home ground.

Irony sharpens Chandler's portrayal of the dark, brush-lined gorges and clefts of Purissima Canyon as an image of the destroying woman. The following description of the designated meeting place for the jade buyback calls forth the short transit from rectum to vagina: "a dirt road winds down into a little hollow and we are to wait there without lights," says Marriott, for whom the dark abandon of sex, previously his livelihood, will mean death. Worried that his expensive phallic roadster will get scratched by the bushes flanking the hollow, he is pounded to compost by Helen's blackjack. Marlowe's recovery of consciousness, like his and Marriott's sappings, evokes sexual associations.

Richly evocative throughout the sequence is the sage that gives off such a wild, intoxicating fragrance before Marlowe is sapped but that materializes as "sticky sage ooze" after he wakes up. This second impression fits with several others that convey the sadness following sex. Like many spent lovers, Marlowe is drowsy, his head aches, and he wants to be somewhere else. The once throbbing, glistening world looks flat and drab: "The dirt road stretched empty, back up the shallow hill . . . . Beyond the low walls of brush the pale glow in the sky would be the lights of Bay City." The first human sound he hears in this dim, gluey world is female laughter. His chastening is complete. The next time he visits the canyon, the drifting scent of sage makes him think of a dead man and a moonless sky. Once redolent of romance, sage continues to call forth loss and pain. The heavy smell of it along a mountain flank assails him in Chapter 24 just before he is knocked out again from a car—by a Bay City policeman. His waking up drugged in a locked room with barred windows from his "pool of darkness" sustains the motif of sex as entrapment and paralysis.

Marlowe's clubbing by Helen in Chapter 9 (where danger uncoiled swiftly from another car parked near naked rock on a sage-scented night) foreshadows his erotic attraction to Red Norgaard. It also reminds Marlowe of the difference between the promise of sex and its grim actuality. Pain and death dominate the seductive Purissima Canyon. The Canyon also materializes Anne Riordan, who, significantly, meets a dizzy, reeling Marlowe near a corpse and threatens to shoot him with the pistol she's holding. She calls him "a sick man" and says he reminds her of a morgue attendant. He will later be called "a very sick man" by an armed Dr. Sonderborg when, again dizzy and reeling, he enters the doctor's office. Perhaps he'll never forgive Anne's humiliating him with her innocent, nervous laughter. Overreacting to the strong mixed image she presents of promise and dread, he resists her throughout. Her prefiguring Dr. Sonderborg's evil with both her words and her gun ruins her chances with him from the start. To reinforce his belief in her unworthiness as a lover or wife, he notes her alleged defects in minute detail—the high, narrow forehead, the unattractively long upper lip, and the too wide mouth. And even though he concedes that her face releases its beauty subtly, whereas Helen Grayle's flashy good looks wilt with time, he remains determined to repel her. His determination costs him a great deal. Anne breaks the case for him, identifying Helen as the owner of the missing jade necklace, showing him her picture, and setting up the meeting with her that leads to her exposure as the culprit. He seems to resent this help. His rudeness to Anne after his escape from the sanitarium clashes sharply with the vulnerability he will display with Red Norgaard the night the two men steal aboard the gambling ship, *Montecito*. Whereas he insults Anne after eating and drinking his fill at her expense, he admits to Red that he's frightened and forces money on him for taking him to the *Montecito*. Chandler makes his boorishness in her presence psychologically plausible. Just as she first appeared to him near a male corpse whom Marlowe resembled in size and build, so does she live within walking distance of Dr. Sonderborg's Bay City clinic, where Marlowe was stowed after being knocked out amid the pungency of wild sage. His second meeting with Anne, like the first, takes place at night, the time when sexual promise explodes into violence. Is she continuous with the threat emanating from the sage-filled canyon where Marriott was bludgeoned? Although Chandler doesn't answer the question, his raising it discloses Marlowe's fears.

Marlowe harbors no such fears with men. As he does with both Norgaard and Randall, he finds Moose Malloy more relaxing company than Anne. In fact, he trusts Moose so much that he receives him at home wearing pajamas and tells him that his killing of Jessie Florian will probably send him back to jail. One wonders why Marlowe takes such chances. Moose's accidental throttling of Jessie recalls a similar killing perpetrated by Lenny Small in Steinbeck's *Of Mice and Men* (1937). Like Small, O'Neill's Yank in *The Hairy Ape* (1922) and Ross Macdonald's Hector Land in *Trouble Follows Me* (1946), Moose reflects his era's interest in the missing link, or evolutionary throwback, stemming from the 1925 Scopes trial in Tennessee. Chandler's portrayal of Moose as a good bad man conveys popular pseudoscientific notions about pre-Darwinian man. These notions show that Moose gives Marlowe a good deal to fear. One source of danger is Moose's deep self-division. As his name suggests, he combines the rankly animal with the highmindedness savoring of knightly quests, imperishable ideals and chaste maids. This identification with medieval gentilesse is only partly ironic. Marlowe's noting of the big man, "His eyes had a shine close to tears that gray eyes often seem to have," provides a correlative for Moose's love for Velma, the novel's leading dramatic idea. Despite his crudeness, this love is always believable. In fact, only when it's thwarted does his brutishness flare out. And flare out it does. His wild anger serves an obsession so pervasive that it outpaces his instinct for survival. But it also recoils on itself. Combining the malignancy and the instinctive wisdom of the primitive, he can't elude his own rough justice. The tension he embodies between the savage and the human implies a person at war with himself. While his heart drives him to Velma, his mind tells him that closing with her can only destroy him. Marlowe's summary of the case shows how these lines of force converge upon Moose with an inevitability the big man foresees but can't prevent: "She[Velma] had turned him in eight years ago. He seemed to know that. But he wouldn't have hurt her. He was in love with her."

His consenting death doesn't surprise Marlowe. Moose had killed two people for disclaiming knowledge of Velma. Although he believed Sam Montgomery and Jessie Florian rationally, his feral self seized the chance to kill them; commiting homicide in Velma's name would warm the trail to her.This mad, destructive logic makes sense dramatically. Velma incarnates death; betrayal, prison, and death are all she offers. Tired of outraging his reason, Moose takes her five bullets without protest. The fantasy his death ended had already consumed him. He would make excuses for her: "Eight long years since I said goodby. She ain't wrote to me in six. But she'll have a reason," he told Marlowe at the outset. His first glance at Florian's showed him that neither Velma nor any other singer had played the club in years: "There ain't nothing left of the joint .... They was a little stage and band .... Velma did some warbling." But his refusal to act on his perceptions riveted him in the old club. By trying to wish things into existence, he created havoc. He crawls out of the past at the end just long enough to die.

Perhaps Marlowe brings him together with Velma at the end to relax pressure. Puzzled by the elaborate preparations for the scene in which the two former lovers meet in Marlowe's apartment, John Cawelti believes that "Marlowe has come to feel that Moose and Velma have earned the right to confront each other without interference."[5] Cawelti's explanation overlooks at least one big point. Velma's evil would have wiped out for Marlowe any rights Velma might claim. Besides, those rights, as Cawelti reads them, clash with her purpose—to repel Moose. Hasn't she been avoiding Moose ever since his arrival in town? She killed Marriott to block the trail between Moose and herself. Then she hired Marlowe to keep the big man at bay. His betrayal of her brings unforeseen grief. Whereas the outdoors scenario for the Marriott murder recalled Keats' "La Belle Dame Sans Merci," the episode in Marlowe's apartment invokes "The Eve of St. Agnes." Marlowe's awareness of how love's promise curdles to betrayal and death, lively enough in the presence of Anne, has vanished in a purple cloud. His actions violate the compassion he professes for Moose throughout. If he's staging Moose's mercy killing, why doesn't he protect Moose's illusions, as he had done those of the dying General Sternwood? The last person he thinks of before sleep in Chapter 39 is Red Norgaard. Soothed by thoughts of both Red and his own moral rectitude, he dozes off quickly. The nightmarish sequence that follows begins with his being awakened by another bruiser, Moose. To prepare Moose for the meeting he has engineered with Velma, he tells the big man that the police know about the Jessie Florian death. Marlowe is trying to get him to use his last hours of freedom to face the truth about Velma and her villainy; he hasn't the time to build a life with her. Then she enters the apartment. To encourage him, Marlowe positions him within earshot when she admits both coming to the apartment for sex and having murdered Marriott. But he has underrated the intensity of Moose's love for Velma. His project of moral reclamation ends disastrously. Knowing the truth about Velma doesn't free the Moose; it kills him. Reuniting with Velma has stripped him of purpose. He dies with his dream rather than grabbing the chance to survive an ambulance driver had given him.

Lt. Randall's obilque condemnation of Marlowe (" 'So you had to play it clever,' was all he said and hung up quickly") upon hearing the news of the shooting death carries into the novel's sour finale two chapters later. Like *The Big Sleep* before it, *Farewell,* ends on a downbeat note. Three months have passed since the Malloy shooting. The case resolves itself in Baltimore, 3000 miles from its origin, and Marlowe, rather than reconstructing the crime, hears about the killer's apprehension and death. His fee falls far short of both the trouble he went to and the battering he took. What is more, the fee is paid by the killer, his client, who might have shot herself to spare her husband the agony of a murder trial. But even though the often cynical Marlowe interprets her suicide charitably, he doesn't claim that justice and love have been served. Velma's motives can't be ascertained from a distance of three months and 3000 miles. Also, the only benefit accruing from the gore and heartbreak disclosed by the investigation comes in the reform of the Bay City police, an action that declares itself late in the day and stays in the background. Finally, Marlowe stands as far from self-knowledge as he did at the end of *The Big Sleep*, when he felt mired in nastiness. In *Farewell*, which includes April Fool's Day in its time schemes, he plays the fool—prying information from Jessie Florian with booze, discounting Anne Riordan, and playing God with Moose Malloy. Not only has he become part of the nastiness; his folly has also covered him with it.

II

The folly reflects a similar lack of control and purpose in Chandler. The critical reputation of *Farewell* is drastically inflated. In a September 1949 letter, Chandler praised the novel unduly: "I think *Farewell, My Lovely* is the top and that I shall never again achieve quite the same combination of ingredients. The bony structure was much more solid,the invention less forced and more fluent." Others have echoed this wrongheaded praise. Durham finds *Farewell* Chandler's "most complex and successfully unified work," Pendo calls it "the best of the writers' novels," and MacShane judges it "a much better book than *The Big Sleep.*" Only Knight has attacked its awkwardness and implausibility. Uncoordinated, padded, and wanting in credible motivation the book is. Much of the trouble inheres in Marlowe's relationship with Moose, the book's dramatic core. Chandler might have been thinking of his failure to develop this promising tie when, in 1950, he called the relationship of Guy and Bruno in Hitchcock's *Strangers on a Train* "an absurdity become real, an absurdity...which falls just short of being impossible.'"[7] This absurdity becomes provocative and productive because of the tension it builds. By contrast, the only time Marlowe sees Moose between the splendid opening sequence at Florian's and the finale in his apartment, he walks past the unsuspecting giant without greeting him. Chandler risks and gains nothing in this limp scene. He gives Moose nothing to do or say at Dr. Sonderborg's. Nor does he explain Moose's presence at the mental home other than to say that the home is a gangster hideout.

How Moose found out about Dr. Sonderborg's profitable sideline is never told, though we can assume that word reached him from a fellow convict in Oregon. This assumption raises problems of its own. Its force hinges on Moose's foreknowledge that his search for Velma would occasion some killings and thus create the need to hide from the police. It also requires the reader to fill in gaps that Chandler should have plugged himself. An author who relies on unreported or undramatized action to explain motives has scamped his work. The whole sequence at Dr. Sonderborg's is shaky and strained. Nothing about Moose's presence there is believable. Chandler has materialized him because doing so fits his narrative intent; he wants to jog our memories. Were Moose to stay out of the action till the end, we might have forgotten him. But Chandler's technique is so poor in the mental home sequence that he creates more problems than he resolves. Among them is the improbability of Moose's movements. How can someone as conspicuous as the Moose remain at large in a city, even for a day? Common sense dictates that he'd be spotted and caught en route from Florian's in downtown L.A. to Bay City. Although his unshakeable love for Velma has endowed him with special powers, his ability to push his big body through security nets set up by city, country, and state police defies belief.

His incredible turn at Dr. Sonderborg's calls to mind other defects in the rest home sequence. When Marlowe lumbers into the main office, he finds the doctor "brooding, with his face in his hands," as if he's expecting the visit. Marlowe, too, acts more like a posed character than a person. So weak from being drugged that he can hardly stand, he plucks up the strength both to crack wise and to trot out learned allusions. Are we to assume that the early April Sunday he rises from his two-days' stupor coincides with Easter? In the next chapter, he tells Randall, "You're not God. You're not even Jesus Christ," as if he coveted these honors for himself. He's not equal to them. Although he has been blackjacked, punched, choked, doped, and straightjacketed, he neither saves nor redeems anybody, including himself. He solves no mysteries, he causes a death, and he watches two killers escape. For salvation he substitutes wisecracks. His rudeness toward Anne and his determination to control the style of his exchanges with both Dr. Sonderborg and the psychic consultant Jules Amthor imply that he has replaced the Holy Ghost with jittery, dark-toned backchat.

These exchanges expose Chandler's failings as a plot builder. The lurid details in *Farewell* don't align themselves in a coherent explanation. Everything connected with Amthor, for instance, is outlandish and uncoordinated. Amthor's very entry into the novel bespeaks tired technique; his calling cards are hidden inside the mouthpieces of some marijuana cigarettes belonging to Lindsay Marriott. Voicing our curiosity, Marlowe asks him in Chapter 21 how his cards turned up in such an unlikely place. Amthor replies evasively. Marlowe's telling Anne seven chapters later that the cards mean nothing explains this evasiveness; the calling cards were merely a device to get Marlowe into Amthor's consulting room, from which he could be taken to Dr. Sonderborg's, site of the second Moose Malloy epiphany. But if the calling cards are merely an excuse to reintroduce an immobile Moose, to pad the plot, and to bring in some bizarre characters who have nothing to do with the outcome, then Chandler has cheated the reader. The hard, bony plot structure he will boast of has splintered and collapsed under layers of gimcrackery; it couldn't support the novel's heightened effects, which exist for themselves rather than for the plot. Amthor's entourage, for instance, is as ridiculous as it is prearranged looking and overly supervised. In addition to Amthor's medium, the grunting stonelike Indian, Second Planting, there is his Asian secretary-wife, whose speech, incidentally, Chandler gets wrong. After referring to her "dark, thin wasted Asiatic face," he has her tell Marlowe, "I weel conduct you"; most Asians would omit the helper, will, most Eastern languages being isolating rather than synthetic in syntax.

The vulgarities of American Gothic also account for Amthor, who, like another dubious God-figure, Sheridan Ballou of *The Little Sister*, makes his sole appearance in the middle chapter of a Chandler novel. Preceded by an array of theatrical effects, Amthor enters his black-and-white consulting room with flourish. The fanfares continue, Chandler heaping one superlative upon another on him. "Ageless," Amthor has "the palest finest white hair" and "one of the most beautiful hands" Marlowe has ever seen. After smiling "the faintest smile in the world," he claims to be in danger "at all times." Such exaggeration impedes novelistic development, as Chandler found out. He removes Amthor from the action after his one spectacular appearance; so wrong footed is the novel that Marlowe reports his arrest in New York while reviewing the case with Anne. The resolution of the Amthor subplot to the side of dramatized action means that Marlowe did nothing to bring it about; the resolution is given, not discovered.

The illustrator in Chandler fights the storyteller again in the episode aboard the gambling ship *Montecito*. The chapters comprising this episode use great gobs of melodrama to little thematic purpose. Marlowe pierces fog and sea mist before scaling the *Montecito*'s "ancient sides"; he circumvents "clumps of rusted chains" and keeps his composure despite screaming rats and armed guards—all to convey a messge he could have mailed, cabled, or delivered by boarding the ship like an ordinary passenger. The lurid, irrelevant colors washing over the episode bespeak Chandler's inability to enrich the novel internally. What is more, Chandler knew that the *Montecito* episode flagged badly. Laird Brunette, the big gambler Marlowe chooses to notify Moose on his behalf, chides the detective: "I don't make you out. You risk your hide to come out here and hand me a card to pass on to some thug I don't even know. There's no sense to it." To his question, "Why didn't you leave your gun ashore and come aboard the usual way?" Marlowe replies feebly, "I forgot the first time." Presumably, Chandler thought he could distract us from the needless trouble and risk Marlowe took to meet Brunette by withholding the contents of Marlowe's five-word message to Moose. This replacement of sound plotting by mystification only makes us more mindful of Chandler's struggling and stumbling. Other mistakes made along the way have also forecast his failure to shore up the ungainly novel; he didn't warm to the challenge of writing *Farewell* as he had *The Big Sleep*.

The bouncer in Florian's who enters the novel wearing suspenders in Chapter 2 is wearing a belt two pages later. Helen Grayle's husband, Lewin Lockridge Grayle, is referred to by Marlowe as Merwin Lockridge Grayle in Chapter 32. Judging from the shock registered on the face of the person Marlowe is talking to, Police Chief John Wax, the mistake is Chandler's. A writer who forgets the basics of his story isn't committed to them. Nor is he enjoying himself; his characters aren't surprising him, and he's not learning fictional technique from the plot, either. *Farewell, My Lovely* distracts more than it enriches. Running downhill after its fine opening on Central Avenue, it ends as a hodgepodge of false starts, loose ends and melodramatic gleams.

Chapter Seven

Thrills Without Form

CHANDLER NEVER LIKED *The High Window* (1942). Five months before the book's publication he told Blanche Knopf, his publisher's wife, "I'm afraid the book is not going to be any good to you .... No action, no likable characters, no nothing. The detective does nothing." The years didn't improve his judgment. In 1949, while telling Canadian journalist Alex Barnes that *Farewell, My Lovely* was his best book, he decried *High Window* as "the worst."[1] These dismissals are too severe. Just as he had overrated *Farewell, My Lovely*, so did he underrate *High Window*. A look at the later novel's plot discloses developments presaging artistic growth rather than decline. By restoring an element he had used before, an author often finds either new tensions energizing it or new resolutions to existing tensions. The carry-over of materials from *Farewell* in *High Window* spurs this kind of growth.

Like Poe's "The Purloined Letter," *Farewell* and *High Window* both treat the recovery of a valuable object from the thief that stole it. Both works also refer to the subgenre, which includes Steinbeck's *The Pearl* (1947), of the story of hidden treasure, whose temporary or would-be owners all suffer. But whereas Helen Grayle's stolen Fei Tsui necklace turns out to be a red herring, the Brasher Doubloon, a rare gold coin minted in New York State in 1787, keeps moving the plot. Its theft also involves motives beyond those of mere greed. Leslie Murdock's stealing the coin from his mother, to use as collatoral against his gambling debts, conveys the breakdown of the American family (which, like Chandler's own half-American family, has already been fragmented by the absence of the father). Leslie gambles to protest the pressures imposed upon him by a domineering mother. The two murders set in motion by the coin uncover, as well, the deathliness of the commercial tradition stemming from America's eastern seaboard in the eighteenth century.

Finally, the key relationship in *High Window* resembles and extends from the one at the heart of *Farewell*. As he did by pitting

147

Moose Malloy against Marlowe, the Chandler of *High Window* also contrasts self-destructive innocence against his detective's cynical swagger. The opposition works better in *High Window* even though shy, little Merle Davis lacks the animal drive and threat of Moose. The improvement comes from technique. *High Window* accomplishes more with its prosaic materials because Chandler keeps Merle in view. Not only is she alive at the close; Marlowe also ends the case by driving her back to her parents in Wichita, Kansas. We've seen enough of her to feel that she needs the attention. Rather than punishing the wrongdoers, Marlowe will try to restore her lost faith in herself. His efforts win our approval because she has won our hearts.

I

The High Window opens well, its first paragraph expressing Chandler's attachment to and gift for realistic detail. As Joseph Conrad did so often, Chandler opens the action with a strong visual image rather than an idea or a dramatic encounter. The practice carries over from his first two novels. Whereas the opening paragraph of *Big Sleep* describes Marlowe and that of *Farewell* showed a city street, *High Window* starts by depicting a large home in Pasadena. A detail in the book's second paragraph brings in further variation. The season is summer. Having set *Big Sleep* in October and *Farewell* in March and April, Chandler will change season once again as he tries to learn his art. To foster artistic growth, he also builds *High Window* around two mysteries. The first of these has two parts, equally provoking. A murder victim is shot with a pistol that turns up under a neighbor's pillow, which, oddly, is where the neighbor kept his own pistol. Though the neighbor had both the means and the opportunity to kill George Anson Phillips, he lacked a motive, presumably never having met him. And what would Phillips' killer be gaining, everybody wonders, by taking the neighbor's gun after leaving the death gun behind? The next murder proves just as puzzling. A package containing what looks like the missing Brasher Doubloon is brought to Marlowe's office by a local messenger service. The same day, Marlowe's client tells him that *she* has the coin.

Chandler sustains the chase for answers to these puzzles by matching character to setting. Chapter Seven describes both a sleazy old building and the wheezing, run-down old coin dealer who rents an office in it. Another older man interviews Marlowe in a parlor whose heavy, ornate appointments hint at the old-world menace that the man, a mafia chief, projects in his speech. One of the *padrone*'s businesses, a funeral parlor, both recalls the coin merchant, who gets murdered, and looks ahead to the suburban Idle Valley Club, a casino in Cahuenga Pass. There's nothing idle or casual about the casino. People go there as full of purpose and anxiety as did the visitors to Eddie Mar's Cypress Club or to Laird Brunette's gambling ship, *The Montecito*. Known locally as a number rather than a name, it represents an extreme of impersonality. The security system protecting it includes a floodlit gate house, armed uniformed guards, and patrol cars. The owner of this para-military network lives in Stillwood Crescent near Bel Air. Jules Amthor's office and consulting room in *Farewell* was located on Stillwood Heights, whose thin air matched the vacuity of both Amthor himself and the goods he was peddling. The calmness conveyed by the name Stillwood Crescent also bespeaks unreality and death. The initials of the former owner of the gambler's house, a convicted criminal, still adorn the property; the gambler's wife entertains her lover at the house in clear view of the servants and the other guests; the house was paid for with profits from gambling, a special phobia of Chandler's. It fuses opulence and sleaze in the usual Chandler mode. Although he doesn't condone Lois Morny's adultery, Chandler extends little sympathy to her gambler-husband. Alex Morny earns his living by flouting civilized process; he can't complain if a contract is violated at his expense, even one undertaken only eight months earlier. Promoting wildness and waste, how can he hope for the stability represented by marriage? His mansion on Stillwood Crescent rests upon dead values.

The narrative vigor Chandler uses to offset this deathliness takes several forms. Verve comes from a pocket treatise on the minting, striking, and molding of coins and from an explanation of, how the materials and techniques used to make golden inlays can also be used to counterfeit coins. To avoid congestion, these two descriptive passages occur twenty-four chapters apart. The organization of the action in the early going also gives the solidness provided by the coining treatise the lively context it needs to serve the developing drama. In Chapter 6, Marlowe makes an appointment with George Anson Phillips, the young detective who cries for help when faced with more trouble than he can handle alone. But Marlowe has several hours to spare. These he uses to visit Elisha Morningstar, the ageing coin dealer, who gives him useful information about coins in general and the Brasher Doubloon in particular. Other issues develop, too. As soon as Morningstar believes himself alone, he phones Phillips. The next time they appear, they're both dead. That Marlowe discovers them focuses the danger and tightens the plot. He can't escape death. The point is neatly underscored. If Alex Morny's gambling club nestles in Cahuenga Pass, Marlowe occupies an office in Hollywood's Cahuenga Building.

Other places where Chandler tightened *The High Window* show him learning from mistakes made in the spongy *Farewell, My Lovely*. Leslie Murdock owes Morny $12,000; his estranged wife, ex-suitemate of Lois Morny, now sings in the Morny-owned casino where Murdock ran up his gambling debt. Such interlocking of motifs not only strengthens plot; it also creates pressure points from which violence can erupt. The novel's quality is enhanced. The tracery of financial and sexual motives formed by the overlapping ties creates a design both rich and exciting without straining plausibility. Further concentration comes near the novel's halfway mark. Within minutes of the delivery of the Brasher Doubloon to his office, Marlowe gets a threatening phone call. Then he discovers Elisha Morningstar's corpse. For variety's sake, Chandler reports the Morningstar death straightaway; in the instance of Phillips' corpse, which Marlowe found earlier the same day, he described some of the physical effects of death, letting the reader infer what had happened to Phillips before pronouncing him dead. Chandler is learning the importance of narrative tempo. He's also learning new skills in narrative design, which is always a function of tempo. The first nineteen chapters of *The High Window* cover one day, nearly matching the novel's chapter division, which breaks in half after Chapter 18. A different balance comes from the arrangement of Marlowe's visits to his client. The detective meets Elizabeth Bright Murdock in Chapter 2 and talks to her next in Chapter 20, the second chapter of the book's second half. What's more, these visits take place on succeeding days.

Marlowe also adds to the reader's pleasure. Chandler erred in saying that he does nothing in *The High Window*. He plays a more active role than he did in *Farewell,* and he displays much more initiative. The earlier book showed him absorbing more physical punishment than he'll do anywhere else in the canon, meeting Moose by accident, and being taken to Amthor's and Dr. Sonderborg's. His meeting with Helen Grayle was arranged by Anne Riordan. The shabbiness with which he repays Anne makes it clear that he has used his options badly; better that he be led by others. For besides disappointing Anne, he also fails to prevent the deaths of Lindsay Marriott and the Moose. By contrast, the Marlowe of *High Window* chooses creatively and does his own leg work, going to Alex Morny's mansion, Morningstar's office, Phillips' apartment, the Idle Valley Casino, and the public library to do important research. As has been seen, he also renounces playing the scourge, both to drive Merle Davis back to Wichita and to help her believe in herself. As the following banter shows, he still can't resist a show of verbal wit (his last words reveal Chandler bending the received standard of glittering backchat, the patter of Oscar Wilde and Noël Coward, to his idea of American vernacular). The bartender's own last words show the exchange dissolving in froth. Yet Chandler kept it in the book because it both provides comic relief before Marlowe's interview with Morny and helps create the pose of indifference Marlowe affects to hide his pain:

> "Your name?"
> "Marlowe."
> "Marlowe. Drink while waiting?"
> "A dry martini will do."
> "A martini. Dry. Veddy, veddy dry."
> "Okay."
> "Will you eat it with a spoon or a knife and fork?"
> "Cut it in strips," I said. "I'll just nibble it." "On your way to school," he said. "Should I put the olive in a bag for you?"
> "Sock me on the nose with it," I said. "If it will make you feel any better."
> "Thank you, sir," he said. "A dry martini."

Marlowe's wisecracking does fret nerves. It jaded Lt. Carl Randall's appetite for coffee in *Farewell*. In *High Window* it baffles and vexes others. In fact, his chatter disconcerts nearly everyone he meets. Elizabeth Bright Murdock orders him, "Please do not be witty"; her son Leslie says, "Your tough-guy act stinks"; her secretary, Merle, advises him, "I wouldn't carry that tough-guy manner too far"; an apartment building manager calls him "a wisey"; a police lieutenant tells him, "Skip the wisecracks"; finally, a chauffeur tied in knots by his chatter pleads with him, "Talk English, Jack." Though Marlowe deserves these retorts, he can also transcend the edgy cynicism that occasioned them. *The High Window* shows that he can be as tactful or as gracious as he wants to be. Respecting Leslie Murdock's determination to preserve his faltering marriage, he refers to Leslie's wife as Linda Murdock both in dialogue and narration. To a crime reporter who gives him some useful information, he says with genuine gratitude, "Nobody could ask for more. Many thanks, Kenny." His courtesy extends to the police. The same good host who made morning coffee for Lt. Randall in *Farewell* mixes highballs for two visiting policemen in *High Window*. As soon as he perceives Merle's trauma, he can't help her enough. When she has a seizure in his apartment, he makes sure she's comfortable, protects her tongue with a handkerchief, and calls a doctor. He then shields her from her persecutor, Elizabeth

Bright Murdock, and from herself. No crusader, he won't try to force-feed her with the truth. But he does present it to her fully and accurately, reconstructing her employer Horace Bright's death eight years before as soon as he discovers how it happened. Though Bright's rough sexual pass gave her the motive and an open window provided her with the opportunity to push him to his death, she remains innocent.

Bright's wife gave him the fatal shove. Marlowe finds a photograph snapped from the street below which clears Merle of guilt. After showing it to her, he destroys it, to confirm his faith in her. Her blacking out at the same moment Bright dropped from the window shows two falls coinciding. But only one of them needs to be fatal. Thanks to Marlowe, Merle eventually escapes from Elizabeth. If her innocence has made her a victim, it also preserves the moral goodness to let her renew herself in Kansas. Life on the middle border with her parents will soothe the pain incurred during her half life in hectic, brutal Pasadena. Marlowe deserves much of the credit for redeeming this innocence.

No longer the dazed, bisexual boy-adventurer he was in *Farewell*, the Marlowe of *High Window* maintains a clear sense of purpose. He matches the powerful Alex Morny sarcasm for sarcasm with Morny's bodyguard standing by. Unafraid of offending a would-be client, he will set the rules for his investigation. And when Elizabeth Bright Murdock objects to the fee he charges for his services, he answers politely but firmly, "I'm just one man and I work at just one case at a time. I take risks, sometimes big risks, and I don't work all the time." He stands fast when Elizabeth explains that she wants him to confirm her prejudices about the theft of the Brasher Doubloon. This integrity and thoroughness win the day for him; he makes it clear that he will investigate in his own way and set his own fees. Although Elizabeth later tells him that she regrets having hired him, she also admits that her son, not the daughter-in-law she wanted to smear, stole the coin.

The theft is both historically and psychologically motivated. Somebody as repressed as Leslie Murdock *would* make an unsuitable marriage to spite his mother. His gravitation to gambling, after his marriage to ex-torch singer Linda Conquest fails, fits the pattern of his masculine protest. Wild, even self-destructive behavior is the only form of assertion he has left, his tyrannical mother having blocked all acceptable outlets of self-expression. The theft of the coin and the killing of his mother's blackmailer reflect the need to compensate for being overly sheltered and bullied. Leslie is as innocent as Merle, his spiritual sister. Convinced of his ineffectuality, he has nothing to lose in recklessness; his movements suggest that he has no job, employment being an activity he would shrink from undertaking lest he fail and confirm his mother's contempt for him. Acting wildly, on the other hand, will make him feel big. Besides, like causes produce like effects. The byproducts of his wildness could hurt the mother who has been denying and discounting him all his life.

Leslie's pain resembles that suffered by others in the book. Rightly, MacShane calls the main subject of *High Window* "the misuse of power and the control of one person by another."[2] In her bullying of Leslie and Merle, Elizabeth violates the hearts closest to her. This false mother has blocked all outlets for growth in both her natural son and her surrogate daughter. She offers no protection, food, or love. Rather than preparing Merle and Leslie for adult life, she tries to solidify their dependence on her. Although she drinks, she never eats; nor does anybody else eat in her presence. She even denies Marlowe the oral satisfaction of smoking (which General Sternwood granted). Her life style shows how this cruel, demanding woman has perverted motherhood. A resident of sunny Pasadena, home of the Rose Bowl, she exudes darkness. Her house is made of dark brick. She first appears in a dark room, the sun room of her cheerless estate, which she has dimmed with heavy drapes. This act typifies her. Despite her middle name (Bright) and her sunny home town, darkness is her natural element. Besides dominating Leslie and Merle, she has outlived two husbands, at least one of whom she killed. Her cheating at solitaire conveys her greed and rapacity; she'll go to any length to achieve her goals. Although Chandler may be overstating his case by implying murderousness from dishonesty at cards, he does display, in the solitaire sequence, Elizabeth's utter lostness. A person who cheats and lies to herself won't blink at deceiving others; a destroyer of her own pleasure, she'll try to crush it in others. Nobody is safe with her prowling around. Even her housemaid, who appears only to admit Marlowe into the estate, is always scowling.

Merle Davis demonstrates Elizabeth's baleful influence more dramatically. Through Merle, Chandler describes how corrosive suffering can be when the sufferer can't protect herself. Introduced as "a thin fragile-looking blondish girl in shell glasses," the wan, pinched Merle drips self-denial. Her paleness, drawn-back hair, and littleness, which Marlowe keeps mentioning, show her need to be held and loved. Elizabeth has robbed her of warmth and wholeness. Molested sexually by Horace Bright, Merle only compounded her troubles by becoming his widow's secretary. That widow has reinforced the pattern of domination and submission initiated by her lecherous husband. By talking for hours about Horace Bright's death, she keeps the trauma it caused alive in Merle's heart rather than quieting it, as she claims. So pervasive has been her conditioning of Merle that, without prodding, Merle also accepts the blame for the blackmailer Lou Vannier's death. She believes that she killed Vannier to repay Elizabeth for her many years of kindness. Leaning more heavily upon psychology than heretofore, Chandler shows the discovery of Vannier's corpse reviving in Merle the horror of Bright's death eight years before; both men had made sexual advances to her, both offended Elizabeth, and Merle learned about the death of both during the daylight hours.

Experience has indeed repeated itself. Though Merle killed neither Bright nor Vannier, in her innocence, she has blamed herself for both deaths. Marlowe tries to purge her anxiety in two ways. He explains that she couldn't have shot Vannier because a shell of the caliber that had been placed in the breech of her pistol would have jammed the pistol's action had the trigger been depressed. Next, he points out that Elizabeth has been persecuting and not protecting her for the past eight years. Whether he drives out the demons haunting her remains unknown. One hopeful sign comes in his shrewd assessment of Elizabeth's power. When he visits his client in Chapter 32, to explain that Merle is resting in his apartment, he faces her across her solitaire table. Noticing that his chair has put him beneath her, he chooses another; he won't give the tough old warrior an advantage she hasn't worked for and earned.

Chandler makes us feel the pain of characters outside the Murdock home who are squeezed by the rich and powerful. Marlowe and Detective Lt. Jesse Breeze discuss the Cassidy case, in which a prominent family shut off a police investigation that would have found Cassidy a drunken paranoic and thus cleared his secretary of committing Cassidy's crime. Moral anxiety stemming from the abuse of power occurs elsewhere in the book. As Merle did after the murders of Bright and Vannier, the dancer Maybelle Masters goes into shock when she learns that her next-door neighbor in the Florence Apartments, George Anson Phillips, has been shot to death. The man she lives with, Del Hench, later pleads guilty to the Phillips murder, wilting under pressure applied by a local mafia chief. The pattern of intimidation takes on a Kafkaesque tint in Chapter 30, when an innocent Lois Morny concurs with her husband's charge that she shot her lover, Vannier.

Chandler attacks the arrogance of power in a style marked by speed, subtlety and evocative range. Like the Cassidy case, the painted Negro jockey on the Murdocks' lawn which Marlowe touches, talks to, and makes a point of ignoring has some of the suggestive range of that other outsider and nonbelonger, the pink bug he finds in an eighteenth-story office of Los Angeles' City Hall in *Farewell. The High Window* also carries forward and builds upon a technique used in *Farewell*—using an epithet both to describe and refer to a character. Wisely, Chandler limits the technique to minor characters to prevent any clash between the breezy tone created by the epithets and any inwardness he might want to unearth. Marlowe dubbed Detective Sergeant Galbraith Hemingway because of his clipped, repetitive speech. In *High Window* such epithets depict several characters. These, like Galbraith, help move the plot, provide atmosphere, and move in and out of the action quickly without needing to be reintroduced. The scowling middle-aged maid who admits Marlowe into the Murdock home is called only Sourpuss. The physical trait that supplies the epithet needn't come from a facial expression. Though the sharp-featured, red-haired manager of the Florence Apartments, where Phillips was staying when he died, has the name Passmore, he lives in our memories as the carroty man, Marlowe's private term for him. An identifying mark also serves as a leitmotif for Phillips, whom Marlowe rarely mentions without referring to his cocoa-colored straw hat and its gaudy print band.

Another stylistic device Chandler uses with new control is the simile. Rather than scattering his similes about, he saves most of them to end selected descriptive paragraphs (the last three paragraphs on p. 343 of *The Raymond Chandler Omnibus* [New York: Knopf, 1969] end with similes). The power of the simile to simultaneously describe and interpret, created by the perspective of distance the simile enjoys over the metaphor, will help clinch an idea or impression. The net curtains in Marlowe's shabby office that "puckered in and out like the lips of a toothless old man sleeping" join Marlowe imaginatively to the elderly Elisha Morningstar, whose death invokes the detective's own mortality. Lois Magic Vannier, the ex-show girl who married rich, hasn't acquired taste along with her new money and property; her heavily mascara'd eyelashes look "like miniature iron railings," and her hair is "as artificial as a night club lobby." *The High Window* also gains stylistically from Chandler's quick and unerring nose. The third paragraph of Chapter 12, with its most powerful and evocative detail coming at the end for emphasis, shows how the rarely used imagery of smell can help build a realistic foreground, enhance poetic effects, and impart an inwardness not accessible through any other trope:

It was getting dark outside now. The rushing sound of the traffic had died a little and the air . . . had that tired end-of-the-day smell of dust, automobile exhaust, sunlight rising from hot walls and sidewalks, the remote smell of food in a thousand restaurants, and perhaps . . . a touch of that peculiar tomcat smell that eucalyptus trees give off in hot weather.

II

Any judgment of *The High Window* must account for the echoes in the book from Chandler's earlier fiction. Although some of this accounting has been done, some still remains. For instance, Leslie Murdock's marriage to Linda makes *High Window* the third straight Chandler novel in which a marriage between a well-to-do man and a nightclub singer goes sour; the paradigm is reinforced by Lois Magic's adultery-plagued marriage to Alex Morny. *The High Window* borrows still other motifs from the earlier fiction. Like *The Big Sleep*, the novel begins with Marlowe arriving at an elegant estate where an older person will hire him to find a missing child-in-law. The missing persons case in *High Window* has a different stinger in its tail from the one in *Big Sleep*. Elizabeth Bright Murdock wants to find Linda, not because she loves her, as General Sternwood did Rusty Regan, but to discredit her as a thief and then persuade her son to divorce her. But Linda's whereabouts turn out to be a red herring. She never pinched the missing coin, and Leslie, who has known where she is living, will probably divorce her without any maternal prodding. Some repetitions are internal and thematic. Chapter Twenty-one ends with a sharp exchange between Marlowe and Elizabeth. The chapter's short last paragraph, which records Marlowe's confusion while exiting Elizabeth's dark sun room, turns the detective momentarily into the groping midwestern narrator featured by Sherwood Anderson:

I gave her a sort of a tired leer and picked my way to the door and opened it and went out. I shut it quietly, holding the knob with a stiff hand and clicking the lock gently into place.
For no reason at all.

The gentle click made by the closing door recalls Marlowe's surreptitious exit from Morningstar's office in Chapter 7 after the detective had overheard Morningstar telephoning Phillips:

I . . . did a rapid glide across the floor to the entrance door and opened it very silently, like snow falling, and let it close the same way, taking its weight at the last moment, so that the click of the catch would not have been heard three feet away.

Marlowe's later "For no reason at all" hides an anger he'd rather not face. Like Morningstar, Elizabeth is an older person who makes him feel anxious. The second time he went to Morningstar's office, after departing quietly the first time, he found the coin dealer dead. The care he takes to shut Elizabeth's door just as quietly conveys his hidden wish that *she* die. The wish, so expressive of his author's complex response to mothers, sets forth exciting lines of psychic development.

But the development is blocked by Chandler's lack of both self-knowledge and artistic technique. An explanation for this blockage lies in his practice of clinging to fictional conventions or motifs from the past rather than testing his imagination. Some of the narrative elements he adopts in *High Window* come, not from his own work, but from that of Hammett. Marlowe's meeting with the apple-cheeked sleuth Phillips in the lobby of the Hotel Metropole recalls Spade's first conversation with the young thug Wilmer Cook in San Francisco's Hotel Belvedere. As a reminder of the similarity, Phillips hands Marlowe a business card bearing a picture of an open eye, symbol of the Pinkertons, the detective agency Hammett both worked for and used as the model for the Continental Detective Agency in his Op stories. *The Maltese Falcon* remains an influence. The delivery of the counterfeit coin to Marlowe's office by a messenger service harks to the arrival of the counterfeit falcon in Spade's office. Spade's words to Brigid at the end of *Falcon*, when he says she's going to jail for murdering his partner, also inspire Alex Morny's snarling, "Yes, angel, I'm going to turn you in," spoken to Lois near the corpse of Vannier, whom Morny believes Lois to have killed. Finally, Marlowe's explanation of his delicate relationship to the police in Chapter 20 recalls both the content of Spade's speech to Casper Gutman about giving the police a fall guy and the style of his words to Brigid about the impermanence of love:

> "I'm working for you," I said, "now, this week, today. Next week I'll be working for somebody else, I hope. And the week after that for still somebody else. In order to do that I have to be on reasonably good terms with the police. They don't have to love me, but they have to be fairly sure I am not cheating on them.... And they have to question anybody they want to question. Can't you understand that?"

These echoes from *The Maltese Falcon* invoke Chandler's famous accolade to Hammett in "The Simple Art of Murder"; Hammett was the "ace performer" of the *Black Mask* stable of writers because he "wrote scenes that seemed never to have been written before." Chandler lacks this invention, and nowhere is his shortcoming more embarrassing than in *High Window*. Impairing the book's timing, technique of characterization, and plausibility, it negates Pendo's claim that *High Window* is "one of the author's structurally superior efforts."[3] Artistic failings of all kinds stem from it and run the work downhill after its promising start. MacShane has spotted the gap that opens and widens in it between aim and execution: "*The High Window* has a curious tone, for it wobbles between burlesque and an expression of anger against ruthless behavior."[4] *High Window* has a good central idea but lacks the art to sustain it. Marlowe is the book's only fully developed character. Chandler's enmity toward Elizabeth Bright Murdock, on the other hand, has reduced her to a caricature. He can't mention her without sneering. His calling her "the old warhorse" and "the old dragon" and his references to "her thick arms," "the rough mannish sound" of her laugh, and "the elephant hide of her cheeks" show his verbal flair defeating him. This volley of degrading details betrays his lack of objectivity. More damagingly, it dwarfs the novel; Elizabeth has no chance either to develop a serious moral statement or enrich the realistic foreground. Chandler won't let her. MacShane objects to her for other reasons. Not only does he find her a parody of a rich society matron; he also argues that she's asked to pull more narrative weight than her cardboard frame permits: "It is asking a caricature to become a fully developed character."[5]

Though apposite, MacShane's complaint applies more strictly to several other characters in the book than to Elizabeth. Marlowe meets Linda Conquest Murdock at the end of Chapter 18 of this thirty-six novel, and his interview with her opens the novel's second half. She doesn't deserve this prominence. She tells Marlowe nothing he didn't already know, she instigates nothing new, and she never reappears. The unmasking of her husband Leslie as the thief of the Brasher Doubloon, which takes place in Chapter 20, ends her thematic usefulness. As has been said, the divorce her mother-in-law is pushing so hard for Leslie will probably grant on his own; Alex Morny, her boss, has his own domestic woes; she never meets either of the murderees. And neither does Eddie Prue, Morny's bodyguard. Like Amthor's ridiculous retainers in *Farewell*, Prue is a melodramatic contrivance who never finds a place in the plot. Marlowe's visual impression of this stalk the only time he appears before us has a frightening photographic accuracy: "A great long gallows of a man with a ravaged face and a haggard frozen right eye that had a clotted iris and the steady look of blindness." This brilliant effect goes to waste; the minor role played by Prue makes Chandler's stylistic flourish irrelevant and self-indulgent. Furthermore, the effect misleads us into looking for Prue to spark excitement that can't happen because he never returns to the action.

The stir and fret emanating from the gigolo Vannier also

subsides quickly. A blackmailer and double murderer, Lou Vannier spends too little time before us to emerge as a legitimate suspect; his capacity for evil lacks enactment. Then he is introduced clumsily; Chandler intrudes a runaway dog into Marlowe's conversation with the Mornys' chauffeur in order to send Vannier to fetch it. The next scene teases out some ideas both germane to the plot and consistent with Chandler's sour view of sexual relationships. But because the three-page scene marks Vannier's only appearance in the action, the ideas never develop dramatically. Lois Morny's first three remarks to Vannier convey both his limited appeal to Lois and his consequent nobodiness. Returning to the poolside patio after retrieving her dog, he is told, "Sit down and rest your sex appeal." The insults continue. When he complains of Marlowe's presence on the patio, she answers, referring to Marlowe, "Big, isn't he? Too much for you to handle, I guess." (Maybelle Masters, Del Hench's live-in girlfriend at the shabby Florence Apartments, is another blonde instigator of violence.) Continuing to browbeat Vannier, she tells him that her dog hates his guts. The showgirl who clawed her way up to L.A.'s suburban gentry even denies her paid lover the affection of her dog.

Any man made to feel lower than a dog will retaliate, especially one created by Raymond Chandler, one of the most fragile egos in modern American literature. *High Window* also shows Leslie Murdock striking out angrily from his wounded pride. Chapter Thirty opens on a protesting note. Fueling the argument that Chandler's men are more complex and vulnerable than his women, Alex Morny takes Lois to the home of Vannier. Besides wringing a murder confession for her, he may also want to build an emotional scene during which she will declare her bad faith, beg his forgiveness, and pledge to remake their marriage. But this issue, consistent enough with Chandler's feline sensibility, never emerges, as neither Lois nor Alex Morny re-enters the action. In a Chandler novel, the crime puzzle counts less than what Marlowe finds along the way and how he reacts to it. Yet the plot of *The High Window* depends more upon chance than upon psychology. Chandler gets rid of characters so quickly that he violates the process of step-by-step participation characteristic of most good detective fiction. What is more, he violates plausibility. The power Louis Vannier gains over Elizabeth Bright Murdock hinges on a wild improbability—that he photographed the high window of the book's title at the very moment Horace Bright was being shoved through it to his death.

Motivation badgers Chandler throughout. He will violate the consistency of a character by reversing an impression or reopening an issue we had believed closed. These surprises aren't the usual treats we read adventure for. Rather than providing excitement, they betray the seams and the joins in the ragged plot. For instance, Lt. Breeze insists that Del Hench didn't shoot George Anson Phillips. The next day, he reports that Hench has confessed his guilt. He adds that Hench was visited in jail by the mafia boss, Pietro Palermo. What neither he nor Chandler makes clear is Palermo's motive for using Hench to bear the legal guilt. Obviously, it lies somewhere in the coils of local politics, which, Chandler implies, puts it beyond our ken. His implication lacks force. Any materials used to unravel a plot must both grow out of and refer to the plot; *High Window* drags them in arbitrarily. Chandler smudges motivation again in his presentation of the Mornys' eight-month-old marriage. When Marlowe confronts the gambler with his wife's infidelity, he's answered with as delicate a moral discrimination as can be found in the canon: "I trust her heart . . . . But I don't trust her judgment." Yet the day after he speaks so tenderly of his wife, Morny announces his intention to jail her for a killer and, to confirm his resolve, smashes her in the face. But the reader, not having witnessed the drama, must infer it from Morny's wrath. Annoying in itself, the inference also distracts the reader from the book's narrative focus, the strife plaguing the Murdock home.

Both to move and resolve the wavering plot, Chandler must again break basic rules of narrative construction. Marlowe eavesdrops at Morningstar's office in Chapter 7 and again at Vannier's Sherman Oaks home in Chapter 30. As he did in *The Big Sleep*, the detective does important legwork and makes important discoveries while away from us; he goes to the library to look up details of dental reconstruction and to study the news reports of Horace Bright's death in 1934. Then he matches the writing on the package containing the counterfeit copy of the Brasher Doubloon with that found in Phillips' diary. This information dribbles out in the last five chapters, during which Chandler sweats and strains to make sense of the plot. Phillips only kept a diary so that it could be inspected after his death; nothing in his personality labels him a diarist. The plot is so far beyond repair at this stage that Chandler's struggles gain him nothing. Marlowe's tedious reconstruction of the case doesn't help. At one point during it, Marlowe says, "I'm afraid it's getting to be one of those long stories after all." He's right. Had Chandler created characters who could act plausibly and take charge of the action, he'd not have needed Marlowe's long, boring rehearsal of the evidence plus the introduction of two new characters at the end and an arrest in Salt Lake City of a third to resolve the plot. So distracted was Chandler by the problem of ending the novel that he forgot a grace period of twelve hours given Marlowe by the police to solve the case when they found out that he had withheld information about the Phillips murder.

A final objection to this thin, parabolic novel refers to Chandler's bad taste. To call Dr. Carl Moss "a big burly Jew with a Hitler mustache" in 1942 was to identify a member of a persecuted group with the group's persecutor. Chandler's fecklessness, intriguingly, parallels that of the repressed Leslie Murdock, whom he resembled physically and may have identified with, since both he and Murdock were controlled by older women. Chandler's description of Dr. Moss also grazes other neurotic identifications set forth in the novel—protection with persecution and subordination with masochism. But like so many other fetching motifs introduced in *The High Window*, the dramatic and logical possibilities invoked by the identification go nowhere, making Chandler look tactless and bigoted. It's hard to defend him against such charges. It's just as hard to pluck up the will for a defense. Speir complains that the two major plot strands of the novel, the death of Horace Bright and the theft and counterfeiting of the Brasher Doubloon, don't knit.[6] Without gainsaying his charge, one can add that it overlooks many other blemishes, flaws, and omissions undermining *The High Window*, an artistic failure that causes special regret because of its fine start and impressive show of both skill and humanity by Marlowe.

Chapter Eight

Mountain Static

THE LADY IN THE LAKE (1943) displays a much more patient, objective Raymond Chandler than was found in his first three novels. Besides trying to correct the mistakes that marred *The High Window*, he also works hard to build on the strengths that distinguished his earlier writing. These efforts he shapes to the curve of the classic English mystery novel; without retreating into orthodoxy, *The Lady in the Lake* stands closer to mainstream detective fiction than does any other Marlowe. The attempt to write a whodunit bespeaks courage, since the form demands a hard, logical structure, and Chandler never pretended to be a structurist. To help shape the plot of *Lady*, he called upon several resources, some of which lay in the past. He built the action around two stories he had published in *Dime Detective*, "Bay City Blues" (June 1938) and "The Lady in the Lake" (January 1939). He set part of this action in Bay City, the urban nightmare of *Farewell, My Lovely*. And as in *The Big Sleep*, Marlowe will accept a missing persons case whose object died a month before the search for him/her begins.

Marlowe searches for Crystal Kingsley during World War II, which is referred to in the book's opening paragraph and casts shadows throughout. Further tension comes from the novel's seasonal time setting. Although *Lady* follows *High Window* by unfolding in the summer, it exploits more of summer's dramatic potential than its predecessor by taking place, in part, in a mountain resort. The freedom and ease promised by Puma Point, Little Fawn Lake, and Camp Kilkare in the Sierra Madres, some fifty miles east of San Bernardino, dissolves in noise and desperation. Like Scott Fitzgerald's Ivy Leaguers, determined to enjoy prom weekend at the Biltmore Hotel a generation earlier, Chandler's vacationers also kill pleasure by gritting their teeth and making a crusade of it. The barking speedboats, nonstop jukeboxes, and humid, overcrowded bars also create a confusion which helps criminals go undetected. As Chandler did earlier in "No Crime in the Mountains," he reminds us, in *Lady,* that these criminals could be foreign spies; the intensity of purpose motivating enemy agents resembles closely enough that of the city vacationers to blur differences.

But perhaps the main virtue of the scenic vacation setting of *Lady* is its influence on the book's style. The mountains, lakes, and forests that add beauty to the region, with their rich array of birds, squirrels and deer, give vent to Chandler's lyricism. "Chandler's descriptive powers are at their height in *The Lady in the Lake,*" says Clive James, and his words hit home. Like Sir Walter Scott's work of the same name, Chandler's novel pulsates with moving descriptions of natural landscape. The rich, detailed scene painting of flora and fauna in *Lady* takes Chandler's artistry beyond the mean streets, cheap lodgings, and low dives of today's city. The freshness and the ringing brightness marking his descriptions of the manless banks of Little Fawn Lake send out vibrations found only in the best nature writing:

> I turned the Chrysler. . . around huge bare granite rocks and past a little waterfall . . . . A bluejay squawked on a branch and a squirrel scolded at me and beat one paw angrily on the pine cone it was holding. A scarlet-topped woodpecker stopped probing in the dark long enough to look at me with one beady eye and then dodge behind the tree trunk to look at me with the other one.
> Beyond the gate the road wound for a couple of hundred yards through trees and then suddenly below me was a small oval lake deep in trees and rocks and wild grass, like a drop of dew caught in a curled leaf.

This lyricism has impressed readers as much as Chandler's new attentiveness to narrative form. Pendo voices a minority position in his disclaimer that *Lady* offers no surprises and that it "rarely rises above any other well-written routine detective story." In contrast, Jacques Barzun calls the work "Chandler's masterpiece," Michael Gilbert judges it "the finest of Chandler's books" and Tuska finds it "the detective novel [of Chandler's] which I feel to be the most engaging."[2] Confirming this majority report is Ross Macdonald's *The Zebra-Striped Hearse.* Not only does this 1962 novel follow *Lady* in its July time setting, its featuring a mountain lake, its showing, near the outset, a growling, irascible business executive with family troubles, and its including in its cast of characters a woman named Fawn King (Marlowe's client in *Lady* has the first name, Kingsley, and he owns a cabin on Little Fawn Lake); Ross Macdonald's ranking of the novel among his favorites[3] also alludes to the crisp action, well realized atmosphere, and stimulating ideas of its source.

I

One of the most intriguing of these ideas stems from Chandler's attitude toward women. The wildness of women in *The Lady in the Lake* torments their men. As happens elsewhere in Chandler, the male psyche is more delicately organized than the female, and, as Moose Malloy showed in *Farewell*, men carry torches that burn brighter and longer than those borne by women. Because love chastens without redeeming, it also causes more psychological havoc in men. Marlowe's statement to a man torn between impulses of love and hatred defines the male heart under stress: "You were in love with her still. You scared her out of town, out of danger, out of reach. But you covered up for her. You let the murder [she committed] ride. She had you that way." This moral ambiguity reaches a crescendo exactly where it should in a well-crafted whodunit—the last paragraph of the next-to-last chapter (excluding the epilogue). Again, Marlowe is describing the suspended policeman who, torn by warring impulses, kills his murderess-ex-wife: "Somebody who thought she needed killing, somebody who had loved her and hated her, somebody who was too much of a cop to let her get away with any more murders, but not enough of a cop to pull her in and let the whole story come out. Somebody like Degarmo." This tension both sharpens and humanizes the investigation. Ambivalence is Chandler's outstanding psychological trait, and nowhere did it rule him more than in his outlook on sex. Writing from his most private self, he doesn't hide his vulnerability behind literary technique in *Lady*. The inner conflict that made Al Degarmo kill Muriel also gripped Chandler or he wouldn't have perceived it or outlined its destructive effects so accurately. Chandler's sexual fear is the starting point. Neither Degarmo nor Marlowe imagines Muriel's evil into life as Moose had done Velma's goodness in *Farewell*. The women in *Lady* are wanton and destructive. Her own father calls Florence Almore "wasteful and extravagant" while still mourning her death. He has judged her well. Florence ran up big gambling debts, drank heavily, and committed adultery. Crystal Kingsley also ruined her marriage by stealing from stores, spending wildly, and sleeping with men.

The third blue-eyed blonde in the novel, Muriel Chess, who is sometimes called Mildred Haviland, outdoes Crystal and Florence in wickedness. She also dramatizes most of the sexual fear permeating the novel. Perhaps she rouses more of Chandler's anxiety than his two most spectacular female destroyers, Velma/Helen of *Farewell* and Eileen Wade of *The Long Goodbye*, because she lacks their beauty and social grace; a woman needn't look stunning to demolish men, runs Chandler's implication. While working as Dr. Albert Almore's nurse, Muriel also killed his wife with a shot of morphine taken from the cache Almore was peddling illegally. She also marries Al Degarmo, a suspended police lieutenant when he enters the book, and Bill Chess, an amputee. The losses of the men she is closest to, a leg, a job and a wife, define her as a castrating wife. Even though Almore is married to another woman and Degarmo has been divorced from Muriel for at least a year, neither man is safe from her. Nor can the bachelor-gigolo, Chris Lavery, escape her wiles. Called "a homewrecker" and "nothing but a professional chaser," Lavery lives in a good residential district without having a job. But he's not content to blackmail his neighbor Dr. Almore. First seen through a Judas window, he also has sex with his wife, perhaps between similar carouses with Muriel, Crystal and Adrienne Fromsett, Derace Kingsley's capable aide.

Marlowe shows astuteness in calling Lavery the central figure of the case; his having bedded the book's four leading women makes him the connection in a book actuated by passion. But his centricity doesn't insure his survival. Like those other gigolos-turned-blackmailers, Lou Vannier of *The High Window* and Larry Mitchell of *Playback*, he gets killed by his author's sexual puritanism or spite. He has overreached himself; the tomcat in Chandler dies because, having pried secrets from the women he makes love to, he knows too much. The weapon Chandler uses to kill Lavery is Muriel Chess. Muriel works her will freely upon Lavery. After sleeping with him in both Bay City and San Bernardino and then luring him to El Paso, she kills him when she sees his survival threatening her own. His animal good looks, his success with women, and the street sense that lets him thrive without working can't protect him. "Smart, smooth and no good" is how an acquaintance describes Muriel; "She had a way with men. She could make them crawl over her shoes." The description holds good. Besides outdoing the homewrecker Lavery in villainy, she also kills him. His being shot to death while taking a shower symbolizes her power over him.

One device this Circe figure uses to turn men into swine is the mask, or disguise. During one of her impersonations she refers to herself as "that frozen-faced little drip." She has intentionally improvised a description that doesn't fit. Her face is both mobile and expressive. This quick-change artist needs only some make-up and hair color to impersonate other women convincingly. Her artistic accomplishment makes us wince when Puma Point's sheriff, Jim Patton, asks in Chapter 39, "Don't you kind of think Bill Chess would know his own wife?" The question raises the wild possibility that Muriel impersonated Crystal Kingsley the day Bill committed adultery with Crystal. Muriel had fooled her husband before. Shortly after meeting Marlowe, Bill said of her, "I'm married to as neat a little blonde as ever you clapped eyes on." He misjudged her again when he said, "Muriel didn't cry down anybody's neck. They left the weeps out of Muriel." Although she divorced Bay City police lieutenant Al Degarmo, she thought tenderly enough of him to hide an anklet he once gave her in a box of sugar. Bill's ignorance of her sentimentality reminds us that, in Chandler, men neither know nor control their wives. The frequency with which wives deceive, desert, and even kill their mates either implies Chandler's fear of being stranded or projects in inverted form his wish to break away from Cissy and start anew. Muriel reflects his malaise. She sleeps with Lavery, Dr. Almore, Bill Chess, and Degarmo. Two of these men she marries and later abandons; a third she kills; the fourth, Almore, she blackmails after murdering his wife.

From the persistence with which Bill Chess misjudges Muriel, one can see why she wants to leave him; he offers her no real adult companionship. The misjudgments go on. Bill mistakes Crystal for Muriel when he sees her drowned body in Little Fawn Lake. Knowing him better than he knew *her*, Muriel tricked him, dressing Crystal in her clothing and putting her necklace around Crystal's neck before stuffing her beneath the underwater planking. She has read his heart perfectly. She deceives him so easily because he feels guilty about his rut with Crystal. The deception scores heavily for her. Besides avenging herself on her husband's lover, she also rids herself of hard-drinking, unfaithful Bill. The plot to drop Bill and kill his bedmate shows her decisiveness. After drowning Crystal, she covers her own tracks. She drives Crystal's car and wears her clothes to San Bernardino's Prescott Hotel, where she makes sure she's noticed by the staff. Her own car she stows in a woodshed near Little Fawn Lake with two packed suitcases sitting in the trunk. The suitcases again express her foresight. Knowing that the police would search the woodshed after the joint disappearance of Crystal and herself came to their attention, she planted evidence that would steer the investigation away from her. The car containing packed suitcases but not driven away adds to the impression that Muriel drowned before she could take her intended trip. The green necklace found on Crystal after she's lifted from the lake recalls both Helen Grayle's missing jade necklace and the jade earrings Carmen Sternwood had on while posing for naked pictures. Green remains Chandler's symbol for sexual license. As Carmen, Helen, and

Crystal show, it also ties in closely with death; instinct untempered by prudence and responsibility promotes death, not life to the morally conservative Chandler.

The green jewelry in *Lady*, though worn by a dead Crystal, both belongs to Muriel and points up her deathliness. Two men intimately connected with her, Lavery and Degarmo, both die, while two others, Bill Chess and Dr. Almore, undergo moral deaths; Lindsay Marriott got murdered while trying to reclaim Helen Grayle's Fei Tsui jade, and Arthur Geiger died within minutes of photographing a naked Carmen. Muriel's deathliness has the same kinetic force; even *she* isn't safe from it. For all her shrewdness and daring, she never finds happiness. She made two stupid marriages, in at least one of which she failed to win her husband's sexual fidelity. Obviously the money she earned, first as Dr. Almore's office nurse and, next, as his partner in a thriving drug racket, couldn't have fulfilled her or she'd not have married Bill Chess and gone with him to the mountains. Perhaps fulfillment and gladness are beyond her. A clue to her failure to get what she wants (or want what she gets) lies in her multinymity and her skill at impersonations. Known as Mildred Haviland and Mildred Degarmo, she also pretends to be Chris Lavery's landlady, a Mrs. Fallbrook, and Crystal Kingsley, changing her garb, hairstyle, and make-up for each role. But she's not the only player in her drama of disguises. A script writer and costume artist, she also arranged to have Crystal impersonate *her*. Revealingly, Crystal acts her part as a corpse. Chandler's point is well taken: loss of self promotes loss of life. Having committed murder, Muriel pretends to be a murder victim. But her imposture only runs its course with her own murder. Yet the deathly drama plays on. Her murderer, who, like her, used an alias at least once, also dies violently. Only a stable, self-accepting person can survive.

Wise enough to know the benefits of self-rootedness, Muriel does try to get in touch with her feelings; she keeps the anklet given her by Degarmo. Even though she couldn't wear the anklet masquerading as Crystal, she lacked the toughness to throw it away. But a murderer can't afford sentiment, as her ex-husband Degarmo learned when he gave Constable Jim Patton a chance to draw his gun after holding him at gunpoint. A murderer must deny all feelings that clash with his/her survival, even the luxury of playing fair. The nostalgia Muriel indulges by keeping the anklet leads to her undoing. The lesson taught by it applies to others, too. Though divorced from Muriel, Degarmo refuses to forget her. His inabilty to put her in the past causes two deaths. He has buried himself too deeply in his obsession to profit from Marlowe's example: "I hate people hard, but I don't hate them very long," says the detective, alluding indirectly to the dangers of clinging to the past. His indirect warning is echoed by Patton's statement, "I ain't a fellow that feels too bad about anything very long." Nobody in the novel could have profited more than Degarmo by breaking with the past. He has already been drawn into the web of unreality symbolized by the impersonation and the alias. Some weeks before the time of the novel, mid-July 1942 (Crystal Kingsley drowned on 12 June, which fell on a Friday in 1942, as it does in the novel, but on other days of the week in 1940, '41 and '43), he drove to Puma Point looking for Muriel and calling himself Lieutenant De Soto of the LAPD.

Other subtractions from self refer to this imposture. Besides losing a wife, he loses his job and finally his life. If his impersonation didn't stem directly from a death, as with Muriel, who killed Crystal, impersonated her, and then contrived to have herself impersonated by the dead woman, it led to a death—his own. Time runs out quickly on Degarmo after he's stripped of those bulwarks of the middle class, a job and a wife. The process occurs without his knowledge. Having gone once to Puma Point under an alias, he never survives his second visit. An impersonation constitutes a denial both of self and of truth. When Muriel introduces herself as her murder victim Chris Lavery's landlady, Marlowe tells her he's a collections agent. Those who lie get lied to in return. Those who lie to themselves, by suppressing their identities, deny life; all truth is personal. Chandler's lesson may be extended. The joys of the past can warm our hearts and enrich our fullness of being. The trials of the past must be forgotten, lest they chip away at and finally break down our identities by duping us into wearing a disguise or mask. This lesson differs sharply from the one taught by Ross Macdonald, who always depicts crisis erupting from the denial or suppression of the past. Chandler's people, like Scott Fitzgerald's, come to grief because they try to relive the past. Moose Malloy thought he could recover the love he believed he shared with Velma eight years before; Elizabeth Bright Murdock denies the forward flow of time by treating her grown son, Leslie, and her secretary, Merle, like chidren; Degarmo's obsession with Muriel neglects the truth that divorce frees a person from being with, talking to or thinking about his/her former mate.

With his heavily lined face and savage animal eyes, Degarmo represents a brutality unrivaled in Chandler's novels. So sadistic is he that he has been suspended from the Bay City's police force, which, with Al or Red Norgaard serving in the army, has reverted to the ruffianism that characterized it under the leadership of Police Chief John Wax. Even Captain Webber of Bay City's homicide squad has no illusions about the integrity of his men. "Are they lying—as usual?" Webber asks Marlowe of two officers who mauled him before arresting him for drunken driving. For Degarmo to be suspended from a police force whose officers slam suspects in the stomach, kick them, blackjack them and force them to drink liquor, he'd have had to resort to butchery. What Chandler shows of him makes such violence feasible. Within minutes of meeting Marlowe, he threatens to beat him up, subject him to the third degree, and put him on a road gang; he does hit the detective in Chapter 21, midway through the book; he strangles Muriel to death and then claws her stomach. This brutality is his answer to the Velmas of the world. Unfortunately, it promotes no dialogue or moral uplift. Not only do Muriel and Degarmo die within hours of each other; the corpses of these two ex-impersonators are distorted beyond recognition, bespeaking their moral sameness. Incompatible in life, they meet in death, but only as parodies of their earthly selves.

Another bully with woman trouble is Marlowe's client, the perfume executive Derace Kingsley. First seen leaving a conference with some business colleagues, he fits best in a corporate context. A minute of talk with Marlowe makes it clear that, despite his gruff manner, fine clothes, and athletic build, Kingsley can't stand alone. His first words are, "I'm a business man. I don't fool around," and his assertion that he expects Marlowe to do what he's told fails to stir the detective. In fact, Kingsley is so impressed with Marlowe for standing up to him that he offers him a cigar. His tough self-assurance is quickly exposed as a facade. Nor does he display a trace of compassion once his mask is removed. He hires Marlowe to find his wife, not because he loves her, but because her wild streak could surface any time and endanger his job. Adrienne Fromsett, whom he wants to marry, thinks so little of him that she won't let him see her home the night Muriel, pretending to be Crystal, asks her for $500 traveling money.

The distress suffered by Kingsley and Degarmo because of women explains Marlowe's sexual reticence. Nowhere in the canon will he show less interest in women than in *Lady*. The quieting of his libido, though, hasn't dulled his spirit. He displays his vitality in other ways, some of them refreshing. A nature enthusiast, he goes out of his way to look at "the finest grevilla trees in the world," on the road between Ontario and San Bernardino; congenial, he offers a cup of coffee to Police Lt. Floyd Greer just as he had to Lt. Randall in *Farewell*. The night before he meets Greer finds him repeating another action he had performed in *Farewell*—driving nearly three hours to enjoy the security of his own bed after a hard day. His nightmare, featuring the hideous changes caused by longterm immersion in water, also discloses his humanity. By turning from sex, Marlowe shares other sides of himself with us. Older, drier and grayer than heretofore, he faces the other characters squarely. He trusts his feelings. Before exchanging a word with slow, fatherly Jim Patton, he decides he likes the sheriff and his good opinion never sours. Cooperating with Patton throughout the investigation, he doesn't compete with him or try to usurp his authority, as does Degarmo, who tries to browbeat both the military and civilian police at Puma Point. Marlowe also resists scoring a point at Patton's expense. Within hours of telling Kingsley that he doesn't do divorce work, he overlooks Patton's jibe about private eyes handling a lot of "smelly" divorce business. His new self-confidence and clarity of purpose has even jaded his flair for witty backchat; incredibly, he censures Lavery for cracking wise.

Less concerned with preening his image than with helping others, he relieves his client's anxiety and helps him avoid scandal; he wins the praise of a Bay City police captain by holding his ground against Degarmo. Marlowe has his priorities right in *Lady*, and he doesn't advertise himself. George P. Elliott's judgment, "Marlowe ... figures out what's wrong with at least part of the world and then remedies it,"[4] describes his effectiveness in *Lady*. All occasions inform against him: witnesses hold back information; the police beat him up, jail him and try to frame him for a crime he didn't commit (the one ethical Bay City cop he meets is called Shorty, expressive of the low place ethics occupy in the police hierarchy). This brutality comes partly from his ability both to outthink and outperform the police. A year and a half before the time of the novel, the Bay City Police stopped investigating Florence Almore's death, and they don't want the case reopened. The intellect and intuition threatening to foil them come forth early—in Marlowe's explanation of why he came to Puma Point to look for the missing Crystal Kingsley: "She started from here. So I started from here." As the case moves ahead, he displays foresight and patience, refusing to dismiss developments that bear only marginally on his search. These developments often surface as a result of his professional skill and experience. The interviews unearthing them reveal his control. He doesn't lose his temper or say more than he needs, even when cornered by hostile, edgy policemen; characteristically, he had set the style for his first talk with Kingsley even though the talk took place on Kingley's home turf, his office. The control that wins him this edge also sharpens his powers of discrimination. When questioned about his alleged theory that Lavery blackmailed Dr. Almore, he points out that the blackmailing is only a possibility, not a theory. The same appreciation of accuracy helps him handle the practical details of detection. "Patton hadn't gone deep enough," he notes of the box of sugar hiding the engraved gold heart along with the anklet chain that Patton had found.

Keen insights into human behavior beyond criminal motives brighten the investigation. In his obligatory mid-book meeting with his client, in the library of L.A.'s Athletic Club, Marlowe rejects Kingsley's offer of a bribe to suppress incriminating evidence related to Crystal's disappearance. He won't let his frightened, desperate client put himself in jeopardy by covering up a murder. Reasoning well, he protects Kingsley over his objections; playing it straight with the law, he argues, will protect Crystal, whom Kingsley probably cares more about than he admits, from being named Lavery's murderer. Honesty and good sense also distinguish his words to Captain Webber in Chapter 21, where the excitement whipped up by Webber's questions might make a less self-assured person panic and incriminate himself. Self-control continues to work for him. In Chapter 31, while he's being held at gunpoint by Muriel, he spoils her advantage by saying that she forgot to release the safety catch. The distraction he creates by pointing out a possible mistake helps him jerk the pistol from her hand and, for a moment anyway, enjoy safety. But his finest moment, which also involves an alternating emotional rhythm of danger and safety, comes in his riveting reconstruction of the case at the end. The precision, fullness and psychological insight distinguishing the reconstruction make *Lady* his best reasoning performance. The deftness with which he slots the different elements of the mystery into place proves Degarmo's guilt. Yet, true to the modesty he displayed during the case, he moves to the background for the finale, as Degarmo and Jim Patton trade both words and bullets.

Patton deserves the dramatic focus, his down-home congeniality, courage and professional skill lifting the quality of the detection in the novel above that found in *Farewell* and *High Window*. Without flinching, he handles the reeking, decomposing corpse of the lady in the lake. His inspecting the Chess cabin for clues and evidence before Marlowe gets there helps him in two ways. Not only does it let him search the cabin first; it also gives him the weight to question Marlowe about his business in the mountains; breaking into the Chess cabin and then looking straight into the beam of Patton's flashlight create a psychological disadvantage Marlowe can't recoup. Patton continues to rule. Playing the ignorant rustic is a function of his experience and expertise. Though his tendency to simplify criminal motives blinds him to the complexities of the case, it doesn't stop him from breaking it. The old man's fumbling slowness underlying his simplicity puffs up Degarmo with false confidence at the end and literally disarms him. So contemptuous is the arrogant city cop of his bumbling, whining counterpart from the sticks that he puts the pistol he had drawn on Patton back in his holster to give Patton an even chance. A mistake; Patton whips out his Colt so quickly that Marlowe never sees him move. The first thing the detective notices after the roar of the Colt is Degarmo's piece flying out of his hand and thudding against the wall behind him.

The sudden shift of power that puts Patton in command of a dazed, bleeding Degarmo is but one of several reversals accounting for the novel's strong sense of motion, change, and thematic build. The scene at the end of Chapter 31 where Marlowe feels safe after disarming Muriel ends with his being knocked out from behind. His fortunes continue to drop despite gleams of hope. When he wakes up in the next chapter, he sees Muriel's corpse and hears a policeman's hard fist knocking on the door. His eagerness to escape doesn't run so high that, preparing to climb through the bathroom window, he can't relieve his anxiety with a joke. Besides providing a Conradian insight into the psychology of stress, his joke also lightens the action with a final stroke of comic relief before the surging final sequence. Chandler's skill in bouncing suspicion from one character to another also adds to the novel's verve and upbeat tempo. The beaching of the drowned female corpse had made Bill Chess the Most Likely Suspect, even though he's innocent and his wife, Muriel, the presumed drowning victim, still lives. Bill claims that Muriel left after discovering his romp with Crystal, but her farewell note to him has been fingered so much that it looks as if it refers to a prior leavetaking.

The following morning introduces another murder, apparently unrelated to the drowning death. Marlowe finds Chris Lavery shot to death in the shower of his Bay City home. The available evidence makes Crystal Kingsley look like his murderer. A telegram presumably sent by Crystal to her husband a few weeks before from El Paso announced her intention to marry Lavery. But when Lavery spoke to Kingsley recently, he denied having gone to El Paso with her. And now the outfit worn in San Bernardino a month ago by a woman answering to Crystal's description has turned up in the dead man's closet.

But the suspicion shifts. Marlowe's search of the death house has uncovered another piece of incriminating evidence—a handkerchief perfumed with chypre (Joel Cairo's scent in *The Maltese Falcon*) and bearing Adrienne Fromsett's initials under Lavery's pillow. "He was quite easy to hate," says Adrienne after learning of Lavery's death, adding, "And poisonously easy to love. Women—even decent women—make such ghastly mistakes about men." Bleakness infiltrates sexual relationships in Chandler; had Velma not loved Moose, she'd never have acquired the knowledge and the power to betray him. The likable person who falls in love with a sexual cheat is a common victim in Chandler. He/she can also inspire Chandler's technical skills. The hidden life that makes Adrienne vulnerable to a Lavery emerges discreetly. Though the brisk, capable career woman wears gray to the office, the monogramed handkerchief found under Lavery's pillow is edged in red. The passion designated by the color red stays to the fore when Kingsley disappears after Muriel's death. But no sooner do Marlowe and Degarmo corner Kingsley at his mountain cabin than the suspicion swings away from him and Adrienne to Degarmo.

Until the final sequence, all had assumed that the drowned body of Chapter 6 belonged to Muriel. Her husband Bill's belief that the corpse is Muriel's created a sense of conviction that Bill confirmed by lifting the corpse from the water and bringing it to dry land. Bill, who later smashes himself in the face, presents an admirably contained image of dismay as he sees the pulpy, decomposed body surface: "Bill Chess held the handrail and his knuckles were polished bones," Marlowe observes just before hearing Bill croak, "Muriel ... Sweet Christ, it's Muriel!" Besides invoking the love-death conjunction so pervasive in Chandler, the metaphor and the absence of a comma between the independent clauses both capture the depth and the intensity of Bill's shock. *Lady* is a hidden identity case. Once the imposture alluded to in the book's title is disclosed, the murder solves itself; Muriel lurks behind all the impersonations in the novel, including her own. Bill's explosive reaction to the lady in the lake has tricked us into identifying the drowned woman as Muriel; the corpse was also wearing Muriel's dress and necklace and had her hair color. Yet, whereas Chandler shrewdly encourages the misidentification, he also keeps skepticism alive; Bill is so guilt-ridden over the death that his judgment must be suspect. But his howls of grief and his white knuckles batter our objectivity; a man should be trusted to recognize his wife, even after a month under water has changed her.

Chandler's allowing Marlowe to ride the current of Bill's tears is a fine piece of literary conjury. But Marlowe has some tricks of his own. At the end, he joins forces with Degarmo, presumably to question Kingsley about Muriel's hotel death of Chapter 31. Chandler has misdirected our attention from the facts of the case by leaguing Marlowe with Delgarmo, who has gained some reader sympathy after his suspension from the corrupt Bay City Police: yes, Degarmo has erred, but his suspension, coming from a sadistic, inept outfit, could count to his credit. Chandler hasn't told us that Marlowe knew of Degarmo's guilt before teaming up with him. Thus we are a step behind when Degarmo blames Muriel's murder on Kingsley.The reversal of his fortunes turns on a nice irony. A man *has* killed his estranged wife, and he *will* pay for his crime. But the stricken couple are not the two we had believed, Crystal and Derace Kingsley.

Connections have been forming from the outset, had we troubled to look. Both of Muriel's husbands are burly, blue-eyed men whom Marlowe meets in succeeding chapters. Muriel can use Crystal to impersonate her because both women are blue-eyed blondes of the same height and weight (as was Florence Almore). Another balance is struck by the revelation that both Kingsley and Bill Chess, whom Marlowe also meets in succeeding chapters, have missing wives. Tight plotting firms up the balance. The fortunes of the missing wives, neither of whom will survive the action, have been linked all along. Crystal's doctor lives across the street from her lover. Muriel, who once worked as the doctor's nurse, murders Crystal, her and Crystal's lover, and the doctor's wife. Her former husband, Degarmo, meets Marlowe outside the doctor's house soon after Marlowe interviews Lavery. No wonder that that master architect of plots, Ross Macdonald, was so taken with the book. The interconnections in *Lady* imply a world that obeys a strict economy while hewing to a clearly marked curve. Enforcing the impression of an orderly, self-regulating world is the frequency with which the false image, or mask, ties in with death. MacShane reads *Lady* as a portrait of a middle-class society fighting to stay together.

The Lady in the Lake is a somber book because it concentrates on those who are caught up in the system of Southern California instead of those who direct it . . . . What Chandler shows us is a society of men and women trying somehow to keep their lives together, but always under pressure and therefore susceptible to violence.[5]

The mask only intensifies the pressure and brings on the

violence its wearer had hoped to fend off. Rating one's image over one's individuality always worsens trouble. Chandler's sermon on the dangers of dissembling covers a wide range. Its title alluding indirectly to Narcissus, the novel recounts the effects of image worship. In our competitive, middle class society, people must maintain a clean facade, a requirement necessitating cosmetics and, in dire cases, murder. Kingsley, we recall, hired Marlowe to begin with to protect his good name, i.e., his job and reputation, rather than to save his shaky marriage. Kingsley also manufactures cosmetics. Besides pandering to vanity, cosmetics are used in impersonations. The Gillerain Company's most touted product, a perfume, sharpens the issue. Creams and powders can brighten and beautify a facade, hiding the flaws beneath. Chandler's keen sense of smell has also helped him show that perfumes deceive to a still greater degree, putting out false scents, encouraging unrealistic hopes, and, because of their power to intoxicate, leading us into danger.

Cosmetics invoke the novel's arch-impersonator, Muriel Chess, even when she's off the scene. Inspecting her room in Puma Point, Marlowe notices an excess of make-up: "There was the usual stuff women use on their faces and fingernails and eyebrows, and it seemed to me that there was too much of it." He doesn't yet know that, as a disguise artist, Muriel needs a great deal of make-up. Cosmetics continue to identify her, but, again, without Marlowe making the connection. Impersonating Chris Lavery's landlady, Muriel improvises a "tone of cockeyed reasonableness"while discussing matters like carpets and furniture. Her improvisation hinges upon make-up. Subtly, Chandler links the motif to Marlowe's earlier discovery of the cosmetics crowding Muriel's mountain cabin bureau. The connecting principle is excess: "She was a slender woman of uncertain age, with untidy brow hair, a scarlet mess of a mouth, too much rouge on her cheekbones, shadowed eyes," Marlowe says of the woman who calls herself Mrs. Fallbrook. To help us connect the Fallbrook imposture with the jars, tubes, and boxes thronging Muriel's bureau, Chandler keeps the cosmetics motif before us. Birdie Keppel, a journalist Marlowe meets his first night in the mountains, works as a beautician during the day.

The motif covers a wide swathe. The quiet, amply furnished library of the Athletic Club, where Marlowe and Kingsley meet to discuss the Lavery death, provides an ideal setting for the members' post-luncheon naps. The sleeping room outfitted as a library represents one more disguise in a novel of disguises, masks, and false images. Also comical but more thematic is Marlowe's pretending to be an H.G. Talbot, after hopping into Talbot's apartment when he finds himself in the same room as Muriel's corpse and hears policemen at the door. Fooling nobody with his impersonation, Marlowe is arrested straightaway. Military authority can also impose itself in a nation at war. So supple and smooth-muscled is *Lady* that it relates the cosmetics motif to its wartime (July 1942) setting. The novel opens:

> The Treolar Building was, and is, on Olive Street, near Sixth, on the west side. The sidewalk in front of it had been built of black and white rubber blocks. They were taking them up now to give to the government, and a hatless pale man with a face like a building superintendent was watching the work and looking as if it was breaking his heart.

Chandler never mentions America's war effort without referring to rubber; besides noting the rubber sidewalk fronting L.A.'s Treolar Building, he twice connects care and restraint in car driving with the conservation of rubber on tires. If creams and powders are used to cover defects, rubber can erase them. Yet rubbing out defects can cause deep damage. The more one rubs, the more one weakens the underlying membrane. Chandler's symbolic warning is clear. A person who relies increasingly on masks will find them overtaking his reality and destroying his essential self. Perhaps the putative superintendent of the Treolar Building looks glum because his private war has helped him understand the problem.

II

The contrast Durham sees between the novel's two settings, Puma Point and Bay City, i.e., Santa Monica, disregards the unity created by Chandler's deft manipulation of the mask motif: "The unsaintly Santa Monica, the town of brutality and evil, was contrasted with the purity of the mountains, where the Sierra Madres cast their spell on the man of action."[6] Though bracing, this mountain freshness provides no defense against crime and criminals. Two horrible deaths, the first and last recounted in the novel, occur near a sparkling blue lake, and both victims are deformed beyond recognition. As the victims show, the path between Bay City and Puma Point is well worn. Disguises are prepared and worn in both places; the process by which self-effacement become self-negation observes no geographical boundaries. Eden was despoiled before Muriel slew Crystal. Chandler's paradox that life, for some, is impossible both with and without a mask refers to Hitler's War. The same national emergency that tears up a rubber sidewalk in Los Angeles posts military guards along the mountain bridge near which Degarmo falls to his death. The manner of Degarmo's death, in fact, completes his transformation from lawman to outlaw. Having refused to obey a guard's order to stop, he violates military security. He had already lost his job, strangled his ex-wife, and threatened to shoot Jim Patton in the belly. The threat reminds us that he also clawed Muriel's belly after choking her. Since the belly, or stomach, is where food is digested and foetuses grow, the violence Degarmo directs to stomachs makes him the enemy of life. His scorn for military security explains his moral darkness in terms vivid to a reader in 1943, to whom saboteurs of our war effort deserved heavy punishment.

Besides noting this patriotic fillip, any critical estimate of *Lady* should also add that Chandler's methods are more restrained and his materials more realistic than those found in his first three novels. In place of Gothic contrivances like Amthor and Eddie Prue, Chandler will substitute irony. The detective and the murderer drive to Puma Point in the same car at the end to solve the case. Degarmo doesn't know he's being lured back to the site where Marlowe started investigating and thus forming a loop, or noose, around himself as the case comes full circle. Irony can also relieve some of the novel's grimness. Although *Lady* leans more heavily upon the mechanics of detection than any other Marlowe, it also presents a more lifelike, naturally toned picture of its narrator-sleuth than had been previously attempted. Marlowe's conversations develop realistically, achieving their own pitch and momentum, as if Chandler is watching his characters be themselves rather than using them to move the plot. The first-person narrative technique serves this new realism; Marlowe responds at several different levels simultaneously rather than melting into his job. During the scene in which Adrienne Fromsett becomes a leading suspect as Lavery's killer, Marlowe relieves the tension by observing of her, "Her upper lip curled a little. It was a long upper lip. I like long upper lips." No digression or indulgence, the observation, with its playful repetition, keeps the scene from peaking too early and strengthens the human foundation of the case; the principals of the case are people before they're witnesses, suspects, or investigators. An unlooked-for incidental can also enrich the novel's flavor, all the more for its remoteness from the matter at hand, as a maverick moment in Marlowe's interview with Florence Almore's parents shows: "I looked hard at Mrs. Grayson. Her hands had never stopped working. She had a dozen pairs of darned socks finished. Grayson's long bony feet would be hard on socks."

Developing in its own good time, the solution to the crime fits the paradigm of the Chandler mystery formulated in 1980 by Stephen Knight: "The threats that are really basic are found to be private ones ... threats that grow on domestic ground. They come from intimate associates, former lovers—from women, above all."[7] Like *Farewell, Lady* has two culprits, one smooth and one rough, who were once linked sexually. Al Degarmo follows the Moose in being a primitive man of passion who kills when he feels robbed of the wholeness and harmony he craves; even Muriel, his ex-wife, must die for breaking up his home. She leads him to kill, just as Velma, Mrs. Murdock, Orfamay Quest, and Helen Wade instigate much of the damage in other Marlowes. Though not legally guilty, in that hard evidence is lacking to convict them of murder, these women voice Chandler's self-doubts and dramatize his fear of sex. Neither Velma nor Muriel wanted to destroy her man; they only sought freedom from them. But does the presence of two murderers in *Lady* weaken the force of Chandler's warning about the dangers of loving a woman? The answer is no. The growing complexity of modern life, symbolized by the violence erupting in scenic Puma Point, has already corroded social and moral guidelines. Nor does Chandler break a rule of literary detection by having a cop commit murder. Degarmo is off the force when he kills Muriel. Next, the Bay City Police will operate more effectively without him in its homicide division, just as society at large has gained peace through the death of three-time murderer Muriel Chess.

As in most classic English detective fiction, the elimination of murderer and murder helps the commonweal in *Lady*. Degarmo's crashing to his death after a bullet shreds his rear tire shows the military finishing the job started by the civilians Patton and Marlowe. The unity of wartime America makes the death inevitable. Degarmo can't live after denying so many civilized values. If retribution doesn't come from those who induced his guilt, it will be performed by a representative of the values he denied, even if that representative, an M.P., is a stranger. But neither Degarmo's nor Muriel's death restores social harmony. The brutality of the Bay City Police, Dr. Almore's drug racket, and the war overseas all show that there was no harmony to be disrupted. Degarmo's domestic and professional woes bespeak a world in chains. Using him, Chandler blurs the line between investigator and suspects to show policemen subject to the same tensions as anybody else. In a world at war, everybody walks the edge, everybody is tempted to seek relief in the mask, and everybody can go wrong.

But no supervening social or cultural malaise keeps *Lady* from being Chandler's best book. The novel lacks a dramatic focus; its plot is advanced by someone who, when she appears at all, pretends to be another person. Chandler acquits himself somewhat by making us think that Muriel and not Crystal drowned in Little Fawn Lake. But he fails to display Muriel's power to win and then crush men. He describes only the effects of her power, not its radiant cause. His omission undermines the fiber of the book. Helen Grayle and Eileen Wade enslave men with their beauty; Mrs. Murdock uses her money and her power as a mother figure to control those around her. Muriel operates from intuition and intelligence. Potentially, these qualities make her more intriguing than her three co-destroyers. But they're more asserted than dramatic; the book gives no reason why we should believe in them. A wonderful stroke of literary conjury, the mask nonetheless violates the realistic undergirding of the book. Even a whodunit needs something more substantial than misdirection as a foundation. Chandler doesn't explore the issues he raises. By displaying Muriel so rarely and introducing her under a different name each time, he mars the sharp contours of his plot and robs his anti-feminism of a footing in anything more solid than his own fears.

Chapter Nine

Hooray for Hollywood

THE LITTLE SISTER (1949) is a further installment in Chandler's extended poison pen letter to women. Marlowe's disclaimer in *The Big Sleep,* that women sicken him, recurs in Chapter 14 of *The Little Sister* in the sour remark: "To hell with all women." Carrying forward from the earlier fiction, *The Little Sister* may bring all women within his and Chandler's fields of fire. Both men had already lined up a number of females in their gunsights. The destructive daughter of *The Big Sleep* yielded to the sluttish wife with a shady past in *Farewell, My Lovely.* Equally deserving of scorn are the corrupt mother of *The High Window* and, in Crystal Kingsley and Muriel Degarmo Chess, the adulteress and man-eating ex-wife of *The Lady in the Lake.* A woman also maddens her former husband in *The Little Sister,* her rank eroticism dividing her from the more calculating Muriel, who used sex chiefly as a tactic or weapon. In addition to the oversexed divorcée, Dolores Gonzalez, *The Little Sister* includes Orfamay Quest, the book's title figure and Chandler's first notable sister-villainess (the wrongdoing of Carmen and Vivian Sternwood bypasses their being sisters). Orfamay has followed her brother Orrin to Hollywood from Manhattan, Kansas to demand a share of his blackmailing profits; his refusal to comply leads her to betray him to the gangster he's blackmailing, an act calculated to kill Orrin.

Humanizing this attack upon women is Chandler's fairmindedness and perhaps guilt. Yes, Orrin is murdered, but not because of his sister's treachery; another gun gets to him before that of the gangster he had threatened to incriminate. And the destructive ex-wife gains her power to maim through the mistakes of others. The celebrated Chandler siren may be less evil than her commentators have acknowledged. Common sense should have told Moose Malloy to leave Velma alone. Had he admitted to himself that her love for him died eight years ago when she betrayed him to the

180

police, he'd have removed her motive for killing him. She never planned his murder. Likewise, Muriel Chess turned from Al Degarmo after divorcing him; they both died because he followed her from Bay City to the Sierra Madres and back. Chandler emphasizes the futility of his quest by making it follow the divorce by a year, during which time she has moved twice, married and left another man. Although Muriel and Velma aren't angels, neither do they deserve all the blame for the destruction breaking around them. Even the Cleveland woman known as Dolores Gonzales affects the Mexican sexbomb because the affectation will help her movie career. Perhaps she erred in opting for movie stardom. *The Little Sister* shows, along with Chandler's other work, that most domestic trouble in Chandler starts with women and that women have learned to survive it better than men. Both Quest sisters outlive their brother, even though all three are tempted by the same prizes. Their mother also outlived their father after denying him the pleasures of tobacco in the two years he survived after his fatal stroke. A smoker himself, Chandler would have felt the sting of this denial.

Yet even here, a small detail—the Quest father's earlier marriage—stirs ambiguities that fall in line with Chandler's own. As Vivian Regan, Muriel Chess and Sylvia Lennox prove, Chandler scorned divorce. Taking a righteous stand, he would have explained divorce as a failure to see one's commitments through and thus an act of moral cowardice. But the cowardice could well have been his own. As is shown in his portrayals of virile young men, he would retreat into moral orthodoxy in order to condemn people for performing acts of boldness he lacked the physique or courage to undertake himself. Arguing from effect back to cause, he may be implying that sexual looseness wrecked the elder Quest's first marriage and thus earned him his deprivation. Like Chandler, the elder Quest, an M.D., was an accomplished man, as was novelist Roger Wade of *The Long Goodbye*, whose defiance of sexual morality hastened *his* death.

Dr. Quest's youngest child, Orfamay, raises no such ambiguities. In her first exchange with Marlowe, she lies, distorts and withholds information. She will also block Marlowe's way to the truth. Self-righteous and disapproving, she calls him nasty and horrid when he exposes her lies. She wants him to find Orrin, who, she claims, came to California a year ago but has since lost his job and stopped writing home. What she has held back, aside from her phone number and address, is her plan to share the money Orrin has been earning as a blackmailer. But not only does she evade and distort. She also tries to beat down Marlowe's customary fee, lets him get arrested and knocked out on her behalf, and leaves town after selling out her brother and sister. Balancing her mincing corruption is the rankness exuded by Dolores Gonzales. The colors Dolores always wears, black, white and red, convey the telescoping of sex and death that fascinated Chandler so much. "Sexy was very faint praise for her," says Marlowe the first time he sees her, reacting with the rapt horror of his puritan-sensualist creator. Her jodhpurs, "like her hair, were coal black. She wore a white silk shirt with a scarlet scarf loose around her throat. It was not as vivid as her mouth .... Two thick braids of her shining black hair lay on each side of her slim brown neck. Each was tied with a small scarlet bow." Later in the interview, he denies intending to rape her but, noting her provocative smile adds, "But I'm sure as hell working up to it." If deliberately provoked, he can't be guilty of committing rape. His *non sequitur* shows that he has been aroused more than he wants to admit.

His arousal pleases her; stirring men is her greatest pleasure. But Chandler disappoves. Suitably, the sexpot who can't talk to Marlowe without inviting him into her bed gets stabbed to death by her former husband. The last hard, elongated object thrust into her body kills her. Denied the right to penetrate her lovingly, her husband avenges himself with a knife. Thus a thwarted passion for an ex-wife proves a motive to murder in *The Little Sister* as it had in *The Lady in the Lake*. But the reverberations sent out in the later book boom more loudly. Unlike the apelike Moose Malloy and Al Degarmo, Dolores' husband, Vincent Lagardie, has an M.D. degree from the Sorbonne. What happens to him after he starts practicing medicine describes the pitfalls awaiting men who follow women in Chandler. Dr. Lagardie gave up his Cleveland practice to follow Dolores to Hollywood. Now he has lost her, and his cheap, nasty Bay City clinic conceals a drug operation. His final appearance completes his degeneration. Having stabbed Dolores, he gazes blankly ahead of him, blood foaming on his lips from his having bitten through his tongue.

Both his bloodshed and his catatonia are dictated by Chandler's psyche rather than by the plot. Chandler's ability to love and hate simultaneously reveals itself in Marlowe's last look at Dolores: "She was exquisite, she was dark, she was deadly. And nothing would ever touch her, not even the law." As in *Farewell, My Lovely* and *The Long Goodbye*, a beautiful woman won't be convicted for the murder she committed. The failure of the law to punish these murderesses worries Chandler. Unfortunately he can't live with his worry. For each of her appearances, he dressed Dolores,

Orrin P. Quest's killer, in gaudy clothes, painted her face with
cosmetics, and gave her stupid things to say with a fake Mexican
accent. Not content to make her look and sound like a cheap slut, he
adds a chapter to the novel so that he can kill her, too. Her guilt has
nothing to do with the family drama underlying *The Little Sister*.
Chandler makes her a murderess for the same reason he sends Dr.
Lagardie to her apartment in the last chapter. He wants to punish
her for her promiscuity. He also wants to avoid being accused of
prudery. Thus he has Marlowe call the police as soon as he spots
Lagardie in the ground floor lobby of her apartment house.
Marlowe's reaction to the murder fails to resolve the tension
between Chandler's instinctive and rational responses to Dolores:
"They [the police] came fast—but not fast enough. Perhaps I ought
to have stopped him [Lagardie]. Perhaps I had a hunch what he
would do, and deliberately let him do it. Sometimes when I'm low I
try to reason it out. But it gets too complicated." Complicated and
simple; Chandler feels the same attraction/aversion that has
maddened Lagardie and stopped Marlowe from following him up
the stairs. But rather than working out his conflict, he foists a
murder on Dolores which he uses as an excuse to kill her. The minor
figure that carries out his punishment for him, Lagardie,
accentuates his moral cowardice. As usual, he has addressed the
subject of sexual politics at a vulgar, adolescent level. By killing
Dolores out of Marlowe's sight, Chandler avoids asking himself
whether he punished her for breaking the moral law or for indulging
pleasures off limits to him.

I

Chandler's inability to decide whether *The Little Sister* was
written out of spite or moral rectitude colors his portrayal of
Marlowe. Some of the skill, instinct, and dedication that
distinguished Marlowe in *The Lady in the Lake* brightens *The Little
Sister*. He investigates with thoroughness and aplomb. A gangster
is killed in a hotel because he owns something his killer wants; a
woman Marlowe discovers in the dead gangster's room holds him at
gunpoint and then knocks him out before slipping away. Though
ignorant of what the woman came for, he does infer the size of the
hidden object or objects from the places she had inspected—a book, a
tube of toothpaste, and a hatband. His patient, systematic search
eventually prompts him to lift the dead man's wig, inside of which
he finds a claim check from a local camera shop. An incriminating
photo moves the plot of *The Little Sister*, just as it did those of *The*

Big Sleep and *The High Window*. Again, Marlowe averts bloodshed by destroying rather than selling the evidence.

Earlier in the action, his ability to resist temptation by money also served him well. He waited for the right moment before confronting Flack, the house detective of Bay City's Van Nuys Hotel, with his theft of $150 from the murdered gangster. His timing and composure break Flack down quickly. When offered half of the stolen cash, Marlowe demands the whole wad. And he gets it. Only after counting the money does he toss it back to Flack and tell him to put it away. Pocketing the wad, Flack says that the exchange has robbed Marlowe of his bargaining power. He's wrong. Marlowe wants something he prizes more than money, and he knows how to apply the pressure to get it. Before leaving the hotel, he learns both the make and the license plate number of the car driven by the woman who knocked him out in the hotel room. This information leads him to the woman, screen actress Mavis Weld, who underrates him as much as Flack did and fares just as badly. Having her sexual advances rebuffed vexes her: "I've seen all the approaches there are. I think I have. If I can't scare you, lick you, or seduce you, what the hell can I buy you with?" Like Flack, she finds that money won't work. She's not as persuasive as she had believed. Losing her temper when Marlowe dismisses her offer of a bribe, she throws a glass at him; he, in the meantime, wins her as a client. His willingness to work for her reflects his practicality; a detective needn't like his client any more than a doctor need like his patients. Marlowe will serve Mavis even after she lies to him, tries to seduce him, slaps his face, and knocks him out.

This detachment is rare. He snarls at Flack, although the hotel detective breaks a rule for him by giving him the key to the room of the murder victim. Later, he bullies the desk clerk of Dolores Gonzales' apartment building because he believes the clerk a marijuana smoker and thus fair game for his worst. A sour, carping Marlowe dominates *The Little Sister*, in sharp contrast to the cool pro of *The Lady in the Lake*. He won't miss a chance to scathe the sexual morals of Dolores like an angry revivalist preacher. Nothing escapes his bitterness. He calls family life "the blatting of the radio, the whining of ... spoiled children and the gabble of ... silly wives." Tending to compare each thing he sees to something seamier and sleazier than itself, he calls California "the department store state." There's nothing about his home state he refers to without derision or disgust. Not even the ocean escapes his malice; in Chapter 13 he refers to "the great fat solid Pacific trudging into shore like a scrubwoman going home .... None of the harsh wild smell of the sea. A California ocean." His malice has fogged his memory. "I used to like this town," he says of L.A. during a traffic jam. "A long time ago. There were trees along Wilshire Boulevard .... Los Angeles was just a big dry sunny place with ugly homes and no style, but goodhearted and peaceful. It had the climate they just yap about now." This nostalgia is ill judged. Marlowe always railed about his city's alleged defects and flaws. The narrative voice of *The Little Sister* resembles that heard in the earlier novels but is more riddled with scorn. What James Guetti said in 1982 about Marlowe's rueful smartness applies more strictly to *The Little Sister* than to any Chandler novel to date:

> Marlowe's characteristic solution, his way of reading ... complicated experience, is to turn it into a slick one-liner .... Such declarations do not solve anything, of course, but they sound as if they do, and they are the most habitual action that this detective takes against the confusions of his case.[1]

In *The Little Sister* the cynical diatribe, a tissue of glib observations, supplants reason, patience, and kindness. More self-conscious than before, Marlowe looks at himself in the mirror twice in Chapter 20 and once again in Chapter 23. Perhaps he doubts his existence. His sarcasm conveys the sneering disapproval of the outcast. Cranky and captious, he will degrade whatever he sees, including himself. Chapter Twenty-five finds him taking a mudbath in self-pity: "I was a blank man. I had no face, no meaning, no personality, hardly a name .... I was the page from yesterday's calendar crumpled at the bottom of the waste basket."

Nor do his spirits improve. His sullenness mirrors the degradation clouding the novel. Ruehlmann judges well when he calls *The Little Sister* "Chandler's strongest—and angriest—book."[2] Much of the book's pungency stems from the moral depletion that has overtaken Hollywood. Marlowe's long catalogs of urban squalor and sprawl convey this sad comedown. Another side is conveyed by Chandler's many references to decay, insects, and other unsavory forms of subhuman life. Recalling General Sternwood's description of Carmen as someone who enjoys pulling wings off flies, Marlowe kills a fly in Chapter 1 before speaking to Orfamay Quest, another destructive innocent. A gunman named Joseph P. Toad later tries to muscle him off the Quest case (in the chapter before meeting him, Marlowe had referred to restaurants with "sweaty greasy kitchens that would have poisoned a toad"). Toad never changes into a handsome prince. Accompanying him is his retarded nephew, Alfred, a sniffing, twitching drug addict, the clip of whose pistol has been removed to stop him from shooting people. Toad's claim that Alfred "wouldn't hurt a fly" lacks conviction but adds to the festering climate pervading the book; such grotesques stand for southern California society at large. Alfred scoops up the $500 his uncle tries to bribe Marlowe with as soon as the uncle leaves the room.

Chandler uses animals elsewhere to record his distaste for modern life. Marlowe calls himself an alligator in Chapter 33, and in Chapter 19 he watches three dogs pissing against a desk in a sumptuous office while their owner throws his cigar into a nearby swimming pool (to the cat lover Chandler, dogs conveyed the same loathing as flies, frogs, and alligators). Marlowe can't escape shoddiness and vulgarity. Though he turns down money offered to him by Toad and Dolores, he learns that the $20 retainer paid to him by the apple-cheeked midwesterner Orfamay Quest proves just as tainted. The taint spreads. As his investigation moves ahead, he stops searching for the missing Orrin. Nor is he concerned with righting a wrong, punishing an evildoer, or keeping a family together. The Quest family has already broken up on the tinsel and celluloid of Hollywood, America's dream factory. Leila rejected her family when she left Kansas to act in movies (under the name of Mavis Weld). Her brother Orrin is so intent on blackmailing her and her gangster-lover that he icepicked two pretenders to the incriminating snapshot he took of them. Greedy little Orfamay, as has been seen, wants to find him so that she can grab a share of the spoils. Called by Lambert "provincial imitators of the endemic fast-dollar dream,"[3] the Quest children have all denied the family as a source of wholeness and stability.

Given Chandler's dislike for Hollywood,[4] it follows that their denial of rootedness should take them there. Hollywood leads people astray, deluding them with false hopes of wealth, glamor, and fame. As he did with the Sternwoods in *The Big Sleep*, Chandler avoids showing any Quest together with any other. This estrangement, a corollary of alienation to the fatherless and deracinated Chandler, shows how Hollywood divides and degrades. Durham's statement, "In no sense is *The Little Sister* a 'Hollywood novel'," is wrong. Although Ruhm overstates his case by calling *The Little Sister* "the best novel about Hollywood,"[5] he has located its nerve center and moral focus. Part of the action unfolds on a Hollywood shooting set; two screen actresses play major parts, while several other performers, an agent, a studio manager, and some minor functionaries fill in the background. These characters are integral. The Hollywood of *The Little Sister* goes beyond studio props, personalities, and publicity campaigns. It peddles false values, rewarding the gaudy and the superficial, and, with its promise of fast, easy money, encourages crime. As if this crime weren't nasty enough on its own, it ensnares gangsters from Cleveland like Weepy Moyer and Sunny Moe Stein, who corrupt the place further. Margolies has shown how the absence of civilized values and controls in Hollywood altered Chandler's technique of character portrayal in *The Little Sister*:

Chandler reverses many of his earlier themes. The "bad guys" come from the "pure" Midwest to exploit and extort . . . . The seemingly naive heroine who supplicates Marlowe for help is really a ruthless blackmailer, the police are sometimes sympathetic, and the rich and powerful seem sometimes quite bewildered.[6]

One rich and powerful film mogul baffled by his success is the studio executive called Oppenheimer. "The motion picture business is the only business in the world in which you can make all the mistakes there are and still make money," he claims. He also proves his point. Although he reasons that owning 1500 movie theaters will bring success, he doesn't know how to amass them. He prefers watching his dogs wet the leg of his office desk to the toil of working out details of film marketing, advertising, and distribution. Perhaps he has been in Hollywood long enough to know that it violates rational expectations. One stumbles into fortune and fame in Hollywood. Everyone, even the successful, is puzzled by the dynamics of postwar Hollywood. The insect and toad images, together with the stink given off by dog piss, create an overall impression of decay, which coexists with splendor and magnificence. Hollywood withers and waxes simultaneously. This paradox gains expression through the god figure, or celebrant, of the film industry, Sheridan Ballou. Appearing but once, appositely, in Chapter 18, the novel's middle chapter, this screen agent personifies an industry which is both an art and a business and which juxtaposes features of dizzy growth and collapse. He finds work as oppressive as Oppenheimer finds it laughable.

Though handsome, stylish, and surrounded by opulence, he has become sick and cranky from overwork. An aide says that he's behind schedule despite working a twenty-hour day, and the aide is right. Ballou has lost track of himself climbing to the top of the Hollywood power structure. Even if he had the energy, he mightn't know how to regain self-control. He can't explain his success any more than the out-of-work and the hangers-on can explain their failure. Called by Marlowe "a decadent aristocrat," he enters the novel in a prone position, too exhausted either to look at or talk to the detective. Being pampered hasn't spoiled him. His words about both the dramatic emotion and the show business personality reveal high intelligence. Yet his wisdom, his executive skill, and the army of retainers that protect him don't spare him from feeling lost and ineffectual. Why should they? His career is built on dreams. Talent, looks and the application of sound business techniques can't build or perpetuate a career in Hollywood. Bellou frets and droops because he has confronted the film industry with the same expectations that inform business arrangements elsewhere. Nor does he pine alone. Just as hangdog and preoccupied as Ballou is Steelgrave, the millionaire gangster from Cleveland who owns a chic Hollywood restaurant. Said to have killed a dozen men, this undersized hoodlum acts meek, dazed and apologetic when insulted by Marlowe during his sole appearance in the action.

Perhaps he blanches because he wants to stay in hiding; Eddie Harwood of *The Blue Dahlia*, another powerful restaurateur who tried to bury his guilt before moving to California, showed his heart and suffered for it. Filmland, where anything can happen and where images build fortunes, encourages its inhabitants to hide their true selves. The concealment operation can take several forms. And, as in *The Lady in the Lake*, they all end in grief. The man calling himself George W. Hicks who was staying in the room leased to Orrin resurfaces as Dr. G.W. Hambleton, an ice pick handle jutting from his neck. Also known as Mileaway Marston and Ace Devore, Hambleton/Hicks already started hiding from himself by using aliases. Then he hastened the process of self-negation by living in a boarding house and a hotel, way stations for the homeless. At the time of his death, he didn't have enough of his essential reality to retard the drift into blackness. His swift, nearly painless death from an icepick neatly inserted in the occipital bulge, below the neck, merely carries forward his practice of self-denial.

Other wearers of the mask have so far escaped his plight. One Peoria Smith, a film studio factotum who has access to the stars' addresses and private phone numbers, fakes a stammer (as if smooth-tracking speech would betray an insensitivity to the pressures of the studio?). He's easily bested by Marlowe when their interests clash; a person in hiding can neither defend himself nor mount an effective attack. The role played by Dolores Gonzales' Mexican charade in her undoing is less easily assessed. Although renouncing her marriage for Hollywood probably hastened her

death, her renunciation may not have included her exchanging a
husband for a Mexican simulation. On the other hand, arguing from
results rather than motives, her simulation and her death knit
logically; adopting the screen persona of a Latin siren has turned
her into a Latin siren. Mavis Weld, or Leila Quest, develops other
aspects of the problem of multinymity or mask-wearing in
Hollywood. Her choosing the last name, Weld, for her film identity,
pays tribute to stability, union, and juncture, virtues lacking in the
"intense and rather disordered lives" of most performers, according
to Sheridan Ballou. Mavis' cool voice and casually fluffed-out hair
help her affect the calm she doesn't feel. Style is all to her, as is seen
in her having learned how to throw a cigarette in the air and catch it
between her lips. Like the search for wholeness captured in her stage
name (and reflected in Oppenheimer's fascination in the order
with which his dogs urinate), her elaborate casualness hides the
pressure she feels as a movie queen whose career has reached a
crucial point. Her flaring temper stems from the suspicion that fame
and money can't replace the harmony she rejected by leaving
Kansas. Violence, the foe of harmony, thrills her. After making sure
that her slap hurt Marlowe, she tells him to kiss her, her hand,
revealingly, clenching into a fist as her eyes soften and melt; Mavis
is at war with herself.

   This internal struggle expresses her need for a persona. Even
before asking Marlowe to kiss her, she had clubbed him from
behind—in the presence of a male corpse sprawled on a bed. Yet her
feigned nonchalance has divided her from her emotions. Unreality
permeates and pollutes everything in Hollywood; the screen star
who projects a romantic image rather than her real identity is
estranged from herself. Hollywood markets shadows, not the
substance. Chandler argues this point through the subtleties of
narrative technique. Conveying the idea that the filmland society
that crushes the individual consists of crushed individuals is the
door. Doors symbolize the process by which motion pictures promise
glamour and glory but deliver heartache. Most of the doors in the
book don't operate normally. Marlowe finds doors within doors,
doors opening to blank corridors, doors without knockers and/or
handles, and doors fitted with dummy doorknobs. Some doors
contain keyholes inside keyholes. Frustrating the normal process of
entry and exit, the double doors to Ballou's office open electronically
from a hidden switch. Then there are doors disguised as something
else. An inner door to Ballou's waiting room looks like a stained-
glass window; the tall, elegant woman seen passing through it, a
Miss Vane, calls up the vanity goading all would-be screen stars;

that a vane also reacts to wind currents invokes the caprice that rules Hollywood careers. The caprice can show a grim edge. A sign suspended over a doctor's door in nearby Bay City, saying RING AND ENTER, belies the truth that the door is locked. And Orrin P. Quest will soon die falling through the door of the doctor's consulting room.

A person *could* die trying to open a door in *The Little Sister*, where doors serve as barriers rather than as aids to communication. The consulting room door was opened by Marlowe, whom Orrin tried to stab while sinking to his death. Because the path between Hollywood and Bay City is so well worn, Orrin's deathly intent and his dying while frustrated by a door help make Chandler's Hollywood as much a dream dump as Nathanael West's in *The Day of the Locust* (1939). Carefree, opulent, and glittering on the surface, the movie industry discourages, rather than welcoming, aspirants. Its doors are hard to open for a good reason. As the Quest sibs prove, family loyalty can't check greed; Mavis' film career entails a denial of her roots. Her brother's blackmail plot against her follows her example of rejecting the family tie. After using her influence to enter a chic restaurant, he takes the picture he later blackmails her with. Hollywood's bogus promise of quick rewards attracts enemies of civilized process—the impatient, the self-denying, the criminal. Those already rewarded do well to bar their doors. A career built on dreams can fall apart overnight. Why introduce a possible disturbance? Let the dreamer be warned. Ignorance of what lies behind a door should discourage gatecrashing. Unfortunately, this warning often comes too late. Inflating to movie-screen size the American's self-image as someone who acts out his feelings, Hollywood fosters an arrogance that scorns caution.

II

Chandler never decided how well these motifs and ideas worked as fiction. His comments about *The Little Sister* are either unfriendly or guarded. He wrote to James Sandoe, on 3 May 1949, that the book "couldn't pretend to be a proper mystery story." He had spoken more boldly in a 10 August 1948 letter to his British publisher, Hamish Hamilton, when he said, "There is nothing in it but style and dialogue and characters. The plot creaks like a broken shutter in an October wind." Whether he tightened, trimmed and polished his creaking plot during the months between the two letters can't be known. The plot, still the weakest element of the novel, may have been past saving. The praise of one of its rare admirers,

Herbert Ruhm, rests on such a shaky footing that it defeats itself. After commending *The Little Sister* as "Chandler's best novel," Ruhm calls it "an inconspicuous reading of an ancient ritual in criminal dress, with realistic details."[7] Ruhm has praised what deserves to be scathed. The classical parallels labored by Chandler prove one of the book's worst embarrassments. Orfamay's name resembles that of Orpheus, and her journey to southern California recalls her namesake's descent into Hades. But she plays no music, and she makes her descent for money, not love. In place of Eurydice, Orpheus' beloved, Chandler substitutes Orrin, whose name, the same as that of the Orestes figure in Eugene O'Neill's *Mourning Becomes Electra* (1931), summons up Aeschylus. But this summoning up is misleading because the Quest parents have nothing in common with the house of Agamemnon, and no soldier's homecoming foments a crisis. Chandler worsens this muddle with an oblique reference to *Antigone* that falls far afield of his theme. Orfamay tells Marlowe, "You left him [Orrin] lying on the floor, dead.... And I don't care what they do to you. If they put you in prison, I think I would like that." She resents Marlowe, not for dishonoring the brother she loved, but because Orrin's death has shut her off from a possible source of cash and Marlowe happens to be handy. Although Chandler studied the classics, he couldn't adapt them to his fiction. His attempt to lend *The Little Sister* a classical grandeur makes him look pretentious and inept.

Such miscues have made *The Little Sister* Chandler's most roundly attacked work. MacShane calls it "an overripe book." Pendo finds it marred by "trivial writing errors and major plot weaknesses," including "one of the most confusing blackmail schemes ever devised." "Not much of an achievement," is Margolies' assessment, and Priestley denies it any merit at all: "The underlying story pattern seems to me a complete failure. It leaves me neither knowing nor caring."[8] These attacks are deserved. *The Little Sister* drifts confusedly in search of a central action. Though rich in dramatic materials, it lacks the dramatic structure to lend them shape and impact. Its underlying family drama doesn't convert to movement and incident because it has no eye for the revealing moment. Most of the scenes that advance the action aren't described, and Marlowe always arrives just too late to prevent murder. Poor timing forces Chandler to smuggle in implausibilities along with his off-stage action. His desperation explains why the blackmail plot confused Pendo. He doesn't make the right things happen. The naming of Dolores as Orrin's killer bypasses Chandler's investigation of the breakdown of the American family.

Chandler made Dolores a killer because he was angry at her. He was probably also tired of the book, which, with its scarcity of intuition and compassion, didn't inspire his best energies. Besides straining our credulity, Dolores' guilt resolves the plot to the side of its main lines of force. Dolores killed Orrin to get back at his sister, Mavis, who had turned the head of Dolores' lover and taken him away from her. This explanation overlooks the point that Orrin was blackmailing Mavis and that his death did her more good than harm—particularly because she didn't have to raise a finger to cause it.

The early chapters contain no hint of the artistic collapse that will ensue. *The Little Sister* begins in the same vein as many classic mystery stories. G.W. Hicks, or Hambleton, checks out of the room registered to the missing person, Orrin. Within minutes of his departure, the rooming house manager gets murdered, and the page from the register for the day Orrin signed in is discovered missing. But then Hicks/Hambleton, the person suspected of committing the first murder, becomes the book's second murder victim, done in, like his predecessor, with a filed-down icepick inserted at the top of the spine. The photograph the two men died for conveys Chandler's ability to jounce our minds. Intriguingly, the photo shows two people eating at a local restaurant called The Dancers. Marlowe must find out why such a harmless-looking photo should cause two murders. He goes about his job with his usual skill, noticing a local newspaper on the table from which a date can be inferred. His sharp eye continues to serve his reason. If the man in the photo, Weepy Moyer, or Steelgrave, was doing time in jail when his ex-partner in crime, Sunny Moe Stein, was shot to death, then he couldn't have done the murder. Yet reports have been circulating that Steelgrave either got a medical pass or bribed a guard to let him leave prison the day of the Stein murder, which is also the day when the newspaper on the table went to press. The photo looks like a grifter's bonanza. Besides containing evidence about the murder, it incriminates the woman eating her lunch, Mavis Weld. Just a film or two away from star billing, the ascendant Mavis has been guarding her reputation carefully. That her brother is trying to squeeze her lends resonance to the drama building around her.

This resonance is silenced quickly. Haphazard and sketchy, *The Little Sister* consists of scraps, fragments, and undeveloped ideas. Orrin's plot to blackmail his sister allegedly turns "his simple meanness into the classic sadism of the multiple killer." But by delaying Orrin's introduction into the novel until five or ten seconds before his death, Chandler misses the chance to describe his shocking downfall. Various remarks made about Orrin along the way, like Marlowe's "very inhibited sort of guy and with a very highly developed sense of his own importance," form notebook entries which never attain artistic growth. Chandler ignores the conflict between family loyalty and the middle-class push to get ahead. Instead of recording the steps by which the missing-person case leads to the four deaths, he builds his plot around characters we've not met, met only briefly under an alias, or who died, like Sunny Moe Stein, before the time of the present-tense action. Some characters wander in and out of the plot before finding a place in it. At the Bay City rooming house where Orrin is registered, Marlowe meets a man armed with a gun and a knife who is counting money on a kitchen table. After a brief skirmish, the man leaves the novel forever. Chapter Thirty consists of a dialogue between Marlowe and a nameless policeman who works nights in order to practice the piano during the day. He, too, disappears from the action after his solo turn. Why is he in the book? Chandler's practice of displaying characters who have no thematic weight to pull shows poor planning. It also suggests an easy way out, as if Chandler had chosen to describe the confusion of postwar Hollywood with confused writing.

Chandler's own confusion will take the form of forgetfulness, as it did in *Farewell, My Lovely*. In Chapter 15, Marlowe reminds Orfamay of her having mentioned to him her sister Leila. Leila's name had not been spoken to him, at least in our hearing. In Chapters 11 and 24, he discusses the icepick murder case with two policemen, Fred Beifus and Christy French. Whereas French is decent, astute, and professional, Beifus peppers his speech with homosexual provocations and sadistic threats. Yet when the two policemen reappear in Chapter 29, Beifus is patient and humane, while a snarling French orders that Marlowe be handcuffed. French is so belligerent during this interrogation of Marlowe that he punches his fellow officer, Beifus. Chapter Thirty-one, where he grins at Marlowe and, without irony, calls him "chum," restores his humanity. But it doesn't erase the impression that some time between his writing of Chapters 24 and 31, Chandler forgot the personality traits he had assigned to his two policemen and absentmindedly reversed them. No other explanation makes sense of the way French and Beifus act so out of character. The impression that Chandler scamped his work in *The Little Sister* occurs elsewhere. Marlowe doesn't detect enough, Chandler shortcutting and even removing complications in plotting by materializing a studio hand and then a journalist to give Marlowe vital information he might have dug out for himself. Then, a major breakthrough results from the same kind of "unaccountable intuition" Chandler attacked in "The Simple Art of Murder." When Marlowe accidentally meets Steelgrave outside of Dolores' apartment in Chapter 12, he tells him, a propos of nothing, "I wouldn't give a damn, even if your name was Weepy Moyer." His explanation for this bullseye shot in the dark, "I never knew quite why I said that. There was nothing to make me say it, except that his name had been mentioned," insults the reader. Steelgrave's very appearance outside the apartment just as Marlowe is leaving is a wild enough coincidence on its own. What is more, Steelgrave, a.k.a. Weepy Moyer, says little that either speeds or deepens the action. Chandler's pushing his luck beyond the breaking point by intruding Marlowe's intuition shows awful judgment. His writer's instinct told him to validate Steelgrave's importance to the plot by giving the reader a look at him. But he'd have lost less by omitting Steelgrave altogether than by introducing him so clumsily. The embarrassment caused by Steelgrave's one-page appearance characterizes *The Little Sister*, which stands a rung or two below *The High Window* and is therefore Chandler's worst novel.

Chapter Ten

Suburban Death Watch

THE LONG GOODBYE (1953) enjoys the highest critical standing of any Marlowe; nearly all who have discussed the book in print speak favorably of it. Voicing typical words of praise are William F. Nolan, who calls it Chandler's "finest, most mature writing achievement," and Jerry Palmer, who judges it "one of the half-dozen best thrillers ever written."[1] Such plaudits would have cheered Chandler. He wrote a great deal of himself into the novel, distributing both his stresses and parts of his personality among his three main characters, as Natasha Spender has noted.[2] This gruelling self-inventory, prompted in part by his wife Cissy's impending death, made him dig deeper into his psyche and push his conclusions harder than ever before. The longest, by far, of his novels, *The Long Goodbye* runs nearly twice the length of *The Big Sleep* and *Playback*. It covers more time, a year or so, and uses more characters than any of its counterparts. It also reaches ten more years into the past and as far as England and Norway for its main impulses.

This new breadth is matched by a new solidness in documentation. *The Long Goodbye* describes the trigger and recoil action of a pistol along with the kind of entry wound made by the pistol when fired from close range. Other details lend definition and power to the detection. The Carne Organization of Beverly Hills, a private security agency which gives Marlowe some important leads, has a personality, a style, and a history in contrast to the detective's vague sources of privileged information in *The Little Sister.*

The high hopes Chandler had for the book express themselves stylistically. Though not indulgent, his prose includes a wide array of rhetorical devices. Showing no signs of strain, he uses hyperbole ("the two steps of the porch were ten feet high"), synecdoche ("'Well, that's one way of doing it,' I told the white coat"), litotes ("Ellen Wade materialized beside me in a pale blue something which did her no harm") and zeugma ("the light went off, and so did I"). He will also use the undramatized set piece to impart both information and solidness. The action of *The Long Goodbye* stops for a gossip columnist's account of a wedding, a farewell letter, a suicide letter, a D.A.'s statement at a press conference and the rebuttal to it in a newspaper, a policeman's diatribe against gambling in Chapter 48 and, most ambitiously, a stream-of-consciousness memorandum in which novelist Roger Wade uses a heavy, incantatory prose and a flood of wild images to take us into his depression. As the Wade brainstorm indicates, each of these set pieces is couched in a different idiom. This variety in both voice and point of view enriches the novel without bogging it down. The set pieces aren't just interesting in themselves; presenting important issues from fresh angles and supplying different emphases, they also deepen, rather than distract from, the book's theme. So sure is Chandler's grasp of character and motivation that he risks nothing by halting the action for a set piece. Thanks to his fine timing, these nondramatic passages convey the same blend of intimacy and formality found in a dramatic monologue.

Timing, as always, makes the difference. Marlowe's ill-timed movements in *The Little Sister* should have told Chandler that he was outgrowing the first-person private eye formula. But he didn't understand this clumsiness as a function of artistic growth and hence failed to profit from it. By contrast, much of the praise won by *The Long Goodbye* refers to the book's richness of design, which stems from the deft meshing of points of view. Symons calls the plot of *The Long Goodbye* "as beautifully smooth in its intricacies as the lock of a good safe"; MacShane believes that *The Long Goodbye* "took the detective story about as far as it could go"; Speir calls the work Chandler's "boldest attempt to exceed the confines of the detective mystery."[3] This praise may also be extended to include the novel's vital signs. The gains *The Long Goodbye* makes in structural consistency it bolsters with penetration of vision. Textured and expansive, rich and resonant, it stands as Chandler's most serious and sustained attempt to establish the truth. Never did Chandler challenge himself more deeply. Autumnal in its darkness, its reflectiveness, and its moody awareness of loss, *The Long Goodbye* portrays midlife doldrums. Its frayed, fragile characters reach out to each other for refreshment and renewal. "Got it all figured out, haven't you, Marlowe?" a lawyer asks the detective. More vulnerable than ever before, Marlowe might have felt tempted to surprise the lawyer by saying that, though skilled in his craft, he remains puzzled by the elusiveness of happiness and fulfillment.

The grudging honesty with which he faces his puzzlement creates a neat dovetailing of form and function. Written by someone who is testing new creative skills, *The Long Goodbye* focuses upon a man who, like his creator, is trying to replace a system of values with a more livable one while he still can.

I

The Marlowe of *The Long Goodbye* is tired. His horizon is clouded, his energy running out, his sense of purpose jaded. To prove to himself that he hasn't slipped in the past ten years, he trades witty comebacks with witnesses, defies the rich and powerful, spends three days in jail, and connives to get beaten up. What is most important, he forms a deep personal attachment, the emotional demands of which finally defeat him and leave him feeling bruised and alone. His isolation worsens his pain. Ageing, scared, and rudderless, he faces the blackness within and the void without. His assessment of this grimness extends to the future, perhaps even to his death. The bitterness that hung about him in *The Little Sister* recurs together with some solid motivation; he sees that if he keeps hiding behind his sarcasm and moral rectitude his life will fade and dry up. MacShane has shown how he renounces the traditional detective's role of catalyst in *The Long Goodbye* to move closer to other people:

Marlowe is a man of feeling who is no longer hesitant about becoming involved with other characters. He is the device Chandler uses in trying to move the detective story into the mainstream of traditional fiction.[4]

Marlowe's problem comes with his knowledge that, although he knows he needs other people, he also understands the difficulty he will have razing the wall he has built around himself. Linda Loring senses his plight at first meeting. When he says at the end of the meeting, "We had quite a fight," she replies, "You mean you had— and mostly with yourself." She has judged him correctly. Though aware of what he wants and needs, he also knows that his commitment to loveless habits of thought are blocking him from his goals. A talk with Roger Wade in Chapter 23 conveys his appreciation of the difference between softness, a defect, and kindness, a cardinal virtue. He also fights great odds attempting to warm his daily behavior with this appreciation. Anybody whose principles differ so sharply from his practice as Marlowe's will waste energy and forfeit inner peace. Just as he had said at the end of Chapter 46, "Cops never say goodbye," so does his last-paragraph envoi imply that everything except for his relationship with the police can be changed and thus improved: "I never saw any of them [the people he met during the novel] again—except the cops. No way has yet been invented to say goodbye to them." Yet behind this implication lies the suspicion that his inner conflict will blind him to the radiance beyond the station house.

The abundance of evidence brought forth in the novel confirms his fears. *The Long Goodbye* takes a longer and closer look at Marlowe than any other Chandler novel. In his attempt to forecast Marlowe's and his own future, Chandler shows the detective alone and with others, describes him working chess problems, serving breakfast in the morning and champagne in the evening, consulting with policemen, interviewing witnesses and suspects in the rich suburbs, and then returning to his dingy, shabby Hollywood office to advise clients. This range of activities displays his worst traits along with his best. He calls the Wades' Mexican houseboy a greaseball and a wetback and then manhandles him. He lies to a helper. He even feels guilty about Roger Wade's death, which occurred with him near enough to prevent it, had he any inkling of it. "I was the heel to end all heels," he frets while tending to Wade after an earlier crisis. A real person, he doesn't embody the classic virtues so much as test himself by them.

If his disclaimer reminds us that a self-scorner can't give or accept love, it needn't imply any failure to work effectively. The Marlowe of *The Long Goodbye* investigates with wit, courage, and skill, using his sharp eye and human understanding to force confrontations the guilty want to avoid. Someone as gentle as Terry Lennox, he reasons, wouldn't have smashed in his wife Sylvia's face, even though he has confessed to the crime in writing. By applying pressure in the right places, Marlowe learns why it was worth Terry's while to confess. Showing grace under pressure, he times his questions well. He also knows the value of silence. His restraint when an angry police captain spits in his face shows him controlling his temper when losing it would have meant getting thrashed. In this scene and elsewhere, he uses his knowledge of the law to protect himself. When accused of being an accessory to murder after the fact, he replies that his accuser would have to prove that a murder occurred and that Marlowe knew about it to make the accusation stick. His reply reflects his tendency to control his exchanges with others. Besides throwing a hostile police captain and then a gangster off stride by responding to their pressure with pressure of his own, he also rejects an anonymous benefactor's offer to bail him out of jail. Better to be a prisoner, he reasons, than to be obligated to the person who secured his release; anyone powerful enough to free him from jail could put him back in if crossed. This same independence got him jailed in the first place. "They [the police] asked me questions I didn't answer—mostly because of the way they were asked," he claims after his release. Like Hammett's Sam Spade, he's wiling to suffer for his belief in the way the law should work. And he'll suffer alone if he must. He keeps insisting that he didn't go to jail to protect Terry Lennox, whom he had driven to Tijuana after Sylvia's murder.

Doth he protest too much? Once out of prison, he refuses to stop investigating Terry's supposed death in Mexico even after being urged to back off by several policemen, a lawyer, a local thug, the Wades' houseboy, and Linda Loring, Sylvia's sister. Nor does he blanch before the warnings of Sylvia's father, the newspaper tycoon, Harlan Potter, who has had the police close their investigation. Marlowe refrains from smoking in Potter's presence, as requested, but he won't quail before Potter's anger, his hundred million dollars, or his great bulk ("he was an enormous man, all of six feet five and built to scale," says Marlowe of Potter). His moral courage and intellectual clarity win Potter's grudging respect. Though accused of rating both his privacy and fear of scandal over any impulse to justice, Potter calls Marlowe "a pretty honest sort of a fellow" and proposes to send him some business one day. The integrity that impresses Potter includes gentleness and patience. "You kept faith ... when it couldn't have been easy," Marlowe is told after bringing Roger Wade home from a four-day drunk. Though Marlowe's words will convey cynicism and anger, his deeds are those of compassion. Compassion runs so high in him, in fact, that it can surface immediately. After being threatened by the houseboy Candy's knife, he snaps an armlock on the Mexican. But a minute later, he lets on that he's impressed by Candy's affection for his chief, Wade. Helping Candy undress Wade, he then washes the unconscious man's head wound and, with the same tenderness, cuts the hair growing near the wound so that he can apply a dressing.

Compassion comes more easily to him in the line of work than it does unsponsored. The difference declares itself in his reactions to Wade and Terry Lennox. The hard-drinking Wade earns big royalties as a novelist; at the time he enters the action, he has already written a dozen best sellers. His success, regular work habits, and athletic build win Marlowe's compassion when the novelist's guilty knowledge that his wife is a murderess breaks him down. Called "a lost dog" by Marlowe, Terry only attracts the detective's pity. Perhaps Marlowe fastens on to him to begin with because he's looking for someone forlorn and pathetic to make him feel strong. When Terry reveals himself as complex and ambiguous, Marlowe flusters, as if having someone to patronize counts more with him than friendship. Yet Terry's degradation offends him, too. Most of the goodbyes in his relationship with Terry, one defined by goodbyes and separations, come from Terry's presumed failure to meet his moral standards. He keeps scolding Terry and walking away from him in high dudgeon. He fumes when he learns that Terry got $250,000 for marrying Sylvia with the proviso that he turn a blind eye to her infidelities. His suspicion that Terry took the blame for her murder, fled to Mexico, and then pretended to be dead to spare his rich father-in-law the embarrassment of a scandal riles Marlowe again. In order to establish Terry's innocence, he publishes a photostat of Eileen Wade's suicide letter, in which Eileen confesses to the Sylvia Lennox murder. But later, he rejects Terry when Terry comes to him. Why?

While handing the photostat to a journalist, he had said of Terry, "I've never really said goodbye to him. If you publish this photostat, that will be it." He's lying. He has used the photostat to lure Terry back to L.A. so he can preach to him. Marlowe can't resist meting out retribution to Terry. The final exchange in the novel shows him blaming Terry for having indirectly caused Wade's death; had Terry stood up to Harlan Potter and protested his innocence in Sylvia's murder, the police would have inferred Eileen's guilt and arrested her before she could shoot Roger. But Marlowe also feels guilty about Roger Wade's death (as he did that of Lindsay Marriott in *Farewell, My Lovely*). If he can forgive himself, why can't he forgive Terry? He says in Chapter 11 and again just before the end that he's not judging Terry. This ridiculous claim rises from his failure either to know what he wants from Terry or to accept the meaning of the impulses Terry has quickened in him. Born in an orphanage, Terry has had to create himself. This challenge he has faced many times, as is borne out in his different aliases and the two plastic surgeries he underwent. Marlowe views these rigors coldly. No amount of change and no wonder of self-creation could teach him to enjoy Terry's friendship. Cherishing his moral indignation, he prefers to analyze and judge Terry than to accept him as an equal.

The first sentence of *The Long Goodbye*, which recalls that of "The Curtain" (*Black Mask*, September 1936), shows that Terry seized Marlowe straightaway: "The first time I laid eyes on Terry Lennox he was drunk in a Rolls Royce Silver Wraith outside the terrace of The Dancers." The sentence captures Terry's main quality, his debauched elegance, an incongruity echoed later in the paragraph in the description, "He had a young-looking face but his hair was bone white." This paradox refers to Marlowe's strong emotional response to Terry. The reminiscential, "The first time" and the compound verb, "laid eyes on," a conscious substitute for the shorter but less evocative "saw" (which appeared in the opening sentence of "The Curtain"), build a mood of nostalgia tinged with sexuality. This ambiguity challenges Marlowe's instinctive preference for the simple, the direct, and the foursquare. A further test comes from the $5000 bill Terry includes in his combined letter of farewell and thank-you note to Marlowe. As soon as he touches it, the bill dominates Marlowe's life. Like his tie with Terry, it raises implications Marlowe finds burdensome, embarrassing and threatening. He has never known how to handle Terry, whom he calls "the kind of guy who always wants to do the right thing but somehow winds up doing something else." This assessment reinstates the ambiguity so upsetting to Marlowe. Appearing in the last chapter, it also defines Marlowe as too narrow and mean to enjoy qualities like gentleness and charm in a man, which he can only appreciate in the abstract. The ordeal of responding imaginatively to Terry defeats him. Like everybody else, he uses Terry and then rejects him.

Terry's most notable legacy to Marlowe remains the $5,000, a sum that exceeds by far any Marlowe had earned for an earlier case. Despite its promise of freedom and renewal, the bill isn't readily negotiable; it can only be redeemed in a bank and, even then, not before some fairly extended and perhaps awkward questions are asked. It also carries the taint of blood money. For Marlowe to accept it implies that he got paid for going to jail and being beaten by the police. Marlowe, who prefers to be self-acting, doesn't know what to do with the bill any more than he knows how to respond to its donor. His unrest shows in his practice of referring to it as a portrait of [James] Madison. Besides chattering nervously about it with a periphrasis, he also takes it out of his safe to show people, as if one of their chance comments about it will quiet the storm it has roused in him. While commendable for its integrity, his returning the bill to Terry during their last conversation also puts closure on his psychic growth. In rejecting Terry, Marlowe denies what is noblest in himself. Drawing the letter of the law has crushed his spirit.

Like Sam Spade, he reverts to the drab and the prosaic in order to survive. But he defines survival more meanly than Hammett's sleuth did. He rejects Terry because Terry let Eileen get away with murdering Sylvia, whereupon she committed another murder, that of Wade. But Marlowe also freed a murder suspect when he drove Terry to Tijuana. His having protected himself legally by forbidding Terry to explain what happened doesn't clear him morally. Had he believed in Terry's innocence, he'd not have silenced his friend. The police don't buy Marlowe's innocence any more than Marlowe bought Terry's. But the police are acting from official, rather than personal, motives. Arresting suspects in a murder case is part of their job. They had found evidence that incriminated Marlowe, and they followed it up. Any suspicions occasioned by the evidence multiplied when he refused to explain his whereabouts during the time of Terry's getaway. Had the police *not* arrested him, they'd have acted wrongly. Marlowe, on the other hand, condemns Terry because he sees in him a projection of his own guilt. In turning Terry away, he's fighting self-forgiveness. The similarity between his initials and those of Paul Marston, an alias Terry used perhaps longer than any other, helps label each of the detective's denials of Terry part of a cumulative self-denial.

MacShane is right to call the subject of *The Long Goodbye* "the need for love and friendship." But he misfires in locating the book's main proposition in the idea that "any man who tries to be honest looks in the end sentimental or plain foolish."[5] Marlowe's isolation damages him more than looking mawkish to himself would have done. Though he had tried to thaw his frozen heart, he didn't try hard enough. His cynicism, like his bogus moral rectitude and self-pity, are all that remain of him. A loner by default, he wants more. The depth of his wish can only be gauged by his openness to other people. Most critics have spoken only of his desolation and depletion. Pendo, for instance, finds "a new note of pessimism" in *The Long Goodbye*: "In the earlier books, amid deceit and corruption, some good managed to survive .... But in *The Long Goodbye* there exist no such cases of optimism .... Hope has disappeared, and this makes the book a depressing one." Tuska seconds this grim outlook in his belief that "Marlowe's isolation, his alienation are more acute, more bitter than ever before." Finally, James adds his share of darkness by calling the novel "the book of Marlowe's irretrievable disillusion."[6] A closer look at the evidence might have convinced these critics that *The Long Goodbye* contains more hope than pessimism. Marlowe's failure with Terry outweighs any success he enjoys with others. But even after conceding this major point, Chandler gives good reason to hope. Much more introspective than heretofore, Marlowe discovers what's wrong with his life and tries to improve it. Nor does he look to better himself by amassing property or money. He sees that, to become fully human, he needs to commit himself to another person. Though his try at intimacy fails, it confirms man's urge to achieve his humanity; people are worth reaching out to. Many of his actions in the book refute Knight's claim, "Human contact for Marlowe is a sterile process where his arid preoccupations about others are constantly reinforced."[7] Life hasn't worn thin for Marlowe; he refuses to remain passive when he learns that others can make him real.

No instantaneous conversion wins him to the human family. The novel bristles with cynicism and those knowing slurs that mask a failure to cope, e.g., "Tijuana is nothing; all they want there is the buck," and "Every cocktail party is the same, even the dialogue." On the credit side, Marlowe begins calling people by their first names. Heretofore called by *his* first name only by Orfamay Quest of *The Little Sister,* he first-names policeman Bernie Ohls, Terry Lennox, and Linda Loring in *The Long Goodbye.* His extending this friendly practice to three people so soon after adopting it argues a new warmth and confidence. These qualities help him redeem relationships that start badly. He and Candy, the Wades' houseboy, for instance, hurdle the mutual anger that marred *their* first meeting. Starting as enemies, the two men become friends, extending kindness and protection to each other. Candy had ordered Marlowe out of the Wades' house, threatened him and then testified against him during the inquest following Wade's death. But he later mixes Marlowe a drink to show his approval of the way the detective has exposed the lies of Eileen Wade; Marlowe's acceptance of the drink after having just refused one offered by Eileen shows *his* esteem for Candy's good opinion. His friendly treatment of Candy continues. Renouncing vengeance, he'll help the innocent even after having been angered by them. Convincing Candy that the police would enjoy blaming the Wade death on him, a Mexican, he then shows Candy how to protect himself. His advice, as it always is to suspects in murder investigations, features honesty: "Don't hide anything, don't tell them any lies . . . . Tell the truth. This time the truth and all the truth." The premium Candy puts on this advice declares itself both in his resolve to act on Marlowe's words and his ending his conversation with Marlowe (the last he will hold with the detective) by calling him "amigo" for the first time.

Marlowe's relationship with Linda Loring is another that begins badly and ends well, the detective moving easily among men and women, Anglos and Latinos, and also rich and poor; *The Long*

Goodbye is the only novel in which Chandler provides a map of all society rather than using the gangster subculture as a metaphor for the urban inferno. Marlowe's having sex with Linda just a few meetings after their disastrous introduction confirms his ability to win faith and trust. That Linda is separated but still married when she sleeps with him shows him extending faith and trust to himself, too. Sexually restrained, if not chaste, he nonetheless relies enough on his feelings for Linda to act on them. He had never made love to a women previously in the canon. His response to Linda's marriage proposal shows the same generosity and confidence. Coming from a married woman who's also a virtual stranger, the proposal deserves to be rejected. But not mocked; when he says that the proposed marriage wouldn't last six months, she answers, "Suppose it didn't. Wouldn't it be worth it? What do you expect from life—full coverage against all possible risks?" Her questioning the traditional concept of marriage as a lifelong tie both relaxes his moral absolutism and alerts him to the value of tentative, as opposed to terminal, values. Any reprieve from loneliness is welcome. If he and Linda can enjoy each other for six months, they are richer than if they hadn't joined forces at all. Each happy day they can spend together has its own beauty and conveys its own lesson. Linda has taught him the wisdom of means-oriented living; live each day at a time. The joy with which he greets her phone call from Paris at the end of *Playback* and his subsequent marriage to her both prove that her relativism has won a convert. Although he takes a year and a half to accept her marriage offer, the firmness of his acceptance proves that he took her seriously from the start.

II

But does he marry Linda to recoup his lost hopes with Terry? He spends more time with Terry than with Linda, has know him longer, and directs more emotional energy to him. Chandler, too, nearing the end of a long marriage, shows more interest in male bonding in *The Long Goodbye* than in exploring the male-female tie. He portrays the commercial, or professional, bond through publisher Howard Spencer and novelist Roger Wade; worried that his best seller won't finish his work-in-progress, Spencer flies to L.A. from New York. Wade and Candy enact aspects of the master-servant drama. When Marlowe begins to spend time at the Wades', Candy warns him, "The boss is my guy. He don't need any help, hombre. I take care of him, see." His jealousy reflects Chandler's awareness that any business tie also makes emotional claims. Possessiveness also informs the friendship of former army mates. During combat, Terry saved the lives of Randy Starr and Mendy Menendez when he picked up a delayed-action mortar shell that had landed in their trench and threw it out. His courage, though, cost him heavily; the shell he threw away exploded in the air above the trench and tore away a side of his face. Ever since Starr and Menendez found Terry after his release from the Nazi prison camp where he had his face rebuilt, they've looked after him. Thus their umbrage when they learn that he asked Marlowe for help instead of them. Thus Marlowe's complex reaction to them; although he condemns Starr and Menendez for being crooks, his admiration of their loyalty and protectiveness softens his condemnation. This ambivalence, so typical of the novel yet also so alien to Marlowe's earlier morality, colors the homosexual tie joining the ageing Dr. Verringer and his violent young charge, Earl. A quack who prescribes without a license or a medical degree and extorts huge fees from his patients, Dr. Verringer nonetheless prizes love above material profit. Perhaps he also prizes it above personal safety. He sells his rest home and the surrounding acreage in order to take care of Earl, who sometimes responds to kindness with outbreaks of violence.

The protectiveness tinted by sexual jealousy that infiltrates most of the male ties in the book controls Marlowe's response to Terry. Perhaps unconsciously, Terry courts it. His charm and battered alcoholic dignity appeal to everyone's protectiveness but also to their sadistic impulses because of his vulnerability. By the time of the novel, he has already suffered hideously. His having survived his ordeals so well, in light of their harshness, makes him a natural victim to those who've never been so sorely tried. The suspicion that they'd have emerged more deeply scarred than he has from his ordeals whets their resentment. They punish him anew for reminding them of their secret shame. Nearly everyone who meets him patronizes, abuses, or tries to control him. Even Marlowe bullies him morally. The proprietary attitude voiced in the following passage from Chapter 11 makes us wonder whether his objections to Terry's failings don't mask the hurt he feels whenever Terry acts independently of him: "Maybe it was like that with Terry Lennox and me," he says; "I owned a piece of him. I had invested time and money in him, and three days in the icehouse, not to mention a slug on the jaw and a punch in the neck."

What Marlowe can't control in his response is Terry himself. He followed an impulse deeper than reason when he rescued an abandoned Terry in Chapter 1. Such impulses had driven him before, notably in "Red Wind," but they had always referred to women. And Marlowe plays the rescuing knight more avidly with Terry than he had with Lola Barsaly in the 1938 story. He gives the parking lot attendant of The Dancers a dollar to help him stuff Terry into his car. The eagerness stirred in him by Terry the next time the two men meet, Terry again reeling with drink, gives the lie to his explanation for taking Terry home from The Dancers: "Terry Lennox made me plenty of trouble. But after all that's my line of work." So anxious is he to nurse Terry that he offers a taxi driver a five-dollar bonus to drive him and Terry to his, Marlowe's, home. The driver, sensing something untoward, snubs the bonus. Later, Marlowe says nothing when Terry announces that a job awaits him in Las Vegas; he wants Terry to stay in L.A. Only when the stab of pain caused by Terry's announcement subsides does he offer to pay Terry's fare "and something over." He won't let Terry leave town without first conniving at his return. Expressing the hurt of the discard, he mutters inwardly, "I just didn't want to see him again. But I knew I would—if only on account of his goddam gold-plated pigskin suitcase." Like the $5000 Terry later sends him from Mexico, the pigskin suitcase left with Marlowe as collatoral on the money Terry borrowed to get to Las Vegas exudes grandiosity (the whiteness of the suitcase invites the term white elephant). Marlowe's discomfort with the suitcase shows in his passiveness; just as he never spends or invests Terry's $5000, so does he stow the suitcase in a closet and leave it there till packing and then handing it to an unwilling Terry at the Tijuana airport; he won't even look inside to inspect the contents he hears rattling about.

Perhaps he refrains from opening the suitcase because he's afraid to face what lies inside; Terry has always given him more than he can handle. The more time he spends with Terry, the more aware he is of the depth of their bond. Life has scarred both men inside and out. Afflicted with homelessness, both seek relief in the same place, the Potter family; Terry marries one of Harlan Potter's daughters and Marlowe, in "The Poodle Springs Story," the other. Besides sharing the detective's initials as Paul Marston, the name under which he married Eileen during the war, Terry has Marlowe's exaggerated sense of honor. He won't ask the Las Vegas hoodlum, Randy Starr, for help because Starr "couldn't refuse." He's too fastidious. He saved Starr's life during the war, a service Starr appreciates so much that he'd be upset if Terry did *not* come to him in a crisis. Terry's refusal to seek him out carries *noblesse oblige* beyond Marlowe's punctilio in returning Terry's $5000, it also reflects the truth that Terry is Marlowe writ large. More elegant, more ransacked, and, finally, more homeless than the detective, he has lived higher and sunk lower, having done in fact what Marlowe has only fantasized doing, like carousing on a grand scale, getting wounded in combat overseas and marrying a woman (Eileen) he loved recklessly. Not only does Marlowe's marriage at age forty-three or -four lack the fire of Terry's wild, doomed wartime union with Eileen; Marlowe also owes his marriage to Terry, who introduced him to the Loring circle and in whose name he visits the bar, Victor's, where he meets his future wife.

Terry's flair for the luxurious and the sophisticated can make Marlowe retreat into the pettiness of moral judgment too. When, at Victor's Terry explains the correct way of making a gimlet, Marlowe says defensively, "I was never fussy about drinks." Terry's suggestion moments later that he look up Randy Starr his next trip to Las Vegas meets the same sniffing disapproval: "Not too likely. I don't like hoodlums." Beekman judged well when he called *The Long Goodbye* "basically a novel about friendship and the emotional combat of human relations."[8] Having pared down his plot in the interests of pyschological realism, Chandler describes the agony of being both apart from and together with one's special intimate. Because Marlowe can't cope with the impulses Terry has awakened in him, he denies their existence in favor of bringing moral judgment. "To say goodbye is to die a little," he also notes sadly. This sentiment, voiced after Linda leaves him to fly to Paris, applies just as strictly to his tie with Terry. He and Linda will meet again; their lovemaking has confirmed their mutual faith in being together. The aloofness marking Marlowe's rejection of Terry, on the other hand, puts so much distance between the two men that they lose touch forever. Marlowe's knowledge that denying Terry will also kill his own best chances for a full life had kept him from postponing this final goodbye. The novel's title alludes to the process by which he avoids, delays, and prolongs this leavetaking. Judging from the same comedown he experienced in the time between *The Long Goodbye* and his reemergence in *Playback*, his stalling tactics showed foreknowledge.

Chandler justifies Marlowe's sharp attraction to Terry, a civilized, urbane ex-war hero with the right amount of reticence; only at the end does Terry allude to the atrocities performed on him by the German prison doctors. Graced with the ease and civility of the public school man, Terry values what is clean and orderly, fit and mannerly. He likes bars quiet, intimate, and free of the noise, smoke, and hustlers that evenings drag in. Chandler includes the following monologue by Terry both to display Terry's sense of manly decorum and to account for Marlowe's fascination:

I like bars just after they open for the evening. When the air inside is still cool and clean and everything is shiny and the barkeep is giving himself that last look in the mirror to see if his tie is straight and his hair is smooth. I like the neat bottles on the bar back and the lovely shining glasses and the anticipation. I like to watch the man fix the first one of the evening and put it down on a crisp mat and put the little folded napkin beside it. I like to taste it slowly. The first drink of the evening in a quiet bar—that's wonderful.

Marlowe has the sensibility to prize this ceremoniousness. But if Terry is beautiful, he's also damned, and his gentleness is tainted by weakness and lack of drive. This mix brings out the worst in Marlowe, and the detective resents him for it. To get even, he wants to punish Terry; he knows that hiding behind his moral rectitude is a piece of escapism. Terry has disoriented him completely. So important is his revenge that he'll debase himself in order to exact it. Whereas his publishing Eileen's confession of murder will erase Terry's guilt, he doesn't intend the confession to represent his last goodbye to Terry, as has been seen. Leon Howard shows how he uses it to create an opportunity to release anger:

His brutal comment to Terry that his former friend would not have come back at all "if I hadn't smoked you out" doesn't suggest the tough front of a man who is hiding a heartache . . . but a real desire to tell Terry that "I won't play the sap for you." For the first and only time in Chandler's fiction Marlowe appears, in these last two chapters, as a man who is himself mean.[9]

Here is Marlowe as his calculating worst. The impulse to destroy has overtaken his judgment. Part of himself, perhaps the best part, dies with his last farewell to Terry. Listening to the sound of Terry's footsteps recede and disappear, he questions his decision to send Terry away. Is his self-image so important that he has sacrificed his inner being to it? As Howard points out, the idea of the detective's refusing to play the sap for an intimate comes from *The Maltese Falcon*.[10] But Spade speaks these words to his lover, Brigid. One can credit Howard's puzzlement over what was going on in Chandler's mind when he was writing the last two chapters of *The Long Goodbye*. Terry was already lost to Marlowe; the detective was probably right in saying that Terry would have stayed in Mexico had Marlowe not dragged him back. Marlowe's motive for restoring him to L.A. looks low-minded. He hasn't yet learned how to give or receive love. He answers Linda's marriage proposal with a nasty crack after spending the night with her. Then he brings Terry back from Mexico both to call him a moral defeatist and to let on that, even if Terry had come back to L.A. on his own to offer Marlowe friendship, he'd have been turned down. Some of the most important truths in the book are unstated but subtly understood. Marlowe's vanity has been wounded. After outraging his moral principles to love Terry, he finds himself rejected—for Harlan Potter's $250,000, no less. His invoking the *realpolitik* ethic of pay-as-you-earn in his final dismissal of Terry evokes the fury of a woman scorned. To call him a Christ figure makes no sense. A martyr only to doomsaying, he extends no charity or forgiveness. *The Long Goodbye* ends in disillusion. Though Marlowe gives Terry a last handshake, he also calls him Senor Maioranos, the alias Terry has adopted to go with the new face given him by plastic surgeons in Mexico.

Marlowe's wounded vanity keeps him from addressing his friend as Terry. Damaged people damage others, especially those who have damaged *them*. Lacking the patience, imagination, and self-esteem to withhold judgment, he gives the impression that he's dropping Terry. He condemns Terry in terms chosen to flatter himself: "You had standards and you lived up to them, but they were personal. They had no relation to any kind of ethics or scruples." He would have Terry believe that principles count more than experience and that received ethics outpace those evolved internally. The belief that morality is imposed rather than intrinsic bespeaks the self-doubter and the prig. Marlowe has staged his finale with Terry to score off of him. Nobody sees this spitefulness more clearly than he; nobody condemns it more. His sorrow at the end comes from his understanding that he's the worst kind of fraud, a lonely one. Terry will know loneliness, too, as he faces the violence of a new start in a strange new country, wearing his unfamiliar new face and speaking in a foreign tongue. But he also transcends Marlowe's nagging puritanism. Entering the novel as Terry Lennox, he uses several aliases in Mexico, calling himself Silvano Rodriguez and Mario de Cerva before settling on Cisco Maioranos. Chandler had already used the motif of multinymity to denote the absence of a stable selfhood; people who use different names, like Velma/Helen of *Farewell, My Lovely* and G.W. Hicks/Hambleton of *The Little Sister* die. Terry's complacency has also robbed him of a firm foothold in life; his practice of giving in to others has drained his will power. He slides into so many identities because his own is so tentative and unfixed.

But his lacking the solid reality to resist others makes him a creature of the imagination. He invades and lives in Marlowe's spirit. The detective learns that the name he used before coming to California, Paul Marston, was also an alias. As a British trooper, he had to fake an identity to marry Eileen Wade; otherwise he'd have been faced with a long wait while his superiors processed yards of red tape before granting him permission to marry. Although Marlowe knows the name he served under, which is also presumably his real name, he keeps it to himself. His discretion restores "Terry Lennox" to mystery, the realm where he belongs, since he exists more forcibly as an imaginative than as a solid presence. Though Marlowe will never see him again, neither will he forget him. Terry has changed the lives of all the major characters in the book, despite his weakness of will. He has already come back twice from death, as well, having been officially pronounced dead during his year and a half in a German prison camp and, recently, again in Mexico; an American lawman even saw what he believed was Terry's corpse before preparing the death certificate. Terry can be spared any more resurrections. Like the man-god who is mutilated physically but survives spiritually, he'll dwell in the psyche of the traitor who loved him.

Grella reads this love as sexual; according to him, Marlowe shares "an inarticulate homoerotic friendship" with Terry.[11] To accept Grella's reading is to define the friendship narrowly. The union does mean more than any other in a book that displays the full range of Chandler's sexual ambivalence. And the ambivalence cuts deeply. The attention given in the book to types and degrees of male bonding is matched by a reductive attitude toward women. As is usual in Chandler, the book's worst troublemakers are women. Coldblooded and deadly, the awesomely beautiful Eileen Wade prepares tea and chats blithely minutes after murdering her husband, who's lying in his blood in the next room. Eileen is a wrecker. Not content to slaughter Roger, she also smirches his name by blaming Sylvia Lennox's murder on him. Her first husband, Terry, she also put to death—by disavowing him after rediscovering him, by murdering his wife (his other self), and by taking away his name and thus his identity; besides calling himself Paul Marston to marry her, Terry also had to become Cisco Maioranos to protect her from being named Sylvia's killer. Perhaps Roger Wade had this self-exile in mind when he blamed himself for having caused the death of a good man. Eileen's destructiveness has made guilt the life line joining Wade, Terry, and Marlowe, all of whom blame themselves for her crimes.

Marlowe acted wisely by not marrying Eileen, a possibility less remote than it sounds. His responsiveness to Terry and Linda shows him to be emotionally vulnerable. Next, a naked Eileen lured him into her room in Chapter 29 and asked him to make love to her. All along, he had been keenly aware of Eileen, who made a stronger first impression on him than any other woman in the canon. The impression persisted. Her husband even tells him to stay away from her. After Wade's death, Bernie Ohls asks him playfully if he's planning to marry her now that she's available. The flip question foreshadows Marlowe's saying ironically, after naming her as Sylvia's and Wade's killer, that he may marry her when things quiet down. Judging from what happened to Terry and Wade, her first two husbands, marrying Eileen would have been suicidal. Yet Marlowe mentions the possibility, however ironically. Spoken in a novel which shows the power of the emotions to overtake reason, his words could be expressing a hidden wish. His feelings romp as wildly as anyone else's in the novel; by marrying Eileen, he would certainly be punishing himself for losing grip. Punishment seems a corollary of sexual activity in the novel. The corpse of sluttish Sylvia is found naked on the bed she committed adultery in the previous night. That she had her face smashed in with a bronze monkey after she was shot to death implies great anger in her assassin, Eileen. It also implies cruelty in Chandler, who has savaged her for indulging in an activity for goats and monkeys. Though Wade wasn't disfigured by a bronze statuette of a monkey, he, too, dies as a result of rutting with Sylvia, but not until he suffers trauma for keeping silent about Eileen's guilt. Marlowe, whom Eileen nearly had sex with, she accused of killing Wade to an investigating policeman.

The link between sex and violence is perhaps stronger in *The Long Goodbye* than in any other Chandler novel. Symbolism helps forge it. Eileen wears an outfit of black and white to the inquest following Wade's death. These hues were worn before. Earl, Dr. Verringer's wild young charge, wears a white shirt with black pants, scarf, and hat in Chapter 16. Marlowe's lingering description of him carries some of the same sexual fascination roused in him by Eileen: "He was as lithe as a whip. He had the largest and emptiest smoke-colored eyes I had ever seen, under silky lashes. His features were delicate and perfect . . . . His . . . mouth was a handsome pout, there was a dimple in his chin, and his small ears nestled gracefully against his head." Marlowe has been smitten. Within minutes of admiring Earl's charms, though, he finds himself under attack from his flashing brass knuckles. Candy is also wearing "a black and white checked sport shirt, heavily pleated black slacks without a belt, black and white buckskin shoes" when he and Marlowe do battle in Chapter 26. The cause of their brawl is jealousy; Candy can look after Wade without Marlowe's help and wants Marlowe to know it. Chandler's dressing him in black and white, the hues worn by oversexed women like Vivian Sternwood and Dolores Gonzales, reflects the belief that any strong emotion stirs some of the same glands as sexual lust and can provoke the same violence.

The strong currents of sexual energy heating the characters reveal some surprises—mostly about Chandler. Though Chandler would have denied that Terry arouses Marlowe sexually, his narrative technique suggests otherwise. Some of Terry's activities parallel those of Mona Mars, or Silver-Wig, of *The Big Sleep*, Marlowe's first infatuation. Both Mona and Terry consort with gangsters. Both marry into money after working in a nightclub. Both leave greater L.A. in order to foil a murder investigation. During their exiles, both change their appearance. Even within *The Long Goodbye* are analogies describing Marlowe's attraction to Terry as sexual. Most of them are provoked by Linda Loring. Linda could be precisely the same age as Terry; she gives her age as thirty-six when she sleeps with Marlowe, who had, in turn put Terry's at thirty-five when the men met about a year before. The year and a half Marlowe waits before becoming engaged to her matches the time Terry spends in a German prison camp. At times, Marlowe seems to treat her as a surrogate of Terry. As soon as he hears that she knows Terry, during their chance meeting in a bar, he invites her to finish her drink in a booth. He's thinking about more than liquor. Her emerald jewelry and jade cigarette holder identify her with green, the color of eroticism in Chandler. This erotic appeal is sharpened by her association with Terry. Marlowe has met Linda in a bar where he and Terry used to drink together. The bar is special. After going there because Terry asked him to, Marlowe finds Linda drinking a gimlet, Terry's drink (which is also green), and echoing Terry's fondness for bars in the late afternoon: "It's a pleasant hour .... In a bar almost the only pleasant hour."

These parallels imply that Marlowe is so fixated upon Terry that he has imagined Linda into life as his female opposite number. The implication holds. In marrying Linda, Terry's sister-in-law, he gets as close to Terry as he can. This closeness vexes him. Just as he had rejected Terry, so does he bicker a good deal with Linda; love means combat to him. Perhaps most revealingly, he tears his bed apart after she leaves it, an act he had performed after finding naked, giggling Carmen Sternwood between his sheets in *The Big Sleep*. The years haven't quieted his sexual rage. Regardless of his protestations, Terry remains the person he needs most. Terry supplies the standards by which he gauges others, and he also drives Marlowe to new emotional heights. Little of this is disguised. The last sentences of his alleged farewell letter to Marlowe include two requests that sound like a parting flourish from a lover:

Forget ... me. But first drink a gimlet for me at Victor's. And the next time you make coffee, pour me a cup and put some bourbon in it and light me a cigarette and put it beside the cup. And after that forget the whole thing.

Needless to say, Marlowe complies with both requests but without forgetting Terry. And not only does he meet Linda during his errand of love to Victor's; he also meets the beautiful Eileen Wade in the chapter following the arrival of Terry's letter. This juxtaposition of events conveys Marlowe's hot response to both women as a function of the impact made upon him by Terry's letter. The residue of the heat fanned in him by the letter ignites his attraction, half perception and half invention, to Eileen and Linda.

This circuit of passion also includes Roger Wade, Eileen's novelist-husband. Wade and Terry both have war records; both drink heavily. Some of their drinking problems stem from Eileen, whom both of them are husbands to, since Eileen married Roger before making sure that Terry was dead. Sylvia Lennox has also played wife to both men; while married to Terry, she receives Wade in her bed. Marlowe adds his own mite to the mix. Like his two counterparts, he's ridden by guilt, and like theirs, his guilt is heightened by Eileen's murder of Sylvia. In addition, he and Wade are both forty-two. He spends three days in jail, and Wade has been missing for three days when Marlowe agrees to search for him. After meeting Eileen, who married Terry in England, he instigates the search and he has a resoundingly English dinner of prime ribs and Yorkshire pudding. Perhaps meeting this outstanding beauty ("seen close up she was almost paralyzing") sharpened his memory of Terry, who also moved him deeply at first sight and who still retains some English ways.

Enforcing the impression that Terry, Marlowe, and Wade represent three aspects of Chandler is the motif of repetition. Most of the repeated experience in the novel centers on Terry, who marries Sylvia twice and has his face redone twice as a result of brutal conflict. These repetitions channel into Chandler's self-exploration. Says Clive James, "Chandler in real life was more Lennox than Marlowe."[12] The feature of Terry that intrigues and perhaps threatens Chandler most is his inability to avoid recurrence. Recurrence has permeated western literature since Oedipus, the key events of whose life happen twice. Freud, yoking it to repetitive compulsion, traces it to childhood regression and, ultimately, to the death wish. Repetition, or recurrence, afflicts the weak, the sad, and the unlucky in Dante and Nietzsche; it works like a death sentence. Chandler voices his own fear of death through his scurvy treatment of doctors. Authority figures, doctors are natural targets for an insecure semi-outsider like Chandler. His treating them as a collective entity detracts from their individuality. In *The Long Goodbye*, three of them, whose last names begin with the letter V, suspected drug peddlers all, feel the sting of his anger. Her doctors couldn't help Cissy, Chandler's wife, who died in 1954, soon after the publication of *The Long Goodbye*. Chandler's feeling of helplessness as he watched Cissy sinking intensified and sharpened his general bias against doctors. Revealingly, a geriatric specialist gets more of Marlowe's abuse than the other two doctors; Marlowe keeps insulting Dr. Varley after ruling him out as a specialist, his last word to Varley being "death." It's also tempting to explain Marlowe's cuckolding of Dr. Edward Loring (whose professional ethics are also dubious) as Chandler's symbolic attempt to even the score with the medical profession for failing to keep Cissy alive.

Recurrence ties in with Chandler's rage against *materia medica* because of the associations physicians have with death. Recurrence also heightens both Marlowe's fear of entrapment and his suspicion that he can't improve his lot. Each repetition of an event tightens the event's hold upon its performer. "There is no trap so deadly as the trap you set for yourself," Marlowe says at the end of Chapter 12, as if his worries have begun to recoil upon themselves. His having bid goodbye to so many people has deprived him of ballast and warmth. But recurrence can cause other depredations. Dr. Loring rebukes Wade for paying too much attention to Linda; then Wade plays the heavy husband with Marlowe. Marlowe and the gangster Mendy Menendez will each feel slighted when Terry asks the other for help. Roles have become interchangeable in L.A.'s freeway culture, blurring identity in the process. In this topsy-turvy milieu, goodbyes convert readily to hellos, a condition that shows why Marlowe always expects to hear from Terry. The dangers of harboring such expectations are great. If each goodbye presumes a future hello, it also chills progress. Characters consoled by the expectation of saying hello again cling to the past and deny the forward flow of time. Locked in a cyclical pattern, they fear the future. Hence reality keeps resisting their formulations and making them grieve. The upshot of living in the past shows perhaps most vividly in Eileen's suicide letter.

I have no regrets for Paul, whom you have heard called Terry Lennox. He was the empty shell of the man I loved and married. He meant nothing to me .... He should have died young in the snow of Norway, my lover that I gave to death. He came back the friend of gamblers, the husband of a rich whore .... Time makes everything mean and shabby and wrinkled. The tragedy of life . . . is not that beautiful things die young, but that they grow old and mean.

The letter explains what makes the finality of a goodbye so dreadful; by withholding recognition from Terry, let alone love, Eileen punishes him for bursting her dream of a wild young love. But the letter also shows the life-denying dangers of taking refuge in cycle. Eileen's death was inevitable. Despite her magnificent beauty, she was living a fiction; to oppose change is to fight reality. The lesson conveyed by her letter pertains to Marlowe, who has worn himself out trying to squeeze reality to the pattern of fictional stereotypes. His attempt is psychologically valid. To throw off literary conventions and then escape into the open induces dread; it's natural to crave the protection provided by structures and systems. On the other hand, to cleave to them after their hollowness has been exposed is to block the flow of life.

Badgered by this problem as much as Marlowe or Terry is their literary foil, Roger Wade. Perhaps Chandler wrote as much of himself into his fellow writer as he did into either Terry or Marlowe. As a writer of historical romances, Wade works in a subgenre as despised by serious readers in Chandler's day as the mystery story. Wade exudes self-contempt. He belittles himself: "I'm a writer . . . . I'm supposed to understand what makes people tick. I don't understand one damn thing about anybody." He maligns his work: "I've written twelve best sellers. . . . And not one of them worth the powder to blow it to hell . . . . I'm an egotistical son of a bitch, a literary prostitute, or pimp." He's also destroying himself because he can't tell the police that Eileen murdered Sylvia. The answers to his problems don't lie in writing. Chandler wouldn't have grumbled so often about being dismissed by the intelligentsia if he didn't suspect their dismissal was correct. Happiness must be found outside of books, perhaps outside of work altogether. After misleading his readers with false romantic ideas, Wade ends his alcoholic, guilt-raked life by taking his wife's bullet. If he stands for Chandler's "bad self," as Natasha Spender says,[13] then Chandler probably concurs with Thomas Mann's belief (dramatized in *Dr. Faustus* [1948]) that artistic activity is subversive, even diabolic. Nobody would endorse this belief more heartily than the tormented Wade. Writing has weakened his hold on life. His work has damaged his self-esteem so much that he can't enjoy the rich byproducts of it. His prestige, money, and elegant suburban home have made him feel fraudulent. These privileges supply no better formula for happiness than Terry's drifting. But whereas Terry manages to survive despite being broke, homeless, and alone most of the time, the rich, celebrated Wade must choose between slow death by the bottle and the quick death offered by Eileen's bullet. Though he may suspect her murderous intent, his guilt erodes his defenses; Sylvia died because she slept with him. Terry was equally defenseless before Sylvia; any demand she made upon him, however unreasonable, he agreed to. That these two society beauties—Sylvia and Eileen—thwart rather than aid their mates' searches for freedom and fulfillment helps make *The Long Goodbye* one of trenchant fictional studies of self-realization of the 1950s.

III

The Long Goodbye gave the American murder mystery a resonance it had never enjoyed before. Taking fictional crime away from the mob and dropping it into the family, the book also anticipated the best work of Ross Macdonald; so clear is Ross Macdonald's debt to it that he gave the family that steers the plot of *Sleeping Beauty* (1973) the name of Lennox. One can credit his wanting to acknowledge the force of *The Long Goodbye*, the only one of Chandler's novels whose insights the reader wants to absorb into his/her own life. The artistry of *The Long Goodbye* enhances this wisdom. Chandler believed enough in the novel to rework and refine it beyond his usual practice. In May 1952 he sent a New York literary agent a late draft of the novel which he expected her to find "slow going" (*Selected Letters*, p. 314). Speeding the action was on his mind. Later in the month, he withdrew the novel from Hamish Hamilton, his English publisher, in order to revise it (*Selected Letters*, p. 316). The speed and vigor of the finished version of the book give the impression that his later revisions helped greatly. The unified plot lets the people take charge of the action and removes the need for Marlowe's self-important forays into *verismo* journalism. The plot's tightness and balance show clearly in Chapters 27 and 28, the middle sections of this fifty-three chapter book. The inwardness of these chapters, which include Marlowe's analysis of motives and Wade's stream-of-consciousness monologue, anchor both Marlowe's long visit to the Wades (covering Chapters 25-30) and the novel itself. Furthermore, the two centerpiece chapters are both preceded and followed by swift, violent action—Marlowe's daredevil ride to the Wades and the murder of Roger Wade.

The murder is well orchestrated. Practicing the art of misdirection, Chandler shows Wade and Eileen struggling for possession of the gun in Chapter 29. The bullet lodged in the ceiling and Eileen's anxiety both make Wade look suicidal, as Eileen claims. Chandler is deflecting suspicion from her in order to give Marlowe's later naming of her as the killer added force. The scene where her guilt emerges does justice to its shocking climax. Its first surprise comes when Marlowe catches her lying about the date Paul Marston (a.k.a. Terry Lennox) was declared missing in action. The petty lie stirs our minds. Why did she falsify such a trifle if she weren't using it to hide something big? Varying the tempo of the encounter, Howard Spencer, the New York publisher who drove with Marlowe to Eileen's, begins questioning her closely. Had Marlowe pressed her hard instead of Spencer, he'd have looked like an avenging tormentor. Spencer, not Marlowe, reminds her that she accused the detective of killing Wade. Marlowe only picks up the questioning after Spencer introduces the idea that she killed Wade herself. Spencer's part in the investigation creates variety without lowering dramatic tension. Eileen's telling him, "You're getting horrible, Howard," echoes her words to Marlowe, earlier in the chapter, "You're a horrible man." Women call men horrible in Chandler after hearing truths that discredit them.

Another scene enriched by levels of dramatic awareness is the book's last, in which Terry, as Cisco Maioranos, visits Marlowe to explain the death in Otoclan of Terry Lennox. At the end of Chapter 51, Marlowe notices surgical scars on both sides of his visitor's face. This observation tells the reader that Terry's disguise has been blown but that Terry doesn't know it. The irony enhances the issues presented in the next two chapters, the book's last. These issues are emotional before they're moral, as the symbolism bears out. Terry/Cisco had come to Marlowe wearing green (sunglasses), and Marlowe's reconstruction of Terry's bogus death refers obliquely to Friar Laurence's ministrations to Juliet in *Romeo and Juliet*. In case we had forgotten, Chandler is reminding us that *The Long Goodbye* is a love story:

You did not take any coffee on any tray up to Senor Lennox's room . . . . But the two Americanos [Menendez and Starr] did go in. One of the Americanos slugged Lennox from behind. Then he took the Mauser pistol and opened up one of the cartridges and took out the bullet and put the cartridge back in the breech. Then he put this gun to Lennox's temple and pulled the trigger. It made a nasty-looking wound, but it did not kill him. Then he was carried out on a stretcher covered up and well hidden. Then when the American lawyer arrived, Lennox was doped and packed in ice in a dark corner . . . . The American lawyer saw Lennox there, he was ice-cold, in a deep stupor, and there was a bloody blackened wound in his temple. He looked plenty dead.

Again like *Romeo and Juliet, The Long Goodbye* describes a doomed love tie whose chief ingredient is absence. But the doom that parts Marlowe and Terry doesn't inhere in the stars. It comes from Marlowe's failure to trust his heart. The first-person narration, so mangled in *The Little Sister*, lets us live the detective's inner drama along with him in the later work; we participate in his hopes, quandaries, and evasions the moment they're experienced. Nor do Terry and the other characters exist as mere sounding boards to him. The various set pieces punctuating the action both supply a sense of Victorian mass and alert us to sources of meaning beyond Marlowe. No one-man or one-note book, *The Long Goodbye* controls its red-hot materials skillfully. In it, Chandler drew upon the anger, hurt and fear imposed by Cissy's imminent death without becoming their devil's advocate. He showed admirable courage by facing his trauma directly and shaping it artistically. Chandler was basically an evasive man. It warms the heart to see his heroic self-confrontation produce a book of such distinction as *The Long Goodbye*. This honest, probing exploration of his inner life unfolds patiently, inevitably, and convincingly. The imagination is thus served.

Chapter Eleven

Past and Beyond

CHANDLER WROTE *PLAYBACK* as a filmscript in 1947. Ironically, it remains the only one of his novels that hasn't been screened. To the critic, it poses perhaps as many problems as it did to the studio executive. No climax to a literary career, it represents a rewrite or a transposition rather than new material. Yet it can also surprise us, for some of its approaches, observations, and characterizations were clearly beyond Chandler's artistic powers in 1947. Other aspects of the book help make it an anomaly. Besides never having been screened, *Playback* (1958) achieves uniqueness in being both the only novel Chandler wrote after Cissy's death and the only one that displays features expressive of so many different stages of his career. Like his first five novels, it begins as a missing persons case; Marlowe agrees to watch and then follow a woman who gets off the westbound Super Chief in L.A.'s Union Station after having fled North Carolina, from which her father-in-law has launched a search for her. Escape hasn't eased the pressure on Betty Mayfield. Well before reaching the west coast, she runs afoul of the archetypal Chandler spoiler, the blackmailer. To run away from the past is as futile as running away from the self, Betty learns, as did Velma in *Farewell, My Lovely*, Muriel Haviland in *The Lady in the Lake*, and Terry Lennox, others, who, like her, have changed both their names and their venues in the hope of beginning anew. Betty, who enters the book as Eleanor King and leaves it as Mrs. Lee Cumberland, finds that running and hiding will wear her down without protecting her from blackmail.

Chandler adapts other conventions from his earlier work. Betty's blackmailer, Larry Mitchell, is slain by his victim, as were Lindsay Marriott of *Farewell, My Lovely*, Louis Vannier of *The High Window,* and Chris Lavery of *The Lady in the Lake*. Setting in

Plackback also functions ironically, as it did before. The motel, the Rancho Descansado, named after the Spanish word for relax, proves as fretful and strife-ridden as the ironically named Stillwood Heights of *Farewell, My Lovely* and Idle Valley of *The Long Goodbye*. The motel's owner, Clark Brandon, harks to Chandler's earlier fiction too. Recalling Eddie Mars of *The Big Sleep*, Brandon is big and tough but dresses and talks quietly. He can afford to. Hired thugs do his dirty work. He also owns the Hotel del Poniente and a Cadillac convertible filled with costly accessories. "Plenty of money, plenty of health ... and wherever he went he would be the owner," is how Marlowe sees him, noting how his ownership is also enforced by the local police. This circuit of power helps give *Playback* the look of an early Chandler. All roads lead to Clark Brandon, as they did to Eddie Mars and to Laird Brunette of *Farewell*. Also resurfacing from Chandler's early novels is the Hammett influence. A corpse disappears in *Playback*, just as in both *The Big Sleep* and in Hammett's *The Dain Curse* (1929). And some of the exchanges between Marlowe and Betty, who, like Brigid O'Shaughnessy, has sex with the detective, sound like a playback of *The Maltese Falcon*. Echoing Brigid's words from Chapter 9 of Hammett's 1930 novel, Betty says, "All right. I'm a liar. I've always been a liar." Marlowe answers her evasions with Spade-like prods such as, "It isn't money I want. It's some understanding of what the hell I'm doing and why."

But neither the Hammett legacy nor the shadow cast by Chandler's early fiction can explain *Playback*. As he does in the novel from Chandler's middle phase, *The Lady in the Lake*, the Marlowe of *Playback* does most of his work about ninety miles from Los Angeles. Distance remains a force. The motif of the investigation whose boundaries extend beyond California recurs from *The Long Goodbye*. *Playback* is both smaller and shorter than *The Long Goodbye*, and it covers less space. A detective from Kansas City, Missouri, mounts an investigation alongside that of Marlowe; he came into the case, to begin with, because Betty was convicted of murdering her husband but then excused by the judge in a trial set in Westfield, North Carolina. From *The Long Goodbye*, but also from its forerunners, *Big Sleep* and *Farewell*, comes a title redolent of both the sweet sorrow of parting and the wish to recover missed chances. Widowed, alcoholic, and suicidal, the Chandler who wrote *Playback* harbored doubts and fears that crept into his last book. His fear of the future and his tendency to cling to the past tugs against the recognition that his happiness depends on facing the unknown. As shall be seen, *Playback* shows him both reaching outward and withdrawing into himself. This internal stress isn't new. The core of feeling in a Chandler novel always comes from a man. *Playback* suffers from weak vital signs because Marlowe's feelings have coarsened, and no General Sternwood, Moose Malloy, or Terry Lennox supplies the missing emotion; the Kansas City gumshoe Ross Goble, the blackmailer Larry Mitchell, and the big-time operator Clark Brandon only want to turn a quick profit. Marlowe doesn't act much better most of the way, even though he's not eyeing his bankroll. After being warned for moving too quickly, he offers Betty a drink from the pint of whiskey he keeps in his glove compartment. But he isn't trying to relax her so she can deliver sex. With scant credit to himself, he tells her that he's not making love to her, but implies that he could do so successfully if he wanted to.

His reluctance is well judged, Chandler's usual equation of sex and death recurring with force in *Playback*. Though women are figures of poetry and romance to Chandler, their allure can take a dark turn. The morning after spending the night with Betty Mayfield, Marlowe learns that she may have murdered her husband. What is more, he and Betty have sex in the same bed in which Ross Goble was found beaten by a hired thug just hours before. The surrender of rational controls can be fatal when violence overhangs sexuality so closely. Even Marlowe adds to the anxiety in the following exchange with Betty: "I kissed her. With my mouth close to hers I said: 'He hanged himself tonight'." Perhaps Marlowe wants to shock Betty lest *he* be shocked and perhaps even seriously hurt by her. Although he doesn't know it at the time, Betty may have killed *both* her husband and her blackmailer by snapping their necks. The attempted beheading symbolized by this neck snapping bespeaks sexual anger. Betty is dangerous. The men who cross her don't just die but also suffer symbolic emasculation. Marlowe is well advised to give her wide berth.

But caution hasn't soured either him or Chandler on sex. Instead of being warned off by the dangers of sex, both men try to anticipate and thus defuse them to avoid being hurt. *Playback* shows them learning self-protection. Characters in the novel affect an ironic speaking style to hide their vulnerabilities. The following passage describes both a young woman's reaction to her new engagement ring, a tiny diamond, and Marlowe's self-protective response:

Lucille held her left hand up and moved it around to get a flash from the little stone. "I hate it," she said. "I hate it like I hate the sunshine and the summer and the bright stars and the full moon. That's how I hate it."

I picked up the key and my suitcase and left them. A little more of that and I'd be falling in love with myself. I might even give myself a small unpretentious diamond ring.

Lucille's phrasing posits the negativity that gives lovers a resisting surface to push against; the negativity infusing perhaps all close ties can enhance and ennoble if controlled. This insight shows Chandler trying to understand and improve human relationships. The softening of the hard shell encasing Marlowe endorses his efforts. Lucille's loving words and Marlowe's flushed reaction to them end Chapter 14, the midway point of the twenty-eight-chapter *Playback*. If love can destroy, it can also comfort and warm. The image of the loving couple, Lucille and Jack, ending the novel's first half carries into the second half, smoothing its cold, jagged planes.

I

These planes sometimes need more than smoothing or heat. *Playback* is tired and flawed. The book starts so shakily that one can see why hostile critics may never have recovered from their initial letdown. Chandler certainly didn't worry enough about making a good first impression. His weak opening chapters rely on false names, on that underminer of sound technique, eaves-dropping, and on a chance meeting. Betty's words to Mitchell, her blackmailer, in Chapter 4, also imply that motivation hadn't concerned Chandler in the early going:

It's nothing but sheer bad luck that you live here and that you were on the train that was taking me here. It was the worst kind of luck that you should have recognized me. But that's all it is—bad luck.

Perhaps Chandler was preoccupied with a problem he usually overlooked—that of narrative structure. Redeeming in part the implausibilities damaging the early chapters is a carefully orchestrated tempo. The book opens in Marlowe's Laurel Canyon home; in Chapter 2, it moves to Union Station in downtown L.A.; most of Chapter 3 finds Marlowe en route from the train station in San Diego to a motel in nearby Esmeralda (i.e., La Jolla). By the end of Chapter 3, he has checked into his room in the Rancho Descansado, where, in the next chapter, he overhears Betty's phone conversation with Mitchell. Mitchell enters Betty's room in Chapter 5, finding Marlowe in bed with her (but still clothed). After a scuffle Marlowe is knocked out and wakes up in Chapter 6 in the presence of Ross Goble. The action of Chapter 7 both balances the opening quarter of the (twenty-eight-chapter) book and points directions. Besides going to a nearby restaurant, Marlowe phones his client, the L.A. lawyer Clyde Umney, whose calls to the detective both open and close the novel. Chandler's strategies of placing Marlowe indoors and outdoors and of alternating public and private settings in the opening scenes build tension for the motel sequence of Chapters 4-6, which focuses the developing drama.

The mystery surrounding Mitchell's death, the drama's chief source of excitement, sustains this intensity. Only hours after threatening Mitchell in public, Betty reports that he's lying on the balcony of her hotel room shot to death with her gun. Her having had means, motive, and opportunity to shoot him makes her the most likely suspect. She enhances this impression of guilt by offering Marlowe $5000 to dispose of the corpse. His aside to the reader, "I wondered if she was really foolish enough to think I'd help her dispose of a body," marks a technical advance from *The Big Sleep* (and from the powerfully influential *Maltese Falcon*, too); Marlowe is explaining that he has broken faith with a murder suspect while pretending to go along with her. His skepticism shows a clear head. After following her to her room, he learns that he won't be needed after all. A reason for her sudden change of heart surfaces immediately. The corpse she wanted Marlowe's help with has disappeared, if it was ever on her twelfth-story balcony in the first place. The questions called forth by her words show how, in the hands of a skillful writer, the absence of a body can build more intrigue than a material corpse. The mystery surrounding Mitchell stimulates Marlowe's detective instinct, but not at the expense of his humanity. Though suspecting that Betty has been lying to him, he turns on the radiator, "not too much," so she can sleep comfortably in the cold room in which she has passed out, either from stress or drugs.

The next major development in the mystery comes in Chapter 21. Eleven chapters after his disappearance or death, Mitchell's car appears on a lonely, obscure road about twenty miles from Esmeralda. Marlowe's explanation of what happened to Mitchell and the nine suitcases Mitchell packed into his car spoil the development and, perhaps, the novel with it. Orel has shown how Chandler mangled the denouement of *Playback* in Chapter 26, where the mystery is solved: "The means of disposing of the body is tiresomely improbable: a helicopter, and the fact that a prime suspect [viz., Clark Brandon] knows how to fly one, are mentioned for the first time."[1] Besides smuggling in Brandon's prowess as a helicopter pilot, Marlowe also surprises us with the news that

Brandon is a fisherman. These disclosures are justified by nothing preceding them; depending entirely upon developments that unfold out of view, they lack conviction. But there is still one more outrageous improbability. Marlowe claims that, as a fisherman, Brandon must have had a "cord" strong enough to support Mitchell's dead body while it was being lowered twelve floors from Betty's hotel balcony to the ground. No rope or man has the strength to lower a person "six feet one and tough and wiry" from a height of 120 feet without the help of a winch.

Like the helicopter that later picked up Mitchell's body in the desert and dropped it in the sea, the engineering marvel by which the corpse was lowered unseen twelve stories faintly resembles the special effects of Ian Fleming and his ilk, who often substitute technology for the rigors of tight plotting. But the denouement of *Playback* is so botched that all the engineering and electronics available to Chandler wouldn't have salvaged the scene. Brandon's motive for disposing of Mitchell's body never surfaces; he probably wanted to help or to blackmail Betty. Further, Marlowe knows that he comes from Kansas City. But he never explains Brandon's midwestern origins or why they matter. Are we to assume that he recognized Goble, his ex-townsman, after spotting him in Esmeralda? The motivation is badly smudged all the way through. While having dinner with Goble in an earlier chapter, Marlowe corrects him: "In Esmeralda they don't say 'ain't seen.' That Kansas City dialect is an offense against public morals here." Marlowe has misused language himself; dialect refers to regional pronunciation, not to grammar. Besides, Brandon speaks grammatically, which means that nothing in his talk could have linked him to Goble. Whatever the tie joining the two men, geographical, phonological or thematic, Chandler has kept it to himself.

Rivaling the denouement in clumsiness is Chandler's treatment of the love interest. But because it includes several scenes, rather than just one, it harms the novel more. The Marlowe of *Playback* makes love mechanically and impersonally. His moral lapse discredits Chandler more than it does him. MacShane notes, "There is ... more sex in the novel than in the earlier books," and Orel explains how degraded this increased sexual activity is: "The sex is gratuitous, and Marlowe turns out to be unexpectedly seedy. One chapter ends with the heroine sobbing, 'Take me. I'm yours. Take me.' It is dreary trash."[2] This wretchedness can't be excused. By cluttering his book with it, Chandler violated his precept that fictional detectives should be catalysts rather than Casanovas:

"Love interest nearly always weakens a mystery because it induces a type of suspense that is antagonistic to the detective's struggle to solve the problem," he said in 1940.[3] More recent statements by him on the impropriety of sexual love in mystery fiction deepen his failure to blend precept and practice. Letters he wrote in the 1950s scathed Mickey Spillane for steering his detective, Mike Hammer, to the beds of so many willing women. Yet some of Marlowe's wooing techniques are as crude as Hammer's; his sexual activity, as Orel says, adds nothing to the plot; the lack of tenderness and reciprocity in the sexual scenes also makes Chandler look as if he knew nothing about intimacy. The impression holds. Ironically, the fervorless sexual bouts in *Playback* don't weaken or distract from the mystery, but for reasons embarrassing to Chandler. Neither Helen Vermilyea nor Betty reappears after sleeping with Marlowe. In fact, the detective finds a taxi waiting for him outside Helen's West Los Angeles house after being told that he won't see her again. *Playback* makes the one-night stand the pattern for sexual relationships. Observing no formalities, Helen becomes available to Marlowe immediately; Betty tells him to kiss her in Chapter 19, and, fearing he hasn't caught her drift, asks him in Chapter 22 for permission to lie down on his bed.

Curiously, the vulgarities, contrivances, and implausibilities marring *Playback* are redeemed in part. Judging from the disasters leading up to the final two chapters, the novel ends surprisingly well. Durham has called Linda Loring and Marlowe's agreement to marry in the last chapter "a pseudo romantic, unrealistic ending."[4] His insight has merit. Linda and Marlowe have only been alone together twice, they only made love once, and any joy that this closeness might have given them was blunted by self-defensive backchat. On the other hand, the structure of the closing chapters validates the last-chapter telephone engagement. Two obligatory scenes in Chapters 25 and 26 reveal Marlowe as a person led by an unseen hand, preparing himself for Linda's transatlantic phone call. First, he rejects Betty; the morning after having sex with her, he returns the retainer fee she paid him when he agreed to work for her, and he also lets her know that he won't see her again. Admittedly, his farewell is a cheat; he walks away from her and makes the leavetaking sound like her idea. But he follows this act of moral dishonesty with several honorable ones. Enhancing the importance of his honesty is the fact that he directs it to men. After parting from Betty he rejects an overture of friendship from the racketeer Brandon. That his interview with Brandon follows the one with Betty recalls *The Long Goodbye*, which ended just after his last encounter with Terry Lennox.

Brandon is only one of four men Marlowe denies in the closing pages of *Playback*. The house detective of the big hotel Brandon owns offers Marlowe $5000, intriguingly the sum he both accepted from and later returned to Terry Lennox and Betty Mayfield; after spurning this offer, he spurns another—from the clerk of the Brandon-owned Rancho Descansado, who is told by his chief to waive Marlowe's bill for a night's lodging. Marlowe knows that his rejection of money also means a rejection of friendship. Enough faith in male bonding still clings to him from *The Long Goodbye* to leave him shaken by his stubbornness. He leaves Esmeralda as soon as his business there is transacted in favor of the security of home. After an overseas operator tells him that Paris has been trying to reach him, he notices that his hand is trembling. "Driving too fast, or not enough sleep," he says inwardly. But he knows he is lying. The hand that put down the telephone receiver trembled in response to the surmise that Linda was calling. When her call does come through, fifteen minutes later, Marlowe learns that she wants to marry him. She backs her marriage proposal with an offer of an airplane ticket to Paris, where she has presumably been living for a year and a half. Marlowe's bombardment by offers in the closing chapters vindicates an argument more consistent with eastern than with western social thought—that all things come to those who seek nothing. But the countersuggestible Marlowe answers Linda's offer with one of his own; rather than flying to Paris on a ticket paid for by her, he offers to fly *her* to California. He has accepted her marriage proposal on his terms. No millionaire's child, like Linda, he digs deeply into his pocket to come up with the airfare betokening his resolve to work at marriage.

A confirmation of the resolve occurs immediately. When his former client, the irascible Clyde Umney, asks for a report of his activities in Esmeralda, he is invited to kiss a duck and the phone is hung up. Nor does Marlowe pick up the receiver when Umney dials him back immediately. His snub reminds us that he also could have ignored Linda's phone call from Paris, since he knew when it was coming. *Playback* represents a psychic, though certainly not an artistic, advance from *The Long Goodbye*. Umney is the fourth man, after Brandon, Javonen the hotel detective, and Jack the room clerk, Marlowe has repelled. He's acquiring a better sense of himself. He knows that his future happiness depends on a close tie with a woman; specifically, he needs Linda to shore up his lonely integrity. The love he has to give he will direct to her, confirming his faith in the man-woman sexual polarity which undergirds human existence. The power generated by this primary contact has overturned his earlier notion of achieving full growth through male bonding. His disregard of Umney's bluster in favor of the harmonies stirred in him by Linda isn't prompted by money. Always an individualist, he told Umney off and hung up in his face heedless of the prospect of taking refuge in Linda's millions. He insisted on paying for Linda's return trip to California because he wanted to declare, at the outset, his financial independence. "The Poodle Springs Story" shows him trying to rent a small office on a side street, even though Linda would have paid for a larger one on the fashionable main street. He has the self-presence to defy Umney; within the past twelve hours, he has turned down two offers of $5000 plus a thousand-dollar air ticket. He attracted these offers because he had made the most of his opportunities. His skill, insight, and experience will create more chances for him. Besides, having already returned the retainer fee from Umney, he owes the lawyer nothing. A man in charge of himself can afford to obey his instincts. No standards will be more exacting than those he has set for himself.

The upbeat ending of *Playback* is unique in the canon. But is it earned? For most of the way, the novel is weary, slipshod, and devoid of hope. The phone call from Linda also turns her into a *dea ex machina;* we distrust both Chandler's judgment and his art. How can Marlowe hope to live harmoniously with a near-stranger he hasn't seen for a year and a half, during which time he has been sexually active with other women? Oddly, this novel that violates so many basic rules of storytelling does justify artistically Marlowe's last-chapter exchange with Linda. First of all, the Chandler of *Playback* could still write with artistic decorum. To show Marlowe together with Linda, smiling and embracing in a novel whose main actions (the deaths of Lee Cumberland and Mitchell) relate sex and death would be inappropriate; Marlowe shouldn't profit from a complicated many-sided transaction in which nearly everyone else loses. Thus Chandler joins him and Linda with a phone call rather than bringing them together in person, and he interposes a year and a half since their last meeting. Like the letters exchanged by Connie and Mellors at the end of Lawrence's *Lady Chatterley's Lover*, the telephone is a mode of communication that qualifies hope while keeping hope alive. Marlowe responds so vividly to Linda's call because he has remained aware of her since their last encounter. This steady, if indirect, awareness has even affected his behavior. Though he will sleep with practically any attractive, unattached woman, he won't do it in his Yucca Avenue house in Laurel Canyon, the site of his one act of lovemaking with Linda. His restraint may not impress all readers; in an increasingly permissive society, he has permitted himself the indulgences he used to object to. Yet by relaxing his sexual puritanism, he has also placed his faith in others; pleasure and meaning come from human interaction. Had Linda not called him, he might have started looking for *her*. His keeping his home, the most intimate of his surroundings, sex free for eighteen months shows him saving a special part of himself for Linda. His carousing never violates his emotional core, which remains hers.

By holding back from other women, he shows that his heart is alive. His responsiveness to the loving byplay of Jack and Lucille, the recently engaged employees at the Rancho Descansado, both reflects his belief that sexual love can bring happiness and helps justify his acceptance of Linda's transatlantic marriage proposal. Still other reactions of his bespeak a gentler, warmer sensibility than he displayed in the novels of the 1940s. In Chapter 17, he sees another couple whose happiness reinforces his belief that, because love can fulfill, it deserves all the help it can get. "Honeymooners," he says to a garage attendant; "They're sweet. They just don't want to be stared at." The negative phrasing with which Lucille conveys the joy borne in her by her new engagement ring reminds him of the importance of indirection; the health of a close human tie depends as much upon policy and prudence as it does upon love. In 1958, Chandler, still aware of the power of words, could use his rhetorical skills to describe Marlowe's aliveness to the life-giving power of indirection. Marlowe is moved by Lucille's euphoria because he sometimes practices her irony to express his own feelings. In Chapter 2, he said that the smoke fouling the air in a just-vacated railway coach is "kind to your throat and nearly always leaves you with one good lung"; he meant that the smoke was burning his throat and nearly collapsing a lung. Parallel phrasing in *Playback* reveals other hidden dimensions. As his reaction at the start of Chapter 6 shows, Chandler will resort to the tough, mannish talk characteristic of conventional hardboiled prose. Yet rather than hewing to the formula, he introduces variations that enrich it:

Ice water was running down my back.... What rattled and thumped was a knotted towel full of melting ice cubes. Somebody who loved me very much had put them on the back of my head. Somebody who loved me less had bashed in the back of my skull. It could have been the same person. People have moods.

His repetition and parallelism convey opposite meanings so neatly because he breaks up the regularity of his syntax with a short, then a still shorter, sentence.

The gift for pacing that brightens both Chandler's rhetoric and his detective's chances for happiness with Linda declares itself in the book's very first sentence: "The voice on the telephone seemed to be sharp and peremptory, but I didn't hear too well what it said— partly because I was only half awake and partly because I was holding the receiver upside down." The brusque voice that has awakened Marlowe at 6:30 in the morning belongs to Clyde Umney, whose last name (Umney—omni) conveys the power and authority so repellent to Marlowe's fierce individualism. The glint of humor in the sentence describing Marlowe being caught off guard delays the clash that will develop between himself and Umney. Marlowe again records the benefit of laughing at himself in Chapter 5, when his ineptness in lighting a cigarette with one hand eases the tension building between himself and Betty. Within minutes, he convinces her to put away the gun she was pointing at him, and soon after that he has unhooked her brassiere.

II

By the time the book ends, he has convinced us that he deserves his chance with Linda. He had plenty of handicaps to overcome before earning this honor. Durham's disclaimer, that he is "hardly more than a caricature of Marlowe in his prime," holds good most of the way.[5] As has been seen, he has sex with two women who mean nothing to him. He wastes no charm on either. During his first meeting with Helen Vermilyea, Umney's secretary, he ogles her legs and peppers her with ill-bred sexual innuendos. When Helen tells him, "There's one thing I like about you. You don't paw," his reply, "It's a rotten technique—to paw," explains that he has refrained from making a rough pass at her not on moral but on technical grounds.

He reacts the same way in Chapter 23 when Betty tells him he could have made love to her the night before: "One thing at a time, if you don't mind." He's pondering the Larry Mitchell death and doesn't want to be distracted. Minutes later he snaps at her, "When I want your beautiful white body, it won't be when you're my client," presuming her unwavering sexual availability to him. His presumption is correct. The cheap, quick sex in *Playback* shows that Chandler doesn't know how single adults relate to each other. In place of courtship and foreplay, he substitutes the snarl. His characters pretend to use sex to assert their independence from, even their contempt for, one another. Betty tells Marlowe, "You're a dirty low-down detective. Kiss me." When he and Helen make a date in Chapter 11, they both reach out for and repel each other. As soon as their date begins, neither party wastes time establishing an agenda; they skip dinner in order to go straight to Helen's for sex. Marlowe concludes his admiration of Helen's driving skill with the following observation: "When a woman is a really good driver she is just about perfect." Mechanical excellence has become a feminine ideal, Helen winning his esteem for the only time in the novel when she's continuous with her purring Fleetwood.

But this display of feminine capability and control loses its appeal quickly. Neither Marlowe nor Chandler feels at ease with the technical adroitness of Helen. Her skill as a driver soon declares itself as a function of her perversity. Robbing her encounter with Marlowe of any delicacy or uplift, she says, "Beast! Could we have a little less light?" and "You bastard. You complete bastard. Come closer." She is telling him that he appeals to her on sexual grounds alone. He can't complain. If he sees her as a machine, she has returned the insult by using him as an animal. More insults follow. To back up her denial of his humanity, she dismisses him immediately after sex and tells him that she'll never see him again.

Nor is he upset by this rejection, perhaps accepting it as normal behavior; the same people who give their bodies freely guard their vulnerabilities closely. Uneasy with her, he may be withholding judgment when he discovers her uneasiness with *him*. Such detachment follows from his conduct elsewhere. After trading insults in Chapter 11, both he and Helen, knowing how ridiculous they're acting, burst into laughter. The sexual maturity which lets him laugh at himself will recur. Willing to settle for less than storybook perfection, he parries Helen's overheated avowal that she doesn't love him with common sense: "Why would you? But let's not be cynical about it. There are sublime moments—even if they are only moments." At age forty-three, he has learned to look at the bright side. That the moments of joy fostered by love don't last raises, rather than lowers, their value; they deserve to be cherished all the more. Imperfect people can create moments of perfection. Marlowe's sexual exchange with Betty also shows that the advice Linda gave him at the end of *The Long Goodbye*, that he seek joy in the moment, has struck home. When Betty tells him, after bed, that she thinks she loves him, he restores the moral balance straightaway. The banal detail concluding his short speech adds the needed note of finality: "It was a cry in the night," he says of his liaison with Betty: "Let's not try to make it more than it was. There's more coffee in the kitchen."

This good sense doesn't mean that his sexual education is complete. His association with Betty ends on a note that indicates he still has room for growth. When he rebukes her for loving Clark Brandon, a crook who hires gunmen to destroy his rivals, she answers, "A woman loves a man. Not what he is. And he may not have meant it." Betty extends charity where Marlowe has brought judgment; the next chapter shows him rejecting Brandon's offer of a cigarette, a drink, and a handshake for the satisfaction of denouncing him to his face. Betty's argument that a woman can love a man regardless of his deeds has gone past Marlowe. In essence, her sentiment repeats that of Mona Mars, or Silver-Wig, in *The Big Sleep*. Marlowe's slowness to learn has left Linda a bigger job of trying to humanize him than she might have imagined. Yet his chief concern in his last encounter with Betty seems to be getting rid of her. Perhaps he feels guilty about having smirched his professional ethics by taking her to bed. (Might he also be condemning the newly widowed Betty for having had sex with both Brandon and Mitchell in addition to himself during the thirty-six hours or so since her arrival in California, a possibility the novel admits without laboring?) Twice within a page, he tries to fob her off on Brandon, and he quickly returns his retainer fee in order to formally sever all ties with her.

The $500 retainer wouldn't have been excessive, had he chosen to keep it. Despite Durham's belief that he's but a ragged shadow of his former self, Marlowe displays some of his old splendor. He gave Betty good value for her money, while he held it. Keeping up with advances in forensic technology, he removes the guard from the wall heater servicing both his and Betty's rooms at the Casa Descansado, and then places a stethoscope against the heating panel. Insight and determination also help him pry information out of an unsuspecting redcap and a garage attendant. With Lucille and Jack at the Casa Descansado, he uses still another technique to help himself. Pretending to be Betty's discarded, yet still devoted, husband, he persuades the loving couple to rent him the room next to the one Betty has just checked into. What he learns from eavesdropping on her phone conversation he builds on quickly but without surrendering his humanity in the process. He follows her to a local restaurant, The Glass Room, to observe her, resisting the temptation to avenge himself on her for knocking him out. He's not to blame if she and the others fall short of the high standards he has set for himself. Yet he won't let these others compromise him. He wants to know her motives for offering to overpay him so grossly; he halts his investigation until his then client, Umney, gives him the information he needs to work effectively; because he disapproves of Brandon, the source of a $5000 check written to him, he makes the check over to the Police Relief Fund (protecting himself by walking away from Brandon's emissary in a humanizing touch that acknowledges his vulnerability).

As his defiance of the powerful Brandon and Umney shows, he preserves his honor without making unrealistic demands on himself. This virtue carries into his conduct with Esmeralda's police force. Expressive of Chandler's growing conservatism, Esmeralda's police are clean and courteous, honest and capable, in sharp contrast to the vicious Bay City constabulary of *Farewell* and *The Little Sister*. Marlowe cooperates with them every step of the way as soon as he goes voluntarily to the station house to report the death of the garage attendant, Ceferino Chang. He also uses tact to let a local police captain know that, whereas he values the captain's humanity, he won't be cowed by him. The same delicacy marks his exchange with a sergeant who accuses him of knowing much more about the pounding given Ross Goble than he has let on. After gently but firmly putting the sergeant in his place, he thanks him for having provided the chance to clear himself. He'll drop his tough pose to thank people for their kindness. Always responsive to the unlooked-for turns in experience, he may have taken special pains with the sergeant because the first thing the sergeant did after entering the hotel room and seeing a battered Goble on the bed was to give the order to call the local hospital.

Such a grace would have gone unnoticed by Goble, the loudmouthed churl whose rudeness and ineptitude parodies Marlowe's compassionate effectiveness. His entry into the novel is well managed. His barking to Marlowe in Chapter 6, "You could tell me where Larry Mitchell is," introduces the promising motif of the investigator under investigation; the remark lets Marlowe know that he, a private eye on a watching case, is being watched. This impression holds. Goble keeps turning up in the same places as Marlowe, sometimes arriving before, sometimes soon after. These coincidences imply a closer connection between the two men than Marlowe credits. Any likeness between himself and the oafish Goble would make Marlowe wince. Goble sits down uninvited at Marlowe's table in a restaurant and tries to bully both Marlowe and the waiter. Misled by his arrogance, he keeps insisting upon his toughness and his brain power. But he lacks the weight to throw around; the worst kind of boor, he plumes himself on his merit. The ease with which a waiter flicks a toothpick from his fingers foreshadows the beating Goble will get when his prying offends the powerful Brandon. Having overrated his chances from the start, he can't even fool a hotel clerk, who describes him as "a little shabby. A nobody." A man who can't impress a hotel clerk or a waiter shouldn't expect to make headway with Brandon, who looses a sadistic henchman on him. "I didn't make it," a battered Goble whines after the henchman bends and bruises him. "Wasn't as good as I thought I was. Got out of my league." That he confesses his shortcomings to Marlowe after having been hammered in Marlowe's motel room raises no self-doubts in Chandler's narrator-sleuth. Neither does it clarify Goble's purpose in the book. Chandler never explains how Goble heard of Larry Mitchell or of Betty Mayfield. He also disposes of Goble too neatly: "All I want is to go back to Kansas City. The little guys can't beat the big guys—not ever," he whimpers before departing the book.

Goble isn't the only character whose place in the action is left vague. At least three others raise issues beyond the thematic range of the book. Intriguingly these issues held great meaning for Chandler. His allowing the three characters, all men, who dramatize them to appear but once skews the novel's plot from its deep structure. The garage attendant, Ceferino Chang, touches on the burdens created by both Chandler's hybrid past and his practice, as a widower, of living in England several months each year: "I'm part Chinese, part Hawaiian, part Filipino, and part nigger. You'd hate to be me." Chapter Twenty, in which he doesn't appear, begins thus:

A man named Fred Pope who ran a small motel had once told me his views on Esmeralda. He was elderly, talkative, and it always pays to listen. The most unlikely people sometimes drop a fact or two that means a lot in my business.

Most of the three-page chapter consists of Pope's description of Esmeralda, the town's history, and a leading philanthropist-citizen. The similarity between Esmeralda and Chandler's home town, since 1946, of La Jolla, makes the set piece, which also includes an anecdote about drinking, a chart of Chandler's present reality as well as a flavorsome recreation of a local type.

The character who conveys some of Chandler's thoughts on the future is the eighty-year-old Henry Clarendon IV. As Fred Pope's monologue in Chapter 20 showed, the mature, widowed Chandler of *Playback* took a sharp interest in the speech of the elderly. Good talkers like General Guy Sternwood of *The Big Sleep* and the coin dealer Elisha Morningstar of *The High Window* reveal that this interest began before *Playback*. The difference between Chandler's earlier impersonations and the ones in his last novel rises from his personal involvement. Marlowe's comment to Betty, "You're my client. I'm trying to protect you. Maybe on my seventieth birthday someone will tell me why," hints at his sixty-eight-year-old author's awareness of ageing. To express his old man's problems, Chandler introduces Henry Clarendon IV. Another elder, the vengeful father-in-law of Betty, Henry Cumberland, has the same first name, the same initials, and the same number of syllables in his last name. Perhaps he was put in the book to remind Chandler of the importance of forgiving. Cumberland follows Betty across the country to reverse her acquittal in the murder trial of his son; his fool's errand ends in futility and embarrassment.

If the line between Cumberland and Chandler is thin, there's no denying that Chandler had himself in mind when he drew Clarendon. Like his author, Clarendon lives in La Jolla, walks with a cane, and wears gloves to hide hands made ugly by a skin disorder. Both men also studied overseas, Clarendon's academic pedigree including Heidelberg, the Sorbonne and Uppsala. And though Chandler never attended Groton and Harvard, as did his garrulous Yankee blue-blood, his attraction to the carriage trade in later life accounts for this harmless fictional social climbing. Clarendon's mandarin background represents but one aspect of Chandler's wish projection. Clarendon is also alive, if somewhat deaf and lame (Chandler isn't asking for the moon) at eighty. He talks about remarrying, a concern of Chandler, who, as Helga Greene's friend, lover and fiancé, introduced characters called Green in both *The Long Goodbye* and *Playback*. Finally, Clarendon speaks wisdom, raising issues beyond the scope of the book which Chandler nonetheless wanted to ponder. Through Clarendon, Chandler's psyche leaps into the open. Discussing God's omnipotence and the suffering of the innocent, Clarendon voices Chandler's metaphysical quandaries; he also takes the mystic's delight in contemplating how small things, like hummingbirds or the buds of a strelitzia, reveal God's hand. Perhaps Chandler used him to voice his hope that the years would bring him answers to such enigmas.

Perhaps too he died disappointed. Though he refers to eighty-six-year-old Patricia Hellwig, one of the town's leading benefactors, he uses neither Miss Hellwig nor any other mature woman to speak for female gentleness and nurture. No comforters, the oversexed Helen Vermilyea and Betty Mayfield (who may also be a murderess) present a stereotyped, degraded view of women. Nor does the only mature woman of importance in the canon, Elizabeth Bright Murdock of *The High Window*, who killed her husband and badgered both her son and surrogate daughter, provide the needed infusion of womanly protectiveness. Never having developed the full range of his potentialities, Chandler probably never found answers to the sexual and philosophical issues goading him. His giving the name of Green to two policemen in *The Long Goodbye* and *Playback,* presumably in honor of Helga, marks a hopeful but wasted first step—an expression of willingness to surrender his autonomy to the woman he loved in order to achieve wholeness.

Colorful word men like Clarendon and his social opposite Ceferino Chang spell out both the intensity and the futility of his struggles; Chandler dug deeply for answers but dug in the wrong place. What is also important, the Dickensian bounce Clarendon and Chang add to the action impart daring and originality. Nearly every critic who has discussed *Playback* at any length ignores this sense of deeper judgment. Pendo's disparaging it as "a poor novel at best," Nolan's calling it "far below par," Tuska's dismissal of it as Chandler's "last and worst, novel," and William Luhr's belittling judgment, "his last, and least, novel,"⁶ have made *Playback* Chandler's most misread and underrated work, just as *Farewell, My Lovely* is his most overrated.

III

Most of the color and drive of *Playback* disregard the plot. Throughout his career, as well, Chandler had little feeling for form, pace, or development; narrative structure in his work rarely points to the solution of the crime. Nor can he be called a memorable creator of character in the full novelistic sense. His people are seen mostly from the outside, by Marlowe's rueful eye, which distances the reader's sympathy. Even his most winning characters, like Moose Malloy and Terry Lennox, are too limited in development to win any great degree of identification. His praise of Hammett in "The Simple Art of Murder" for having created memorable scenes again and again slights the truth that Hammett invented a new way of writing detective fiction. Instead, it describes him in terms flattering to Chandler himself. Marlowe's epigrammatic remark to Betty Mayfield, "Guns never settle anything .... They are just a fast curtain to a bad second act," and others like it throughout the canon reveal Chandler thinking in thematic sub-units like the act, the scene, or even the one-liner. Chandler's impact comes from a poetic dimension of language that turns his characters into human beings struggling with reality rather than pawns in a mystery-puzzle. But the characters often lack a fertilizing core. In place of a plot that can both actuate and control them, Chandler substitutes a series of episodes, each one of which stands apart from the others. His inability to think big, perhaps to theorize, robs his work of the richness and intensity of great art. It also explains his inconsistency. Out of his twenty-five published short stories, only one, "Goldfish" (*Black Mask*, September 1936), deserves to be called superior. And he never wrote two good books in a row. *The Big Sleep* (1939), his novelistic debut, called by Stefano Benvenuti and Gianni Rizzoni in 1981 "one of the greatest books in the history of criminal fiction,"[7] was followed by two misfires, *Farewell, My Lovely* and *The High Window*. Succeeding the solid, capable *Lady in the Lake* came his worst book, *The Little Sister*. Finally, so depleted was he by the time of writing *The Long Goodbye*, his major work, that, rather than moving ahead, he took the movie script of *Playback* out of the cedar chest, where it had been drowsing for ten years.

Why is Chandler still read and admired? The lack of staying power that weakened both his individual works and a writing career that included only seven books hasn't stopped him from becoming a classic. Few writers have crafted sentences so immaculately. Few literary detectives have the power to rivet us as Marlowe does, as he moves in a corrupt, brutal world armed only with his code of honor. His ability to gauge the worth of a milieu, its inhabitants, and its rites also uncovers something essentially American—the weakening of the frontier sinew that pioneered and peopled America in the nineteenth century. Chandler's people are heirs more than homesteaders. In their childlessness, they symbolize a country whose days of growth have ended but which hasn't yet learned to channel its energies into problems of maintenance rather than progress. Eileen Wade of *The Long Goodbye* grabs, cheats, and kills rather than living within civilized limits; Eddie Mars of *The Big Sleep* sends his wife away because his devotion to the American ethic of getting ahead has taken away his ability to cultivate his nest; his easy money dream costs him more than he can afford. Most of Chandler's destroyers, like Mars and Eileen Wade, operate alone. The belief in progress as a function of self-help has stirred in them a primordially American suspicion of groups and dogmas, exalting, in their stead, the goal of winning at any price. But adherence to this goal often confuses victory with defeat. Moose Malloy dies within moments of finding his little Velma, but he dies with no regrets. Because neither religion nor family can brake the drive to win, Chandler's people recall the poisoners and stabbers of the

Renaissance, another vigorous age which exalted the individual. A person actuated by love like the Moose, Tony Dravec of "Killer in the Rain" (*Black Mask,* January 1935), or Steve Skalla of "Try the Girl" (*Black Mask,* January 1937), hasn't a chance among such brutal opportunists. Chandler even makes these men look grotesque before killing them to show how out of place they are in their milieu.

But he doesn't mock them. Chandler sympathizes with people in trouble while appreciating the ease with which trouble has claimed them. Marlowe's practice of withdrawing from the scene of the crime after providing a solution doesn't erase the fact that he's a member of the Guilty Community. Yet the guilt, if not redeemable, needn't spread. One recurring feature in Chandler is the way one person's guilt is usually prevented from becoming another's bonanza. Chandler knows life to be hard enough without our having to worry about others waiting to profit from our mistakes. The deaths unfailingly meted out to blackmailers, usually by their victims, show those victims transgressing again to win freedom. Chandler approves of this rough justice. Most of the blackmail in the canon derives from sex; Henry Clarendon IV says in *Playback,* "A man who lives on women always blackmails them." Characters in the earlier novels describe this process. Weak rather than wicked, the women in Chandler take lovers because they feel blocked. Velma's husband is too old for her; the career of Crystal Kingsley's mate in *The Lady in the Lake* has drained all his time and energy; a war casualty, Betty Mayfield's husband in *Playback* drinks and wears a neck brace. These men have unintentionally connived at their wives' offenses. The blackmailer's evil is all pitiless and calculating; for him, money cuts across and then destroys sexual love. The deaths inflicted upon his brotherhood express Chandler's pity for the unwary and the misled. Though cracked marriages in Chandler don't mend, the integrity of the marriage bond is affirmed with the death of each blackmailer; human values haven't worn thin for Chandler. Marlowe's never having tried to arrest a blackmailer's assassin shores up Chandler's belief in the value of social solidarity (as did Sherlock Holmes' excusing the murderer of Charles Augustus Milverton, his blackmail victim, shore up Conan Doyle's). A constant in the fiction, the execution of the blackmailer calls to mind other merits in Chandler.

Like his poetic justice, his diagnosis of the venality and demoralization caused by greed, his marvelous vernacular style, and his readable, relevant, Marlowe all deserve serious attention. Chandler, if not a major writer, is certainly important enough to have outlived his time.

Notes

CHAPTER ONE

[1] W. Somerset Maugham, "The Decline and Fall of the Detective Story," in *The Vagrant Mood* (Garden City, N.Y.: Doubleday, 1953), p. 129; George Grella, "Murder and the Mean Streets: The Hard-Boiled Detective Novel," *Contempora* (March 1970), p.8; Eric Partridge, "A Letter," *The Listener,* 11 Oct. 1951, in Philip Durham, *Down These Mean Streets a Man Must Go* (Chapel Hill: Univ. of North Carolina Press, 1963), p. 77; Frank MacShane, *The Life of Raymond Chandler* (New York: Dutton 1976), pp. 1, 269; Jon Tuska, *The Detective in Hollywood* (Garden City, N.Y.: Doubleday, 1978), p. 302.

[2] Jerry Speir, *Raymond Chandler* (New York: Ungar, 1981), p. 1.

[3] In MacShane, p. 185; Stephen Knight, *Form and Ideology in Crime Fiction* (London: Macmillan, 1980), p. 138; W.H. Auden, "The Guilty Vicarage," *Harper's Magazine*, May 1948, p. 408; MacShane, p. 269.

[4] Julian Symons, "Raymond Chandler: An Aesthete Discovers the Pulps," *Critical Observations* (New Haven: Ticknor and Fields, 1981), p. 158; John Houseman, "Lost Fortnight: A Memoir," in Raymond Chandler, *The Blue Dahlia,* ed. Matthew J. Bruccoli (Carbondale, IL.: Southern Illinois Univ. Press, 1976), p. x.

[5] Natasha Spender, "His Own Long Goodbye, *The World of Raymond Chandler,* ed. Miriam Gross (New York: A & W Publishers, 1978), pp. 131-32.

[6] Tuska, p. 302.

[7] *Ibid.,* p. 336.

[8] Spender, p. 141.

[9] *Ibid.,* p. 132.

[10] J.B. Priestley, "Close-up of Chandler," *New Statesman*, 16 March 1962, p. 380; Eleanor Anne Ponder, "The American Detective Form in Novels and Films, 1929-47," Ph.D. Diss., Univ. of North Carolina at Chapel Hill, 1979, p. 34.

[11] William Ruehlmann, *Saint with a Gun: The Unlawful American Private Eye* (New York: New York Univ. Press, 1974), p. 84; Gavin Lambert, *The Dangerous Edge* (New York: Grossman, 1976), p. 213; Russell Davies, "Omnes Me Impune Lacessunt," in Gross, ed., p. 32.

[12] Priestley, p. 379.

[13] Miriam Gross, "Preface," in Gross, ed., n.p.

[14] Davies, in Gross, ed., p. 33.

[15] Dennis Porter, *The Pursuit of Crime: Art and Ideology in Detective Fiction* (New Haven: Yale, 1981), p. 170; Clive James, "The Country Behind the Hill: Raymond Chandler," in *First Reactions: Critical Essays 1968-1979* (New York: Knopf, 1980), p. 209.

[16] Stephen Pendo, *Raymond Chandler on Screen: His Novels into Film* (Metuchen, N.J.: Scarecrow, 1976), p. 15.

[17] MacShane, pp. 139, 130.

[18] Ross Macdonald, "The Writer as Detective Hero," *On Crime Writing* (Santa Barbara: Capra, 1973), p. 19.

[19]Lambert, p. 217; Porter, pp. 63, 64.

[20]Paul F. Ferguson, "The Name Is Marlowe," *Literary Onomastics Studies*, 5 (1978), 220-31.

[21]Patricia Highsmith, "Introduction," in Gross, ed., p. 4.

[22]Julian Symons, "The Case of Raymond Chandler", *The New York Times Magazine*, 23 Dec., 1973, p. 22.

[23]MacShane, p. 5.

[24]*Ibid.*, p. 12.

[25]Speir, p. 16.

[26]Houseman, pp. ix-x.

[27]Pendo, p. 96.

[28]MacShane, p. 4.

[29]Dorothy Gardiner and Katherine Sorely Walker, "The Crippen Case," in *Raymond Chandler Speaking*, eds. Gardiner and Walker (Boston: Houghton Mifflin, 1962), p. 196.

[30]Spender, in Gross, ed., p. 150.

[31]Houseman, p. ix.

[32]Durham, p. 85.

[33]Davies, in Gross, ed., p. 35.

[34]Michael Mason, "Marlowe, Men and Women," in Gross, ed., p. 93.

[35]George P. Elliott, "Country Full of Blondes," *Nation*, 23 April 1960, p. 358.

[36]In Tuska, p. 329.

[37]Ruehlmann, p. 82.

[38]Frederic Jameson, "On Raymond Chandler," *Southern Review*, 6 (1970), 629.

[39]Max Lerner, *America as a Civilization* (New York: Simon & Schuster, 1957), II, 704-05.

[40]Peter J. Rabinovitz, " 'Rats Behind the Wainscoting': Politics, Convention, and Chandler's *The Big Sleep*," *Texas Studies in Literature and Language*, 22 (1980), 238.

[41]Knight, p. 157.

[42]Mason in Gross, ed., p. 90.

[43]MacShane, p. 244.

[44]Lambert, p. 233; John G. Cawelti, *Adventure, Mystery, and Romance* (Chicago: Univ. of Chicago Press, 1976), p. 153.

[45]See Mason in Gross, ed., p. 97.

CHAPTER TWO

[1]In James Pepper, ed., *Letters: Raymond Chandler and James M. Fox* (Santa Barbara: Neville, 1978), p. 2.

[2]MacShane, p. 58.

[3]Symons, "The Case of Raymond Chandler," p. 13.

[4]Jacques Barzun, "The Illusion of the Real," in Gross, ed., p. 162.

[5]See Howard Haycraft, ed., *The Art of the Mystery Story* (New York: Grosset & Dunlap, 1946), pp. 7-17, 189-93, 194-97.

[6]Cawelti, p. 165.

[7]Macdonald, p. 17.

[8]Lambert, p. 226.

[9]Speir, p. 130.

[10]Ralph Harper, *The World of the Thriller* (Cleveland: Case Western Reserve, 1969), p. 45.

[11]James, pp. 200-01.

[12]R.P. Blackmur, "Parody and Critique: Mann's *Doctor Faustus*," *Eleven Essays in the European Novel* (New York: Harcourt, c. 1964), p. 110.

[13]Brigid Brophy, "Detective Fiction: A Modern Myth of Violence?" *Hudson Review* (Spring, 1965), p. 29.

[14]Durham, pp. 53, 58.
[15]Lambert, p. 217.
[16]*Ibid.,* p. 220.
[17]James, pp. 203, 201.

CHAPTER THREE

[1]Speir, p. ix.
[2]Macdonald, p. 22.
[3]*Ibid.,* p. 17.
[4]E.M. Beekman, "Raymond Chandler and An American Genre," *Massachusetts Review,* 14 (1973), 166.
[5]Jerry Palmer, *Thrillers* (London: Edward Arnold, 1978), p. 30.
[6]Speir, p. 37.
[7]Ponder, p. 18.
[8]R.W. Flint, "A Cato of the Cruelties," *Partisan Review* 14 (1947), 328.
[9]Grella, p. 10.
[10]Harold Orel, "Raymond Chandler's Last Novel," *Central Mississippi Valley American Studies Association Journal,* 2 (Spring 1961), 59.
[11]Speir, p. 36.

CHAPTER FOUR

[1]MacShane, p. 53.
[2]Tuska, p. 166.
[3]Durham, p. 24.
[4]Tuska, p. 306.
[5]Speir, p. 101.
[6]Durham, p. 35.
[7]Speir, p. 102.
[8]*Ibid.,* p. 103.
[9]Durham, p. 28.
[10]Symons, "Raymond Chandler: An Aesthete Discovers the Pulps," p. 162.

CHAPTER FIVE

[1]Dilys Powell, "Ray and Cissy," in Gross, ed., p. 83; Rabinovitz, p. 230.
[2]Ruehlmann, p. 80.
[3]Ferguson, p. 222.
[4]Porter, p. 39.
[5]MacShane, p. 72.
[6]Walter Wells, *Tycoons and Locusts* (Carbondale and Edwardsville, IL: Southern Illinois Univ. Press, c. 1973), p. 73.
[7]Raymond Chandler, "Farewell, My Hollywood," *Antaeus* (Spring-Summer 1976), p. 29.
[8]Rabinovitz, p. 230.
[9]In Pepper, ed., p. 29.
[10]Porter, p. 49.
[11]*Ibid.*
[12]*Ibid.*

CHAPTER SIX

[1]Edward Margolies, *Which Way Did He Go? The Private Eye* (New York: Holmes & Meier,1982), p. 39.
[2]Wells, pp. 84-85.
[3]Raymond Chandler, *Selected Letters of Raymond Chandler* (New York:

Columbia Univ. Press, 1981), p. 270.
⁴Jameson, p. 645.
⁵Cawelti, p. 179.
⁶Durham, p. 38, Pendo, p. 11; MacShane, p. 90; Knight, p. 150.
⁷Chandler, *Raymond Chandler Speaking*, p. 134.

CHAPTER SEVEN

¹Chandler, *Selected Letters*, pp. 20, 165.
²MacShane, p. 97.
³Pendo, p. 86.
⁴MacShane, p. 97.
⁵*Ibid.,*
⁶Speir, p. 44.

CHAPTER EIGHT

¹James, "Country Behind the Hill," p. 205.
²Pendo, pp. 62-64; Jacques Barzun and Wendell Hertig Taylor, *A Catalogue of Crime* (New York: Harper & Row, c. 1971), p. 113; Michael Gilbert, "Autumn in London," in Gross, ed., p. 104; Tuska, p. 319.
³Ross Macdonald, "Introduction," Matthew Bruccoli, *Kenneth Millar/Ross Macdonald: A Checklist* (Detroit: Gale, 1971), p. xvii.
⁴Elliott, "Country Full of Blondes," p. 356.
⁵MacShane, p. 102.
⁶Durham, p. 94.
⁷Knight, p. 156.

CHAPTER NINE

¹James Guetti, "Aggressive Reading: Detective Fiction and Realistic Narrative," *Raritan*, II (Summer 1982), 138.
²Ruehlmann, p. 84.
³Lambert, p. 228.
⁴Chandler's quarrel with Hollywood, articulated in "Writers in Hollywood," *Atlantic Monthly* (November 1945) and "The Hollywood Bowl," *Atlantic Monthly* (January 1947) is summarized in two letters. To fellow crime writer and *Black Mask* contributor George Harmon Coxe, he wrote (9 April 1939), "Personally I think Hollywood is poison to any writer, the graveyard of talent" (*Selected Letters*, p. 6). Writing more expansively, he told Charles Morton, an editor of *Atlantic* (28 July 1948), "I simply don't want to do any more work for Hollywood. There is nothing in it but grief and exhaustion and discontent. In no real sense is it writing at all. It carries with it none of the satisfactions of writing. None of the sense of power over your medium. None of the freedom, even to fail" (*Selected Letters*, p. 121).
⁵Durham, p. 70; Herbert Ruhm, "Raymond Chandler: From Bloomsbury to the Jungle—and Beyond," in *Tough Guy Writers of the Thirties*, ed. David Madden (Carbondale and Edwardsville, IL: Southern Illinois Univ. Press, 1968), p. 173.
⁶Margolies, p. 47.
⁷Ruhm, pp. 182, 184.
⁸MacShane, p. 149; Pendo, pp. 115, 118; Margolies, p. 47; Priestley, p. 379.

CHAPTER TEN

¹William F. Nolan, "Portrait of a Tough Guy," *Xenophile,* 38 (March-April 1978), 17; Palmer, 48.
²Spender, in Gross, ed., pp. 128-58; esp. pp. 134-35.

³Symons, "The Case of Raymond Chandler," p. 25; Frank MacShane. Introduction, *Selected Letters of Raymond Chandler*, p. xvii; Speir, p. 65.

⁴MacShane, *The Life of Raymond Chandler*, p. 198.

⁵*Ibid.*, pp. 198, 193.

⁶Pendo, p. 140; Tuska, p. 328; James, p. 208.

⁷Knight, p. 147.

⁸Beekman, p. 167.

⁹Leon Howard, "Raymond Chandler's Not-So-Great Gatsby," *The Mystery and Detection Annual* (Pasadena, 1973), pp. 10-11.

¹⁰*Ibid.*, p. 6.

¹¹Grella, p. 9.

¹²James, p. 207.

¹³Spender, in Gross, ed., p. 151.

CHAPTER ELEVEN

¹Orel, p. 62.

²MacShane, *The Life of Raymond Chandler*, p. 253; Orel, p. 62.

³Chandler, *Raymond Chandler Speaking*, p. 70.

⁴Durham, p. 141.

⁵*Ibid.*, p. 142.

⁶Pendo, p. 8; Nolan, p. 17; Tuska, p. 319; William Luhr, *Raymond Chandler and Film* (New York: Ungar, 1982), p. 74.

⁷Stefano Benvenuti and Gianni Rizzoni, *The Whodunit: An Informal History of Detective Fiction*, trans. Anthony Eyre (New York: Collier, 1981), p. 133.